Financial Crises and Recession in the Global Economy, Fourth Edition

This book is dedicated to Julie Absey, Olivia Absey-Allen, and Biscuit

Financial Crises and Recession in the Global Economy, Fourth Edition

Roy E. Allen

Professor of Economics, Saint Mary's College of California, USA

Cheltenham, UK • Northampton, MA, USA

Published by
Edward Elgar Publishing Limited
The Lypiatts
15 Lansdown Road
Cheltenham
Glos GL50 2JA
UK

Edward Elgar Publishing, Inc.
William Pratt House
9 Dewey Court
Northampton
Massachusetts 01060
USA

A catalogue record for this book
is available from the British Library

Library of Congress Control Number: 2016949923

This book is available electronically in the **Elgar**online
Economics subject collection
DOI 10.4337/9781785361111

Printed on elemental chlorine free (ECF)
recycled paper containing 30% Post-Consumer Waste

ISBN 978 1 78536 110 4 (cased)
ISBN 978 1 78536 112 8 (paperback)
ISBN 978 1 78536 111 1 (eBook)

Typeset by Servis Filmsetting Ltd, Stockport, Cheshire
Printed and bound in the USA

Contents

Figures

Tables

Preface and acknowledgements for the *Fourth Edition*

The *Third Edition* of *Financial Crises and Recession in the Global Economy* was published in 2009, and it included case studies through the initial phase of the 2007– global financial crisis and 'great recession' of 2007–09 as it was called in the US. Written in 2016, this *Fourth Edition* explains the continuing effects of the 2007– crisis, including, especially, as it surfaced to become the ongoing European financial crisis. And, using its common-pattern analysis, the *Fourth Edition* discusses China's 'turning point' and rising financial challenges in 2016 after decades of 'boom'. Otherwise, the *Fourth Edition* retains the various case studies of financial crisis and recession from previous editions, organized in chronological order for the reader.

The goal of this edition, as per previous editions, is to provide a comprehensive history and explanation for the major financial instabilities and trends in the global economy since the 1970s. In this regard, some 'new thinking' from the literature and also from my 'human ecology economics HEE' framework gives some further context.

Coincidentally, and unexpectedly, as I mentioned in the *Third Edition*, I found myself watching up close when the 2007– crisis surfaced near my Silicon Valley and San Francisco Bay Area home—along with other regions of California and the US. That crisis began with the bursting of a housing bubble and a sharp rise in home foreclosures in the US during the fall of 2006, which spread to become a more broad-based global financial crisis within a year. Several of the counties in the San Francisco Bay Area ranked in the top ten nationally for home foreclosure activity, with, for example, a rate of foreclosure activity in the third quarter of 2007 equal to one for every 70 households.

And now, as the US has, by many macroeconomic measures, recovered from that crisis, while other regions of the globe continue to struggle, I am watching international financial inflows surge back into the San Francisco Bay Area—to such a degree that housing and other indicators are once again signaling boom, at least locally. Capital flight from China and elsewhere into the US dollar 'core' of the global financial system remains an obvious trend whether observed close up or afar.

Once again special thanks go to Philip Cerny for his encouragement and editing of the first edition of this book, which helped to locate this work within the various disciplines (an interdisciplinary process that continues). Private correspondence and a review of the first edition by G. Carchedi (1996) helped me understand the long-standing debates over economic value and wealth creation (also a process that continues), and Robert Laurent at the US Federal Reserve is to be thanked for his encouragement and helpful correspondence regarding the puzzles of money supply and demand. Various colleagues at Saint Mary's College of California are to be thanked for their support over the years, especially Wilber Chaffee of the Politics Department, Asbjorn Moseidjord of the Economics Department, and Donald Snyder of the Business Administration Department.

Edward Elgar and his outstanding staff are also to be thanked for continuing to support this book.

Most importantly, this book is dedicated to Julie Absey and Olivia Absey-Allen, who have been great supporters at my side in all the ways that really count. And, to Biscuit, a new member of our household, who was a companion near my feet for much of the writing.

Roy E. Allen
May, 2016
Oakland, California

Introduction

This book discusses large-scale economic crises since 1980, including in developed countries (e.g. the global recession of 1982, the global stock market crash of 1987, Sweden's financial crisis of 1991, Japan's after 1989, US and Europe 2007–), and in less developed countries (e.g. Latin America 1982, Mexico 1994–95, Asia 1997). Despite a rapidly growing literature on financial instability and boom–bust processes, some of the more important patterns underlying these crises are only now being identified. For example, a good historical data set on severe financial crises was developed only recently, by Carmen Reinhart and Kenneth Rogoff (Reinhart and Rogoff, 2007, 2008, 2009). Interestingly, they find that since 1800 the percentage of years that advanced economies have spent in severe banking crises is 7.2 percent, and emerging economies 8.3 percent; and those numbers only change to 7.0 percent and 10.8 percent in the time period since 1945. Their results indicate that the 2007– crisis was actually 'overdue' in terms of average historical frequency in advanced economies. Furthermore, since World War II, there has not been any greater ability to avoid severe financial crises compared to the period since 1800.

However, for most observers and participants in the 1980s and 1990s, and even into 2008 after the recent crisis hit the US and Europe, 'this time was different' and confidence in institutions remained high. Heightened awareness of the possibility of a large-scale global crisis only began to surface in the mid-1990s. In 1996, the International Monetary Fund (IMF) indicated that approximately three-quarters of its more than 180 member countries had encountered 'significant' banking sector problems between 1980 and 1995, one-third of which warrant the definition 'crisis' (Lindgren et al., 1995). Then, in 1997, unexpectedly, the East Asian financial crisis struck, which was followed by the Russian and Brazilian crises in 1998 and various others, such as the Argentine crisis in 2002. These crises, even prior to 2008, began to generate a flurry of policymaking activity. Initiatives at the IMF and elsewhere in 2000–05 came close to, but did not realize, a 'bankruptcy procedure' for countries, which was a stark contrast from the famous, and uninformed, quote of less than four decades ago (shortly before the 1982– Latin American debt crisis) from the Chairman of CitiCorp that 'countries don't go broke'.

Unlike the well-researched national banking crises that have been resolved under domestic regulations, there has been no comprehensive international law or policy that sets out the procedures for the international community to follow in international crisis episodes. The ad hoc rescue fund provided to Mexico after its crisis at the end of 1994 was unprecedented in size—approximately $50 billion—as well as in international political scope, given the ways that it involved the IMF, the US Treasury's Exchange Stabilization Fund, the Bank for International Settlements, and a variety of independent countries. Ad hoc financial bailouts offered to Korea and Indonesia in 1997, and Brazil in 1998, were similarly large. And, the eurozone's ongoing efforts to prevent sovereign debt defaults, as discussed in Chapters 4 and 5, have yet to lead to a sustainable financial architecture.

Complicating efforts by the IMF, central bankers and others to prevent and resolve country crises and to advance a better international financial architecture has been disagreement on how recent financial crises are related to the recent 'globalization' of economic activity. When the author published the first edition of *Financial Crises and Recession in the Global Economy* in 1994, a member of the US Federal Reserve Board concluded (in *Choice* magazine, January 1995) that the author 'grossly overstates [that financial globalization] is the principal cause and explanation of various events that Allen exaggeratedly refers to as crises'.

This book thus has two major goals: (1) to summarize the common patterns underlying severe economic crisis as well as their common explanations in the literature; and (2) to present some 'new thinking', which helps explain why we have not made much progress in avoiding crisis. Along the way, 'a new political economy of financial crisis' and a 'human ecology economics (HEE) framework' are advanced to guide research and policymaking in the future.

Regarding the new thinking presented in this book, key financial variables are shown to be driven somewhat more by subjective, even transcendental ('transcendental' of observable GDP or 'real' processes) psychological and social constructs than is commonly understood. Since the 1980s, structural changes in evolving financial markets, especially driven by advances in information-processing technology and government deregulation, have allowed a greater separation of financial market processes from GDP processes. Specifically, the demand for money-liquidity for financial market participation has become, especially during episodes of chaotic structural change, an important source of money demand which absorbs money-liquidity away from observable GDP uses. As a related process, monetary wealth can be created, transferred, and destroyed across time and space more powerfully and independently of observed GDP processes than is commonly understood. Also new to the literature, expanding our understanding of financial crisis is shown to be assisted by evolutionary and complex systems approaches, especially ones that privilege the role of interactive knowledge and belief systems. The relative rise and fall of interactive institutional and technological systems, or 'meso structures' in the language of evolutionary economics, is seen to play a key role in driving boom–bust patterns as well as other non-equilibrium episodes.

Sorting out these money supply and demand puzzles with econometric analysis, identifying key structural changes in historical financial trends, and delving further into the nature and uses of money, credit, capital, and wealth, all lead the author to the following conclusion: the recent crisis after 2007 arose from a 'long boom' dating from the early 1980s to its peak in 2006, and the 'bust phase' that began in 2007 will thus take longer to unwind—on a global systems basis—than predicted by those who saw the boom phase as a more recent and smaller bubble. The resources that the US Federal Reserve and US Treasury used to respond to the crisis, along with their counterparts in other countries, are extraordinary, however, and will likely have no historical precedent in magnitude. The economic recovery of the US and parts of Europe and elsewhere has come relatively quickly, but recovery is accompanied by expansion of central bank and Treasury deficits that are unprecedented in size and impose other challenges for long-term financing of governments.

Ironically, the many 'lesser' cases of financial crises and recession presented in earlier editions of this book cover the same time period as the long boom associated with the recent 'greater' crisis: the last two decades of the twentieth century and the very beginning of the twenty-first. Thus, smaller boom–bust patterns have occurred around the world while the recent greater boom progressed. Perhaps an even longer-scale 'super' financial cycle is now occurring within which the recent 'greater' crisis plays a lesser role. However, that longer-scale research is left to others such as Reinhart and Rogoff, and this *Fourth Edition* sticks with the period since 1980.

The organization of this *Fourth Edition* is chronological. Chapter 1 presents various processes of financial globalization since the 1970s, with emphasis on the institutional changes during the 'explosive 1980s' that are specifically relevant to finance. In light of the material in Chapter 1, Chapter 2 discusses financial trends and instabilities in the 1980s, Chapter 3 discusses financial trends and instabilities in the 1990s, Chapter 4 presents the recent crisis, especially 2007– in the US and Europe, and Chapter 5 summarizes this material while advancing a human ecology economics (HEE) approach to orient us toward the future and more effective policymaking.

This book is rooted more in the international economics, macro-economics, and international political economy literature than in other disciplines, but the author hopes that it is useful to a wide range of social scientists, practitioners, and policymakers. For the most part, case studies and explanations are not tailored to a particular discipline or professional interest group. If the reader has some practical experience in the international economy or some academic training in economics and related fields, then most of the discussions should be accessible. Unlike most scholarly books, there are many citations from periodicals such as *The Wall Street Journal*, *Financial Times*, and *The Economist* in addition to academic references. Of course, news of the latest financial crises floods these types of periodicals, and there is plenty of topical material to read. With this book the author hopes to provide the reader with a good historical perspective and academic framework through which to 'channel this flood' of financial news.

1. Financial globalization since the 1970s

Since the 1970s, the rapid expansion and globalization of financial markets shadows most other recent developments in international economics. This chapter documents and defines financial globalization and discusses what caused it: developments in information-processing technologies; government deregulation; and the more global nature of all economic activity. International interest rate and financial strategy 'parities' are presented as new, dominant, dynamic patterns in the global economy. Also in this chapter, it will be argued that financial market globalization has been a driving force behind recent imbalances in trade and investment between countries, and that the self-adjustment mechanisms within the global economy have been irreversibly changed by financial globalization.

An understanding of these recent structural changes provides a necessary introduction to subsequent chapters, where it will be argued that financial globalization processes are behind most of the major financial instabilities, trends, booms, and busts since the 1970s. In particular, what the author presents in Chapter 4 as 'the long boom' that extended from the early 1980s to its peak in 2006, as well as the recent global economic crisis that followed this boom, were both driven by financial globalization processes.

Richard O'Brien provides some helpful definitions of globalization processes, which can be applied to non-financial as well as financial markets:

> *International* means activities taking place between nations ... *multinational* describes activities taking place in more than one nation ... *global* should refer to operations within an integral whole, if it is to have a separate meaning from the foregoing terms. Global combines the elements of international and multinational with a strong degree of integration between the different national parts ... A truly global service knows no internal boundaries, can be offered throughout the globe, and pays scant attention to national aspects. The nation becomes irrelevant, even though it will still exist. The closer we get to a global, integral whole, the closer we get to the end of geography. (O'Brien, 1992, p. 5)

For the purposes of this book, O'Brien's definition of globalism is useful—operations taking place within an integrated whole whereby geographic boundaries are not important. Given the dramatic financial opening of China, the Soviet Union, and others since the 1970s, the 'integrated whole' increasingly includes most developing as well as developed countries.

I. THE RAPID EXPANSION OF INTERNATIONAL FINANCE, 1970–

Beginning in the 1970s and continuing at least to a peak in 2006 of 'the long boom' that preceded the recent global crisis, there was a continuing rapid expansion of international financial activity. The London Eurodollar market, now the major market for the world's largest financial institutions, was in its infancy several decades ago—turnover in the entire year of 1970 was $59 billion. But by the mid-1980s it was turning over $300 billion of financial capital on an average working day. This volume was many times the total reserves of the world's central banks and at least 25 times the value of world trade in merchandise and services. The Euromarket for all currencies (in which securities issuers avoid home country regulations) grew to several trillion dollars of outstanding securities by the late 1990s (Federal Reserve Bank of Kansas City, 1997, p. 300).

From 1980 to 1985, global foreign exchange trading volume doubled to a level of $150 billion per average working day, which was at least 12 times the value of world trade in merchandise and services. By 1990, the average volume of foreign exchange trading had reached $600 billion per day[1] and during the European currency crisis in late 1992, $1 trillion per day. Since 1992, daily trading has averaged over $1 trillion (Federal Reserve Bank of New York, 1995). Because each foreign exchange transaction involves two or more payments, it may be that $3.2 trillion moves through the foreign exchange settlement systems each day.[2]

Virtually every type of international financial asset experienced a similar explosion in trading, especially in the 1980s or 1990s, and the list of such assets seems endless. Notably, the cross-border trading of corporate stock, which had increased from $100 billion in 1980 to $800 billion in 1986, recovered from the world stock market crash of 1987 to reach $1.6 trillion by 1990 (ibid.). Short-term commercial paper borrowing by corporations, often with bank guarantees, grew from $40 billion in issues in 1970 to $700 billion in 1997 (Federal Reserve Bank of Kansas City, 1997, pp. 263–4).

The US government securities market, with $3 trillion of securities outstanding by the end of the 1980s and a daily turnover of more than $100 billion, became the largest single-asset capital market in the world. The certification of foreign firms as primary dealers gave this market a boost in the 1980s. Primary dealers, the first-round traders with the Federal Reserve Bank, have an advantage because large institutional investors prefer doing business with primary dealers. Because the buying and selling of government securities by the Federal Reserve Bank is the main instrument of US monetary policy, foreign firms and their foreign clients began to play an active role in US monetary affairs. Up to 30 percent of new US government borrowings were supplied by foreign, especially Japanese, firms by the mid-1980s. To downplay the significance of this, the Japanese securities firms were quick to point out that more than half of the clients for whom they traded US government securities were US citizens.[3] Currently, in mid-2016, approximately $20 trillion of US Treasury securities are outstanding, of which approximately $13.5 trillion are marketable all over the world.

International financial transactions denominated in US dollars increased, until by the late 1980s dollar holdings by foreign investors reached $1 trillion, over 60 percent of which were in Japanese banks. To put this number into perspective, $1 trillion was the annual amount being spent by the US federal government in the late 1980s, and equal to 20 percent of US annual gross domestic product (GDP).

The growth of 'offshore financial markets' since the 1970s as discussed below makes this type of data increasingly difficult to measure. But, it is likely that non-US-owned savings in dollars of almost $300 billion per year were made available for new uses in the global economy in the late 1990s compared to less than $150 billion per year in the early 1990s. Sixty percent of the world's money supply in recent decades has been provided by the US dollar, and more dollars circulate outside the US than inside.

By the end of the 1980s, global financial markets were generating a *net* international flow of funds of more than $3 trillion each month, that is, the flow of funds between countries which reconciles end of the month balance of payments data. The *gross* monthly flow was several orders of magnitude higher than this net flow, and it is increasingly impossible to measure given the often unregulated use of electronic funds transfers. Of the $3 trillion net monthly flow by the end of the 1980s, $2 trillion was so-called stateless money, which is virtually exempt from the control of any government or official institution, but available for use by all countries.[4]

Derivatives and other new exotic 'off-balance-sheet' contracts, which are based on underlying balance sheet assets such as stocks, bonds, and commodities, have also added to international finance. The Bank for International Settlements estimated that over-the-counter trading in derivatives, worldwide, was $1 trillion in 1995, based upon outstanding contracts worth $40.7 trillion. Outstanding contracts increased to $55 trillion by the late 1990s, and regulatory authorities had not yet found a way to get companies to account for derivatives on their balance sheets.[5] Also, daily turnover of exchange-listed (as opposed to over-the-counter) interest rate and futures derivatives contracts was even higher, based upon outstanding contracts worth $16.6 trillion (Bank for International Settlements, 1995). Of course, the rise of subprime mortgage securities, collateralized debt obligations, and other more recent bundled securities played a key role in the 2007– global crisis, as discussed in Chapter 4.

Eurodollars (dollars held in accounts outside the US), and many of the other new money and financial accounts and forms that have been created since the 1970s, often do not have reserve requirements in the banking system; therefore quasi-money and loans can be created based upon these accounts almost without limit. The rise of 'offshore finance' has encouraged this process, because offshore accounts usually do not have reserve requirements. Offshore finance can be defined as 'markets where operators are permitted to raise funds from non-residents and invest or lend that money to non-residents free from regulations and taxes'. Once money is raised, then without a reserve requirement it can be loaned, deposited, re-loaned, re-deposited, re-loaned, and so on in offshore markets without limits imposed by the banking system.

Offshore markets are generally categorized into three types: 'spontaneous' offshore sites, as in the UK and Hong Kong; 'International Banking Facilities' (IBFs) as in New York and Tokyo; and 'tax havens' as in the Cayman Islands and Switzerland. London became an offshore site 'spontaneously' after the new Thatcher government abolished foreign currency exchange controls in 1979. In the UK, minimum reserve requirements were then abolished in August 1981 for onshore banks. The Bank of England wanted to maintain them, but the commercial banks lobbied successfully to abolish them so that they could compete in the Eurocurrency business with non-British institutions.

IBFs, which are more stringently licensed and controlled, were allowed in the US after 1980 in order to compete with London and the tax havens of the Caribbean. Tokyo followed suit with its IBF in 1984. All offshore sites can have tax advantages, but the typical tax haven is inhabited by 'letterbox' or 'brass plate' companies who exist mostly on paper, with the real activity taking place in 'proper onshore' financial centers. Tax havens struggle with respectability and anonymity in order to both attract deposits and avoid regulations. The Bahamas, for example, was identified by the International Monetary Fund (IMF) as the third largest international financial center in 1983 after Britain and the US, in terms of foreign liabilities, but after much publicity about drug trafficking and corruption it slipped to seventh place. The net worth of assets held in offshore markets has been difficult to estimate, but through the 1990s and until the start of the recent crisis as late as December 2008, it was estimated at $6 trillion or approximately 20 percent of world GDP.[6]

Since the 1990s, according to some estimates, 'as much as half of the world's stock of money either resides in, or is passing through, tax havens' (Kochen, 1991, p. 73). According to IMF data, the Caymans and the Bahamas together held approximately $400 billion in foreign liabilities in 1990, which compared with $1,073 billion in foreign liabilities held in the UK, $659 held in Japan, and $584 billion held in the US (of which the New York IBF held $333 billion). Much of the money in tax havens is held by 'residents', and is therefore not included as part of foreign liabilities. The nine tax havens of the Caribbean have been home to half of the world's insurance companies and 15 percent of the world's merchant shipping companies. In addition, individual private savings of $500 billion was held in tax havens in 1993—an amount of money approximately equal to the entire savings of the world's 'super-rich' (Norton, 1993). Thus, Lord Rees-Mogg (1993) warned:

> The world has never seen anything quite like this before. Governments are unlikely to recover their control of finance . . . Any future attempts to restore capital controls or regain taxing power are quite implausible . . . American and European welfare systems which depend on high tax may become insolvent. In the new world 'tax the rich' has ceased to be an option; the rich are not going to sit around waiting to be taxed.[7]

More recently, The Boston Consulting Group reckons that on paper roughly $8 trillion of private financial wealth out of a global total of $123 trillion sits offshore, but this excludes property, yachts and other fixed assets. And, over 30 percent of global foreign direct investment (FDI) is booked through havens.[8] And, financial assets held in all of the world's 55–60 offshore banking sites could be as much as $20 trillion.[9]

Since the 1990s, when international trade data is added up for all countries, world export revenues have fallen short of import expenditures by approximately $100 billion per year. Economists agree that much of this $100 billion represents a true shortfall (not just measurement error) of money which is not repatriated but instead is added to offshore finance. When combined with other flows that add to the stock of money in offshore markets, it may be that offshore markets are directing as much money as onshore markets.

Through the mid-1990s, approximately 60 percent of the world's official money reserves was held in US dollars, 20 percent in German marks, and 10 percent in Japanese yen. This dominance of the dollar, and this 90 percent dominance of the 'big three' did not change much after the euro replaced the mark and other European currencies at the end of the 1990s.

Table 1.1   Sources and uses of foreign savings in dollars ($billion)

	1992	1993	1994	1995	1996
Sources					
Accumulating in offshore financial markets	45	50	55	65	75
Non-US purchases of dollar bonds and notes	10	20	25	30	45
Capital flight	35	40	50	55	40
Direct and equity investment in the US	10	60	50	60	85
Net flows out of the reserves of:	0	40	80	65	20
Industrial countries[1]					
LDCs[2] Fuel exporters	0	0	−20	10	5
Non-fuel exporters	40	30	15	10	15
Total	140	240	255	295	285
Uses					
Net financing in dollars by:	−35	−100	−20	−20	−25
Industrial countries (ex-US)					
LDCs Fuel exporters [3]	10	20	25	25	15
Non-fuel exporters	35	55	30	50	50
US direct and portfolio investment abroad[4]	60	160	70	80	90
US current account deficit	70	105	150	160	155
Total	140	240	255	295	285

Notes:
1. Additions to the US Treasury's holdings of foreign currency subtract from this total.
2. Less developed countries (LDCs).
3. Mexico is included under this heading.
4. US purchases of foreign currency bonds are added to this total.

Source: Brown (1996, p. 119).

In offshore financial markets, compared to the entire global economy, the US dollar has an unknown, but significantly larger share of the *stock* of money reserves. What has been possible to estimate is the yearly *flow* of foreign (non-US) savings of dollars. Table 1.1 shows a rare estimate of the annual sources and uses of US dollar financial flows outside the US, for 1992–96.

Table 1.1 estimates that, in the 1990s, there was a flow of more than $50 billion dollars per year into offshore financial markets from international transactions wherein money was not repatriated (or measured) through official national balance of payments statistics. This flow is then a non-US *source* of dollars that can be used for just about anything in the global economy, and it is increasing. The same comments apply to the separate category of capital flight, which also adds approximately $50 billion per year into the available supply of non-US-held dollars.

By definition there is no firm data for capital flight, because it describes funds which leave a country in secret or disguised accounts to avoid taxes, political risks, inconvertibility risks, and so on. Other sources of non-US-held dollars, which are made available to the global economy each year, include dollars held in other countries which 'materialize' from private sources to buy dollar bonds, notes, direct and equity investments, and dollars which are 'freed-up' in other countries from official national reserve accounts. The grand total of non-US-held dollars, which were made available for use in the global financial markets each year, rose from an estimated $140 billion in 1992 to almost $300 billion in 1995 and 1996.

Because of the rise of offshore finance, perhaps a quarter of the world's money stock (m) is not subject to significant reserve requirements. Thus, quasi-money, loans, and effective money flow can be created on the basis of a process of deposit lending and added to the world system almost without limit—the offshore financial markets can expand as long as the players remain profitable. Many of the players are limited by national regulations where they do other business, and they cannot expand off-shore business beyond a certain share of onshore business. However, some players have no such regulations, and they are the modern-day equivalents of private goldsmiths in the European Renaissance. Dollar-credits today, just like gold-notes in the Renaissance, can be issued almost without limit, that is, as long as all private parties to the issuance profit from the use of those notes.

Central to this book, including explanations for the financial crises and recessions discussed in later chapters, is the existence and use of what the author would call this 'global money and credit pyramid', or what was called the 'global savings glut' by Federal Reserve Board Governor Ben Bernanke (Bernanke, 2005). As the volume and speed of international money and credit transfers increases, the risk of more dramatic boom, turning point, and bust stages of large-scale money-liquidity crises also increases.

II. THE GLOBAL INFORMATION REVOLUTION AND GLOBAL FINANCE

A financial transaction can loosely be defined as any business arrangement where money changes hands but the only other thing that changes hands is documentation. Both money and documentation are moved by information technologies; therefore financial market activity is enhanced by advances in those technologies. Expanding use and performance of electronic and regular mail service, telephones, computers, fax machines, image-processing devices, communication satellites, fiber optics, the internet, and so on creates better opportunities and more profits in financial services.

In fact, no sector of the global economy spends more on information technology than financial services: $500 billion globally in 2009, compared to (in descending order) $433 billion spent on information technology by the global manufacturing sector, $390 billion spent by governments, $211 billion spent by retail and wholesale trade, $202 billion spent by communications companies, and so on.[10]

The explosion of information technologies in recent decades did parallel the explosion of international finance as discussed in the previous section. For example, in 1946 the world had only one widely recognized computer, the ENIAC, built at the University of Pennsylvania, weighing 30 tons, utilizing 18,000 vacuum tubes, standing two stories high, covering 15,000 square feet, and costing several million dollars. In 1956, there were 600 computers in the US, in 1968, 30,000, in 1976, half a million, in 1988, several million, and by the end of the century half of all the households in the US had a free-standing computer.

Transistors were invented at Bell Laboratories in 1947 and integrated circuits—the ability to put large numbers of transistors on one silicon chip—were developed in the late 1950s. But by the late 1980s one memory chip could hold as many as one million bits of information. Computer technology benefited from the convergence of three breakthroughs: artificial intelligence, whereby computers solve problems by manipulating symbols and decision rules, making inferences and other probability decisions, and generally simulating human methods of intelligence; silicon compilers, which allow the complete design of integrated computer circuits on a computer by any computer-literate person with a $50,000 work station; and massively parallel processing, whereby many computer operations occur simultaneously. Carver Mead of the California Institute of Technology, one of the industry experts and the inventor of the silicon compiler, estimated that these and other developments resulted in a 10,000-fold increase in the cost-effectiveness of information-based computer technology over the last two decades of the twentieth century.[11]

Other major scientific developments that fueled the information revolution were the development of fiber optic cables, a few pounds of which can now carry as much information as a ton of copper cables; and continuing development and deployment of communication satellites, which bounce information around the world at nearly the speed of light. A single communication satellite now displaces many tons of copper wire, and this displacement factor is increasing. By the mid-1980s approximately 60 percent of the trans-Pacific foreign currency trading and 50 percent of the trans-Atlantic foreign currency trading were done via satellite transmissions,[12] which allowed for a greatly increased global flow of funds.

In the late 1980s, the telecommunications industry became the largest source of new jobs in the US and perhaps the world. Although the jobs were so scattered among equipment manufacturers, installers, and users that they were hard to keep track of, it was estimated in 1986 that more than 2 million were employed in this industry in the US, and the number was growing by 200,000 each year.[13] In the US fewer letters were written in the 1980s, but there were more telephone calls—an average of four calls per day per person. More calls were made through computer modems to retrieve information from databases. In 1980, very few US homes had modems, but by the late 1980s close to one million homes had them.[14] This technology and others, including the facsimile (fax) machine, enhanced the efficiency of legal and business documentation. First generation fax machines from the 1970s took six minutes to send one page of documentation, but by the late 1980s the transmission time was down to three seconds and the popularity boomed. In 1987, 460,000 facsimile machines were installed in the US, compared to 190,000 in 1986.[15] By the early 1990s, there were over one million installations per year. By the late 1980s, more than $100 million worth of video teleconferencing services and equipment were sold in the US each year, and prices were declining by an average of 15 percent per year. Many corporations began using full-motion images, such as those of a sporting event, in their teleconferences. To handle all of this growth in the late 1980s, the capacity of international data circuits had to rise by 40 percent per year.[16]

By the year 2000, private bank telecommunications networks included Manufacturers Hanover Trust's T1 (high-speed) backbone network between its US locations which linked with its global X.25 packet-switching network based on Telnet (now Sprint) hardware and software that connects 52 cities in 27 foreign countries. In the 1980s, Citibank developed 100 separate private networks covering 92 countries, which were combined into an integrated global information network (GIN) in 1992. Chase has a similar network provided by Tymnet, which is owned by British Telecom, and Bank of America has a similar network to support its World Banking Division. Bankers Trust (purchased by Deutsche Bank in 1998) is noted for preferring earth-based to satellite links in its system in order to avoid several-second delays. In Europe, the Belgian-based Society for Worldwide Interbank Financial Telecommunications (SWIFT) was handling message volumes that rose from 3.2 million in 1977 to 604 million in 1995.

Changes in communications have always affected the structure of finance, but these developments of the last few decades were responsible for the truly global nature of today's financial markets. As participants used these new technologies and networks, linkages were formed between various national and international sub-economy financial markets. New international opportunities have occurred for centuries, but only recently has inter-dependence become so pervasive to merit the word 'global'. The transatlantic cable was completed way back in 1867, and the price of the dollar in London could then be found out in two minutes rather than two weeks. Even further back in the history of information finance, the Rothschilds used carrier pigeons to gain advance (and therefore profitable) news of the Napoleonic wars. Perhaps no single example of new international financial technology in the last few decades is more important than these, but thousands of lesser examples have been collectively more important in the globalization process.

The switching of financial markets from paper-driven trading floors to computer screens, as with America's NASDAQ and its hookups with London's 'off-(the London Stock) exchange market', is one example of how a new computer-based technology encouraged global trading. It was estimated that between $200 million and $300 million of foreign stock shares changed hands daily in London's off-exchange market in the UK's 'Big Bang' deregulation year of 1986, roughly double the levels of 1981, with half of that volume in US stocks.[17] That level equaled as much as half the volume on the London Stock Exchange, which also trades many non-British securities.

By 2000, networks which handled staggering amounts of money included the Clearing House Interbank Payments System (CHIPS) run by private banks out of New York. CHIPS mostly handles foreign exchange and other large-value, wholesale-level international transactions, and the net settlement of its transactions is in dollar reserves through the Federal Reserve Bank of New York. Transfers through CHIPS increased from $16 trillion in 1977 to more than $310 trillion in 1997. The Federal Reserve's Fedwire is its electronic facility, which transfers reserve balances among private banks through dedicated wire and is the favored system for large domestic transfers. Transfers through Fedwire increased from $2.6 trillion in 1977 to more than $225 trillion in 1997. On a daily basis, CHIPS and Fedwire now move more than $2 trillion. Retail systems such as credit and debit cards transfer an additional several hundred billion dollars per day. These daily recorded flows amount to half the entire broad money (m3) stock of the US, and more than one-third of the US gross domestic product for the whole year (Solomon, 1997, p. 7). Compared to the US, Europe uses even more electronic transfers; for example, its GIRO credit transfer system sends money directly from the buyer's account to the seller's and accounts for 19 percent of transactions, whereas indirect and debit-based checks account for only 2 percent.

Countless other new technologies which enhanced the opportunities in boundary-less electronic finance include automatic transfer machines (ATMs), electronic points of sale, telephone banking, interactive screen communications between financial intermediaries and their wholesale and retail customers, ever more innovative debit and credit and smart cards, and even electronic wallets. Computer, telecommunications, and other 'non-bank' firms have begun to enter these markets. The Discover card was originally offered by the retailer Sears in the 1980s, and then sold to the brokerage firm Dean Witter. Shortly after, AT&T's Universal credit card began offering Visa or MasterCard through Universal Bank. Globalization of plastic payment cards is now being realized. Worldwide spending at merchant locations on general-purpose cards totaled $1.47 trillion in 1995, and increased to $3.26 trillion in 2000 and $6.43 trillion in 2005. Of the 1995 total, the US had a 47.5 percent share, Europe 25.8 percent, and Asia/Pacific 18.0 percent.[18] Perhaps globalization of payment systems will move from plastic to the internet with alliances between companies like Microsoft and banks, as per Bill Gates' vision of 'frictionless capitalism' on the internet (Gates et al., 1995).

Most recently, 'blockchain' technology and 'distributed ledgers', which underpin the decentralized digital currency bitcoin, are being used as databases that are maintained collaboratively by all users, rather than by a single authority such as a bank. However, central banks are exploring the possibilities of virtual currency supported by these technologies, which could save on printing and administrative costs, be tougher to counterfeit, and be harder to use for illicit activity.[19]

Electronic banking programs have been used for as long as the internet has been popular—approximately three decades. The phrase that stuck was 'electronic funds transfer' (EFT), and EFT systems have allowed 'fast money' or 'hot money' flows, and now 'virtual money'. Virtual money is a catchphrase for a host of innovative payment forms such as electronic (e-) cash and digital money. As with internet communications, virtual money deliveries can be non-centralized and 'non-physical' beyond the 0–1 on–off digital switching of computer systems.

Virtual money systems are not always subject to banking regulations. For example, in Hong Kong, by the end of the 1990s, the Octopus card system had created HK$4 billion ($516 million) of electronic money in an economy with approximately HK$100 billion of currency and coins circulating. E-money transactions in the Octopus system amounted to HK$17 billion per day. Octopus cards, owned by two-thirds of the local population, are easily read by sensors without waiting. The Octopus system is run as a joint venture by various transport companies, and is not technically a bank, but the companies are free to 'reuse' and invest most of the HK$4 billion in customer deposits. Whether risk management and funds on hand are sufficient to cover reliably customer redemptions of the float is continually under review by the Hong Kong Monetary Authority.

What remains to be seen is the degree to which new virtual money systems create new money stock, versus the degree to which these systems merely move around 'real money' which already exists in bank accounts in deposit form. Chapter 2 develops this issue further, by relating the money stock and its velocity of circulation to the 'real' growth of financial and non-financial markets. Increasingly, it is difficult to know whether economy-wide growth in total transactions is being accommodated by increased money stock or increased velocity of circulation of money. Perhaps the distinction between money 'stock' and 'circulation of the stock' will become less useful as the monetary system co-evolves with new information-processing technologies.

More of the money stock moves as electromagnetic waves or photon particles. The average retail user of money still depends mostly on paper money and plastic cards, but the multinational corporation or financial institution or trader relies mostly on satellite and fiber optic routing. The large wholesale amounts are transferred electronically. In 1995 the US Federal Reserve estimated the *value* of US electronic transactions at $544 trillion, check transactions at $73 trillion, and currency and coin transactions at $2.2 trillion; however, the physical number or *volume* of currency and coin transactions was estimated at 550 billion, check transactions at 62 billion, and electronic transactions at 19 billion.

III.   GOVERNMENTAL DEREGULATION AND INTERNATIONAL FINANCE

The globalization of financial markets has also been encouraged by government deregulation. In the 1980s, especially, governments began abandoning financial market protectionism, deciding instead that the benefits provided to their citizens by the new international opportunities would outweigh any losses to previously protected groups.

Linked together with new information-processing technologies by the 1980s, borrowers and lenders were completing transactions in new international markets that were more profitable than any opportunities within the old domestic markets. Governments recognized the value of giving their citizens access to the new international markets, especially before other countries extended the same opportunities to their citizens. As with any profitable new markets, those who were able to participate first were often the most successful. Eventually, as competition increased, the profitability was reduced to more normal levels.

A threshold was reached by the early 1980s: governments began rushing toward financial market deregulation and internationalization in order to capture a large share of the new profitability for their own money centers, and in order to attract new international funds into their own economies. Policymakers removed ceilings on interest rates, reduced taxes and brokerage commissions on financial transactions, gave foreign financial firms greater access to the home financial markets, allowed increased privatization and securitization of assets, and took other steps which allowed money to move more freely and profitably between international and national markets.

Much of the global deregulation movement came from the Reagan/ Thatcher supply-side movement of the early 1980s in which the private markets were encouraged to take the lead—often without a clear understanding of what 'free markets' mean in international finance. Speaking to the author's class years later, the early 1980s US Comptroller of the Currency stated that he, Reagan, Federal Reserve Chairman Volcker, and others 'believed in the principle of free market finance, but we could not have possibly imagined the long run consequences'.

Deregulation was advanced under the consensus that financial market protectionism had failed. For example, The US Interest Equalization Tax of the 1960s was a form of protectionism; various US lenders were taxed for lending overseas, and immediately reduced their foreign activities and increased their domestic business. A long-run problem with protectionism, however, especially in financial markets, is that businesspeople usually find a way around the protectionism. The Interest Equalization Tax reduced taxable capital outflows from the US to negligible amounts in 1964, but non-taxable outflows rose to fill the gap by 1966. The tax encouraged the development of international financial markets, especially in Europe, that US banks could lend from, but which US policymakers could not regulate. New 'non-European' bond issues in Europe increased from less than \$200 million in 1962 to nearly \$1.5 billion in 1966.[20] The Interest Equalization Tax was finally removed in 1974.

Other regulations that had shifted US bank activity to the Euromarkets were Regulation Q on interest rate ceilings, the Foreign Credit Restraint Program, and rules of the Office for Foreign Direct Investment. These types of regulations were dismantled in the 1980s.

On 1 April 1986, the US government ended the 5.5 percent interest rate ceiling on passbook accounts as the last stage in its deregulation of consumer interest rates paid by banks and savings and loan institutions. Especially important in this process had been the creation of automatic transfer services (ATS) in 1978, negotiable order of withdrawal (NOW) accounts in 1981, and Super NOW accounts in 1983. These are checkable 'money' accounts which, for the first time, offered interest rates high enough to attract funds which otherwise would be put into 'non-money' financial assets such as stocks, bonds, and money market funds (MMFs). By 1984, 8 percent of all checking accounts at US banks and 30 percent of all checking accounts at US thrifts were Super NOW accounts (Fortier and Phillis, 1985), which were able to pay interest rates almost as high as MMFs.

Also in 1986, three of Japan's biggest securities firms were allowed to become primary dealers in US government securities. Nomura and Daiwa Securities Companies were then able to trade directly with the New York Federal Reserve Bank as part of their battle for global markets. Additionally, the Industrial Bank of Japan gained this privilege via its purchase of primary dealer Aubrey G. Lanston & Co. On that date five other foreign firms—one Canadian, one Australian, one from Hong Kong, and two British institutions—already owned primary dealers.[21]

The US Glass–Steagall laws of the 1930s, which separate commercial and investment banking, were also slowly dismantled in the 1980s and 1990s despite some attempts at re-regulation during each financial crisis. US banks could then trade stocks for their customers, but non-bank commercial enterprises could not generally own banks. Of course, since the 2007– financial crisis re-regulation has been significant, including conversion of all remaining investment banks in the US into bank holding companies (allowing greater Federal Reserve benefits and oversight), and some restoration and oversight of the lines between commercial and investment banking (i.e. the 2010 Dodd–Frank Wall Street Reform and Consumer Protection Act, and a new section 13 to the Bank Holding Company Act of 1956, which is commonly referred to as the new Volcker rule).

UK financial deregulation in the 1980s paralleled that in the US, and due to the international dominance of New York and London as financial centers, these two countries influenced financial developments elsewhere. In October 1979 the UK removed all inward and outward barriers to capital flows. Consequently, Britain experienced an annual portfolio investment outflow for the 1980–83 period that was 1,800 times higher than in the 1975–78 period (Taylor and Tonks, 1989).

Finally, on 26 October 1986 London's 'Big Bang' financial market deregulation scrapped 85 years of fixed commissions for brokers as well as separation of powers between brokers. As stated by John M. Hennessy, chairman of Crédit Suisse First Boston Ltd., a leading international investment bank based in London, 'Big Bang is an attempt to generate a few global competitors among the British institutions'.[22] Competition increased immediately. Forty-nine firms, including American, European, and Far East financial giants, had signed up before 26 October to market British stocks and government bonds; only 19 companies had been doing this trading previously.[23] In addition, after 26 October commissions charged by financial intermediaries dropped as much as 50 percent.

Recognizing the more integrated and global nature of their financial system, the European Community Commission began moving toward a unified financial services market for the 12 Common Market countries (by 1992), including uniform lending restrictions and reporting of large loans.[24] Also, as of 1992 all international banks subject to the auspices of the Bank for International Settlements (most developed countries and in the future some LDCs) must meet common capital adequacy targets—the first real attempt at a global standard for banking.

Anxious not to lose business to New York and London, other countries embraced the international financial markets in the 1980s. On 4 December 1986, the Ontario, Canada, government announced that it would open the highly restricted Canadian securities industry to unrestricted access by foreigners and Canadian financial institutions. Previous law prohibited foreigners and Canadians outside the securities industry from owning more than 10 percent of a securities dealer. Under the new regulations, foreigners could own 50 percent of a Canadian securities dealer after 30 June 1987 and 100 percent after 30 June 1988.[25]

By 1984, Japan had given US banks virtually free access to many of the Tokyo financial markets including the underwriting of Japanese government bonds. The Japanese government had decontrolled most national interest rates by the late 1980s, thus finishing a process started in 1979, when increased competition was created between Japanese banks, securities firms, and insurance companies. Notably, Japanese reform of the Foreign Exchange and Foreign Trade Control law in December 1980 allowed these companies greater ability to issue bonds, buy and sell securities, and hold foreign currency deposits. While the holding of foreign securities by Japanese insurance companies has been restricted, statutory limits have not been binding, and these insurance companies have increased their holdings. And, by the mid-1980s, US securities firms had become active players in the Tokyo market. Paine Webber opened a large Tokyo branch office in April 1986; Morgan Stanley & Co. at that time had built a Tokyo staff of 160; Goldman, Sachs & Co. had 60 people; Salomon Brothers had 80; and Merrill Lynch had 260. And, what has been called Japan's 'Big Bang' occurred in April 1998 when the Foreign Exchange Law abolished the remaining restrictions on international financial transactions.

Mr. Yusuke Kashiwagi, chairman of the Bank of Tokyo, correctly prophesied during an important lecture to the IMF in Washington in September

1986, that Tokyo would be linked with New York and London to form a 'three-part axis of global finance'.[26] Tokyo sits in a time zone between New York and London and it makes a natural bridge for 24-hour-a-day trading. Mr. Kashiwagi estimated that the American financial market had an annual volume of $7.1 trillion in 1986, Japan was second in the world with $2.2 trillion, and Great Britain was third at $1.6 trillion. Between 1970 and 1985, Japan's financial markets grew at the rate of 18.3 percent per year, Great Britain's at 14.5 percent, and the US's at 8.8 percent. Integration between these markets has more recently made it difficult to estimate separate statistics. The US Federal Reserve Bank's funds transfer business day has been extended to now begin at 9:00 p.m. (Eastern time) on the preceding calendar day (rather than 8:30 a.m. on the calendar day of the transfer) and ends at 6.30 p.m. so that the system can receive and process foreign exchange transactions while both European and Asian markets are also open. Related initiatives by banks from most large industrial countries have also created limited-purpose banks to clear foreign exchange transactions and thus remove payment delays in CHIPS.

Germany's major deregulation was its liberalization of foreign exchange controls in March 1981. International capital movements were also encouraged when Germany abolished its withholding tax on interest payments to foreigners in August 1984—one month after the US had removed its withholding tax, and during the same several months that Japan reciprocated.

The process of financial globalization was further encouraged in the 1980s where there was a need to reduce budget deficits, because governments now had a ready source of funds in the international privatization of their assets. For example, after Mitterrand's socialist revolution lost support in France and Chirac was elected Prime Minister in 1986, the center-right coalition embarked on an ambitious denationalization program to privatize ownership of many large companies. An unexpectedly popular $40 billion sell-off of government corporations to the private sector seemed to mark the end of the socialist revolution. The denationalization program allowed foreign investors to buy up to 20 percent of the newly privatized firms. In October 1986, the British broker Morgan Grenfell Securities International placed a $100 million package of French securities with US and British institutional investors, the biggest transaction of its kind in French history.[27] By January 1990, France had completed its piecemeal liberalization of foreign capital flow regulations.

Even the historically closed China and USSR began developing links with global financial markets in the explosive mid-1980s. In November 1986, a group of top Wall Street executives met with high Chinese political and financial officials in Peking for talks on how securities markets should be run and on how financial capital can be raised. Stock trading in China began on 26 September 1986 for the first time since the Communists took power in 1949: the Jingan-district branch of Shanghai Trust & Investment Co., China's main venue for stock trading, eventually had to move in December 1986 from a branch office measuring only 430 square feet to a new location five times as large.[28]

Besides beginning to trade local issues in securities markets, China also sold more than $2.5 billion of debt securities on international markets in 1985 and 1986 and began developing a modern banking system.[29] China's five-year plan for 1986–90 resulted in approximately $30 billion in new foreign loans, which increased China's foreign debt from $14 billion to $40 billion over that period. China issued its first Eurodollar bonds in August 1987, two months after settling a 38-year dispute with the British government over defaulted bonds and British assets that were seized during the Communist uprising in 1949.[30]

Perhaps the most significant economic change in the USSR during the Gorbachev period was the increased access to Western financial markets. In 1987 the USSR settled czarist debts with Britain and Switzerland in order to gain access to the European bond markets. In 1988, the USSR had its first public bond offering on the international capital markets and owed $25.9 billion to Western commercial banks compared to $11.3 billion in 1985.[31]

In non-Soviet Eastern Europe, also like the USSR suffering economic decline in the 1980s in most regions, regulatory reforms and attempts to sustain economic growth in 1990 were defined largely by a new dependence on foreign debt. Western grants and low-cost credits of more than $1.5 billion were provided for non-Soviet Eastern Europe in 1990, and additional, non-concessional Western bilateral and multilateral credits of $5.3 billion were arranged for 1990–92 (Allen, 1991, p. 477). To raise funds, in the spring of 1990, Hungary, Poland, and Czechoslovakia began selling hundreds of state-owned enterprises to private international enterprises, and international joint business ventures in non-Soviet Eastern Europe increased dramatically after 1989 to a total, in 1990, of approximately 500 in Czechoslovakia and well over 1,000 in both Poland and Hungary. Approximately $100 billion of business assets in non-Soviet Eastern Europe were identified for sale in the early 1990s, an amount approximately equal to the foreign debt of this region before the revolutions of 1989 and 1990.[32]

IV. INTEREST RATE AND FINANCIAL STRATEGY PARITIES

The globalization of financial markets has meant that borrowers, lenders, and other investors have increased ability to make inexpensive international contracts through financial intermediaries. Globalization is encouraged by the information revolution, which makes businesspeople and financial intermediaries more aware of, and networked to, all the international opportunities, so that the financial markets become more dynamic and price competitive. Dynamic means that the reactions of market participants are quickly provoked and accommodated. Price competitive means that no businessperson or financial intermediary has a strong pricing advantage over others for a significant period of time. For example, each must accept the interest rate for certain types of transactions that the global market produces.

Some efficiencies result from the dynamic, price-competitive nature of the globalized financial market. Financial intermediaries must adopt the cheapest information-based technologies that can reliably perform the necessary services if they are to profitably survive. Embracing the information revolution is crucial to them. Also, financial intermediaries must be well informed about the needs of their customers. If they do not supply the mix of financial services which their customers are most willing to pay for, then they will also be competed out of the global market.

With fewer restrictions on international financial transactions, interest rates—or more precisely the total expected return including foreign currency risk—for similar types of loans are more uniform around the globe, and these new global interest rates are lower than the average of all the old national interest rates. The new global interest rates are lower, because low interest rate lenders have dramatically expanded their international business outside domestic markets, which has also expanded international loan volumes. There has been a net expansion of the volume of loans because more people have borrowed at the lower global interest rates. The issuers of the low interest rate loans have profitably expanded to accommodate these new borrowers.

For example, the high interest rates in international markets in the early 1980s were in US dollars, and the low interest rates were in Japanese yen and German marks. Then, as financial markets were rapidly deregulated and integrated between 1983 and 1988, the dollar's share of international lending fell from 72 percent to 53 percent as US banks and thrifts were outcompeted, the yen's share increased from 3 percent to 10 percent, and the mark's share increased from 5 percent to 10 percent.[33] In addition, the volume of international lending increased faster than at any time in modern history, as average interest rates in the global economy were cut in half. Also, interest rates in the major currencies moved closer together during this period. Long-term dollar interest rates adjusted for inflation had reached a peak of 10 percent in the middle of 1984, but then declined steadily to 3.5 percent at the end of 1986. But the comparable yen and mark interest rates rose slightly over this period.

An important equilibrium position of globalized financial markets is called 'interest rate parity' (IRP). First, IRP requires that national and international interest rates for the same types of loans in the same currency have to be equal. Otherwise, arbitragers would simultaneously borrow in one market and lend in another and make tremendous profits, profits much greater than could ever be attained from merchandise and services trade. In the early 1980s, financial market arbitrage became much more profitable on the margin than merchandise and services trade. Therefore, the fully arbitraged IRP-seeking equilibrium position of financial markets became the driving force that merchandise and services trade conformed to. This dominance of IRP beginning in the 1980s differed from more traditional thinking whereby financial transactions were instead believed to accommodate merchandise and services trade.

Using the equality of national and international interest rates in the same currency as a measure of the globalization of national financial markets, it is clear that many types of financial transactions between the major industrial countries became fully globalized in the early 1980s. For example, between October 1983 and May 1984 the average differential between three-month Eurodollar interest rates and the corresponding rates in New York was only 0.1 percentage points. The same test comparing Deutsche mark interest rates in the Euromarket and German markets showed a differential of 0.04 percentage points.[34]

Frankel (1989) has shown that domestic versus international own-currency interest rate differentials for Germany collapsed in 1974 when most capital inflow restrictions were removed. The differential for Italy and France collapsed in about mid-1986 when capital outflow restrictions were removed in those two countries and the European Monetary System (EMS) was realigned. Also, Artis and Taylor (1989) have shown that this differential tended toward zero in the UK after inward and outward capital controls were removed in October 1979.

Japan's case study also shows the relationship between financial market deregulation and globalization in the early 1980s. Between 1975 and 1979, before Japanese deregulation, the differential between three-month yen interest rates in the Eurocurrency and Japanese markets averaged a large 2.06 percentage points. The Japanese government began removing the restrictions on its financial markets in the early 1980s, and in 1984 this interest rate differential had been reduced to 0.31 percentage points. Finally, in 1985, Japan's financial markets, with respect to these statistics, had become as globalized as those in the US, UK, and Germany—this yen interest rate differential had dropped to 0.05 percentage points (Artis and Taylor, 1989).

Second, IRP requires that the same types of loans, which have been insured against foreign currency risk, produce the same total return for the investor even though they are denominated in different currencies. Currency risk can be covered or hedged away via transactions in the forward-looking markets.

For example, suppose that dollar interest rates were currently 8 percent, euro interest rates were 13 percent, and the current spot market exchange rate was $1 for 1.5 euros. Suppose also that one could agree today to swap $1 for 1.57 euros one year from now. If an investor had his/her savings in dollars today but wanted his/her savings converted into euros one year from now, should he/she (a) convert on the spot market today at $1/1.5 euros and begin earning 13 percent on his newly acquired euros; or (b) agree today to convert one year from now at the $1/1.57 euros future rate and continue earning 8 percent on his dollars until that time; or (c) continue earning 8 percent on his dollars and convert them into euros one year from now at whatever the spot market exchange rate happened to be then?

Ignoring commissions and any other transactions costs, options (a) and (b) would produce the same euro savings one year from now with certainty. For example, savings of $100 under option (a) would be converted into 150 euros today and earn (150 euros × 0.13) = 19.5 euros in interest for a total of 169.5 euros one year from now, and under option (b) savings of $100 would earn interest of ($100 × 0.08) = $8 for a total of $108 one year from now which would then be converted with the futures contract at $1/1.57 euros. The $108 would thus be converted into (108 × 1.57) = 169.5 euros one year from now. (Note: these calculations are approximate, and exact equations are developed in textbooks.)

The risk-free equivalence of options (a) and (b) demonstrates the IRP equilibrium for different currencies, and it is summarized as follows: the current interest rate differential between currencies (in this case a 5 percent differential in favor of the euro) must be eliminated by the difference in the spot versus forward exchange rate (in this case the dollar carries a forward premium against the euro of approximately 5 percent from 1.5 to 1.57) to yield the same total return for options (a) and (b).

For the major currencies with well-developed, forward-looking market opportunities, such as those that are actively traded in the Eurocurrency markets, 100 percent of the deviations from (a) and (b) equivalence could be accounted for by commissions and other normal transactions costs by the late 1980s (Taylor, 1988), a result called 'covered interest parity'. When arbitrage eliminates differences in national versus Eurocurrency interest rates on the same currency, it also eliminates differences in the risk-free total return on different currencies. In the above example, money would be moved between dollar and euro loans until interest rates and/or forward versus spot exchange rate differentials adjusted to produce the equivalence. Non-equivalence could not be sustained because of the tremendous profit-seeking flows of capital that would exploit the inefficiency until equivalence was produced.

Option (c) in the above example would expose the investor to currency risk, unlike options (a) and (b), and therefore may or may not be used given his/her risk tolerance. If used, option (c) would result in a superior return to options (a) and (b) if the spot exchange rate for $1 appreciates above 1.57 euros at year-end, and option (c) would produce a lower return if the dollar ended the year lower than 1.57 euros. In other words, whether or not the spot rate ends the forward-looking time period above or below today's risk-free forward rate will determine the benefit of speculating as per option (c) versus hedging as per options (a) and (b). Therefore, beliefs about future spot rates may also lead to tremendous profit-seeking flows of capital and realignment of interest rates and exchange rates until investors believe option (c) to be equally desirable to options (a) and (b).

If option (c) produces the same return as (a) and (b) the result is called uncovered interest parity. However, most research indicates that substantial errors in predicting future spot rates does not allow for uncovered interest parity (Frankel and Froot, 1989). In other words, the risk-free forward rate is not a good predictor of the future spot rate, and speculators must assume substantial risk when accepting option (c).

As currency exchange rates adjusted as part of the process whereby IRP was achieved in the 1980s, international currency-adjusted prices for merchandise were pushed substantially out of alignment, as discussed later in Section V of this chapter. Therefore, trade balances have fluctuated wildly as driven by these financial processes, and historic relationships between currency exchange rates and trade balances have no longer prevailed. Purchasing power parity (PPP), the theory that currency exchange rates move up or down to equate national and international prices of merchandise and services (and thus trade is always rebalanced), has become unreliable for forecasting purposes. For example, no longer does a country's currency necessarily increase in value if it has an export price advantage and is selling more merchandise and services to the rest of the world than vice versa. If an export-driven country is able to lower the interest rates on its currency, its currency could even depreciate due to a substantial outflow of investment funds to higher interest rate currencies.

*Table 1.2   Purchasing power parity exchange rate levels of one US dollar
            (versus actual exchange rates)*

	1990	1993	1995	1997
Japan (yen)	195 (134)	184 (112)	169 (103)	163 (130)
Germany (mark)	2.09 (1.49)	2.10 (1.73)	2.02 (1.43)	2.00 (1.79)

Source: Organisation for Economic Co-operation and Development (OECD).

Table 1.2 shows just how much the exchange rate of the US dollar devi-
ated in the 1990s from its PPP levels relative to the Japanese yen and the
German mark. These PPP exchange rate levels equate the average prices of
tradable merchandise and services between the US, Japan, and Germany.
There was no stability or convergence of exchange rates to PPP levels.
The yen and mark remained persistently overvalued against the dollar
in the 1990s, yet the US current account balance first improved and then
worsened (see Figure 2.6).

The IRP equilibrium discussed above equates the total expected return
on different sources of international borrowing and lending. Money moves
between the globalized countries and currencies until, on the margin,
the market for borrowing and lending is efficient. Arbitragers are then
indifferent between countries and currencies for their next transaction.

Borrowing and lending are associated with debtors and creditors—those
who exchange bonds, commercial paper, certificates of deposit, and other
fixed-income IOUs. It is for these types of financial transactions that IRP
has been statistically verified. Total expected returns on these 'pure debt'
instruments have indeed converged. However, IRP can be more generally understood as financial strategy parity (FSP). For those globalized
countries and currencies subjected to IRP in the 1980s, a more general
convergence of financial strategies also occurred as participants were presented with more similar opportunities in other, non-pure-debt markets.
Specifically, corporations began choosing more similar debt versus equity
financing strategies. Also, there was greater convergence of price to earnings ratios across increasingly internationalized stock markets. As arbitragers and other participants compared returns and risks on a more global
spectrum of financial assets, the best common strategies were chosen.

A.   International Debt to Equity Ratios Converge

Much of the increase in US corporate debt in the 1980s can be seen as a
convergence toward desirable international debt to equity ratios. Before

financial markets became rapidly globalized, that is between 1972 and 1982, the percentage of total debt in the capital stock (machines, factories, etc.) of Japanese and German manufacturers averaged 66 percent and 64 percent, respectively, more than twice the 30 percent of US manufacturers.[35] Although popular sentiment disagreed, it is likely that this lower debt-position of US corporations at the time disadvantaged them relative to their Japanese and German competitors before 1982; and it is likely that the increase in US corporate debt after 1982 was a move in the right direction.

An argument defending the increase in US corporate debt after 1982 proceeds as follows: US managers, especially in the post-1982 period of 'nuclear finance', impatient owners, and hostile leveraged buyouts of companies, needed to insure high short-run returns on machines, factories, land, and so on that are owned outright (i.e. the equity or stock of the firm) in order to maintain high stock prices. High stock prices, prices that fully reflect the replacement value of the machines, factories, land, and so on, please the current owners and discourage hostile corporate 'raiders' from buying stock and gaining control of company assets. In other words, during the boom years for financial markets in the early and mid-1980s, it became popular to radically reorganize the ownership of business assets, and those assets had to be well-presented for marketability—high short-run returns and prices.

However, managers did not need to insure such high short-run returns on debt-capital, because it is not the equity of the firm, but of the lending institution. Debt-capital need only produce enough revenues over the long-run to justify the loan which financed it. Debt-capital was not so marketable or so subject to new ownership as equity-capital (at least in the 1980s), and thus debt-capital has been more insulated from disruptive reorganization by nuclear finance and corporate raiders. From 1972 through 1982, the average before-tax, gross return on capital for equity-biased US manufacturers was 21.1 percent, compared with 14.2 percent and 15.7 percent in debt-biased Japan and West Germany, respectively.[36]

Gross returns on capital should not be confused with corporate profitability for four reasons: (1) they are before-tax returns, and tax systems vary; (2) other non-capital expenses such as wages affect profitability; (3) the gross return on capital becomes institutionalized as a cost of capital, for example to the newer firms who must buy or lease it away from competing uses—in 1981 the cost of raising capital in the US was 16.6 percent, which compared unfavorably with 9 percent in Japan and West Germany;[37] (4) the profitability or net return on a firm's capital operations should be measured as the difference between the gross returns and the costs of raising capital. This calculation indicates that profit rates on capital in Japan and West Germany were one to two percentage points higher than in the US before the rapid globalization period beginning in the early 1980s.

The capital cost disadvantage of US industry worsened in the early 1980s. Economists at Georgetown University concluded that in 1985 US industry spent 19 percent more than Japan to service its capital, that is, raise it, depreciate it, and pay taxes on it. Taxes were identified as the key reason, because Japan was found to tax its capital formation at a 37 percent lower rate than the US.

> If the Japanese system [including higher debt, non-existent taxes before 1986 on the dividends and capital gains of individuals, etc.] were adopted in the US, the cost of US capital . . . would fall by 16 percent. This is the equivalent to an increase in profit margins on output of 5 percentage points [about double our present rate] and is an amount larger than total US corporate income tax receipts.[38]

The lower US profit rates on machines and factories compared to Japan and Germany in the 1970s and early 1980s, due to higher taxes and less debt, meant that fewer corporate investment projects could be justified in the US compared to Japan and Germany. Especially hard hit in the US were investments in product innovation and the opening of new industries and markets. These endeavors are risky and expensive at first, but are very important to the long-run competitiveness of industries in an increasingly international marketplace.

Due to the lower profitability, 'gross fixed capital formation' as a per-centage of gross domestic product was lower in the US than in most other large industrial nations in the 1970s and 1980s—the US ratio averaged 18 percent compared to 23 percent in West Germany and 32 percent in Japan.[39] Also, less economy-wide capital formation in the US during this time period allowed less improvement in industry competitiveness, as measured by output per worker (productivity).

Despite popular sentiment at the time in the 1980s, much of the increase in US corporate debt was desirable, because US capital costs could be lowered at least as much as the gross return on capital. Increased profit-ability on capital occurred, more investment in US industry was justified, and worker productivity improved, *ceteris paribus*. There was less chance that US corporations had the liquidity problems and low stock market values which invited hostile takeovers and disrupted long-run strategies. Instead, the corporations' bankers had more control over the corporation, and a greater self-interest in seeing that the corporation was successful in the long run. As acknowledged by Benjamin Friedman (in Feldstein, 1991, p. 20):

Some observers have argued that most of the [US] substitution of debt for equity in recent years has occurred in the context of reorganizations that are likely to promote business efficiency and hence provide the higher earnings with which to service the added debt; also, that these transactions are explicitly designed to minimize conventional bankruptcy problems in the event that the anticipated higher earnings do not materialize. Others have pointed out that even after the refinancings of the 1980s, US corporations on average remain much less highly leveraged than their counterparts abroad.

Also, the globalization of financial markets in the 1980s provided the greatest benefits to the borrowers who had historically paid the highest interest rates. In the 1970s and early 1980s, before the globalization of financial markets, it was the US interest rates which were the highest. Therefore, it was US borrowers, especially those who creatively took advantage of the new international opportunities, who found the greatest savings with globalization. American corporations realized the benefits of increased borrowing, especially from the new international markets: Eurobonds issued by American corporations grew from $7 billion in all of 1983 to $35.1 billion in only the first ten months of 1986.[40]

By 1990, the globalization of debt and equity markets had already led to similar debt–equity ratios between the US, Japan, Germany, and others. Within the more commonly shared financial environment, corporations were choosing more similar financial strategies. For example, in 1990 the average debt–equity ratio of companies listed on the Tokyo stock exchange was approximately equal to the average debt–equity ratio of all US companies.[41] Computing this ratio was extremely problematic because many newer financial instruments have both debt and equity characteristics, but it is likely that average US and Japanese corporations had approximately equal debt to equity ratios of 50 percent by 1990.

With reference to the 1972–82 statistics presented above, Japanese companies thus reduced their debt levels in the 1982–90 period just as significantly as US companies increased their debt levels until corporate debt burdens were approximately equal in the two countries. Rather than seeing increased US corporate debt in the 1980s as a worrisome development originating in the US, therefore, it seems better to view this increased debt as a natural and healthy process of convergence or globalization. US, Japanese, and other corporations settled upon similar financial strategies in their new commonly shared financial markets.[42] Initially, more attractive takeover targets were found in the equity-biased US capital stock, that is, until the late 1980s when globalization had brought international debt–equity ratios closer together, and when financial markets became more similarly regulated and accessible.

B.   International Price/Earnings Ratios Converge

A natural process of convergence or globalization also occurred in the 1980s with international price/earnings ratios of corporate stock.

Different investors are willing to pay different stock prices for the ownership of corporate assets, depending upon expectations about the size and riskiness of future dividends and other cash pay-outs; preferences for having more cash in the present versus the future; availability of cash; and the availability of alternative investments. For example, in the Japanese stock market in the 1980s, investors were willing to pay an average of 50 dollars for corporate stock for every one dollar of current annual earnings generated by the stock, that is, a price/earnings ratio of 50. For Nippon Telephone and Telegraph, which had a total stock market value of $320 billion on 31 March 1987 (more than the entire West German stock market), investors paid a remarkably high price/earnings ratio of 261.7.[43]

In the US stock market, investors in the 1980s were willing to purchase stock at an average price/earnings ratio of 15, less than one-third of the Japanese stock market ratio, indicating a combination of the following structural conditions, labeled (1)-(5):

1.   Future earnings and therefore cash pay-outs were not expected to be as high on US corporate stock compared to Japanese corporate stock.
2.   Investors as a group felt that the dollar was likely to lose some of its exchange value relative to the yen, and they had not fully hedged away this currency risk.
3.   In Japan investors were willing to pay a higher price and commit more savings for the expectation of future income compared to the more consumer-oriented US. Also, savings had been given more favorable tax treatment in Japan than in the US.
4.   The Japanese tendency to retain earnings within the corporation rather than pay it out as dividends, and other institutional differences meant that a significant amount of Japanese earnings was hidden from the statistics.
5.   There was more cash 'bottled-up' in the less deregulated Japanese financial markets, and there were fewer attractive alternatives to stock ownership compared to the US, such as home ownership.

In the 1980s, structural conditions (1)–(5) maintained the average prices of Japanese corporate assets at levels more than three times higher than US corporate assets, relative to the current income generated by those assets. These structural impediments, which maintained separate institutional and behavioral identities for the world's two largest stock markets, became less significant as financial globalization progressed, however. Consequently, there was a trend toward more similarly priced corporate assets in the US and Japan.

Structural condition (1) became less significant with the increased participation in joint ventures and overseas production by US and Japanese firms, the dual-listing of corporate stock in both exchanges, the recovery of US companies, such as those in automobiles, from exceptional Japanese competition of the early 1980s, the maturation of the Japanese economic miracle, the increased use of debt-financing in the US, and the massive net inflow of foreign funds into the US beginning in the 1980s which lowered interest rates and the cost of capital in the US while increasing them in capital-exporting Japan.

Condition (2) became less significant with the widely perceived bottoming-out in the decline in foreign exchange value of the dollar in the late 1980s, and with the rapid development of futures markets where foreign exchange risk can be hedged as per covered IRP discussed earlier. Condition (3) became less significant with the removal of various tax incentives to save within Japan since 1986, and as the Japanese economy became more consumer- and leisure-driven. Condition (4), which is more a statistical oddity rather than an economic condition, became less significant with the more standardized accounting techniques used by more internationalized (especially Japanese) corporations. And, condition (5) became less significant with the rapid deregulation and integration of the US and Japanese financial markets and increased learning, especially by Japanese investors, about foreign opportunities.

As these structural differences between the world's two largest stock markets began to lose their importance in the 1980s, perhaps especially as (5) became less significant, it was inevitable that Japanese investors began to purchase a lot of US stocks. In effect, the reasons for maintaining higher prices for corporate assets in Japan relative to current corporate earnings began to lose their importance, and the lower US price/earnings ratios became quite attractive to Japanese investors.

Thus, the reduced importance of structural conditions (1)–(5) explains the Japanese 'buying of America' in the 1980s. However, the removal of structural differences and impediments between financial markets everywhere encouraged a more general foreign buying of America. For example, German purchases of US business assets in the 1980s rivaled purchases by the Japanese, but neither country maintained as large a historic claim on US assets as Britain or the Netherlands. Both Japan and Germany made major long-term capital investments into the US in the 1980s. However, 'the channels from Japan to the United States are more direct than those from Germany to the United States', which might explain some of the greater attention paid to the Japanese purchases at the time.

Structural integration of stock markets began to encourage the rapid foreign buying of American business assets in the mid-1980s. For example, foreign investors purchased $5 billion of publicly owned US corporate stock in 1985, $25 billion in 1986, and $30 billion in 1987. The world stock market crash of 1987 slowed this upward trend only temporarily. By 1989, 11.1 percent or $500 billion of America's $4,550 billion total business assets were foreign owned.

As structural impediments between the major equity markets continued to erode, and as portfolios were appropriately reallocated, price/earnings ratios converged toward something like 20:1. Adjusting for differences in institutions and accounting rules which remained, a 1992 study found that 'true' price/earnings ratios for Japan, the US, Britain, France, and Germany were, respectively, 22.1, 26.5, 19.6, 14.5 and 19.1.[44] Compared to stock market levels of the late 1980s, and assuming reasonably constant growth rates of corporate earnings in the US and Japan, this convergence required a doubling of US stock market prices and a 50 percent decline in Japanese stock market prices from the late 1980s to 1992—which was exactly what happened. The Japanese financial crisis that emerged in 1989 as part of this adjustment is discussed in Chapter 3.

V.   SAVER AND DISSAVER COUNTRIES

Unexpectedly large trade and investment imbalances developed between the US, Japan, and others during the 1980s, which have continued. From 1984 to the mid-1990s, the US had a trade deficit averaging more than $100 billion per year, and as a necessary counterbalance the US received a net inflow of foreign investment of more than $100 billion per year—both of which increased in the wake of the 1997 Asian crisis to approximately $200 billion per year and then further to a maximum of $800 billion in 2006 at the peak of 'the long boom' (Chapter 4) before beginning to decline in 2007 and 2008 following the recent crisis.

Despite intense focus on this topic by the economics profession, there has been disagreement over the international adjustment mechanisms and key variables that link trade and investment flows. For example, the general consensus of Paul Krugman and others in Bergsten (1991) seemed to be that imbalances in US trade and finance could be appropriately reduced by movements in currency exchange rates and government policy responses such as protectionism:

The need to reassess became especially acute in the late 1980s as widespread disappointment emerged over the continuation of sizable imbalances despite large changes in exchange rates and other policy measures aimed at reducing the imbalances. (p. xi)

[However] once we clean up the data, it seems possible to argue that trade flows have responded to exchange rates in just about the way that an economist who had avoided listening to any new ideas [since 1970] . . . would have expected. (p. 11)

Yet Robert Mundell, among others, argued that currency realignments and trade barriers play no useful role in improving trade balances and may even be harmful in the US case:

The claim that [favorable consequences] will follow from depreciation is sheer quackery. It is closer to the truth to say that a policy of appreciating the yen and the European currencies relative to the dollar will cause deflation abroad, infla- tion at home, a larger dollar deficit, and vast equity sales to foreign investors. Ownership of factories, technology, and real assets will be exported to finance an even larger trade deficit without there being much, if any, real expansion in exports or reduction in the dollar value of imports. US assets will be sold abroad at bargain-basement prices. If the American dog gets fed better, it will be by eating its own tail. (Mundell, 1987)

The Mundell side has been taken by those, for example from the Japanese perspective during the 1980s–90s, who argue that only the US can improve its trade deficit, when it saves and invests more and improves its productivity:

The fundamental causes of the dollar's depreciation [over 1985–95] are the US budget deficit and an unfavorable balance of payments which shows no sign of improving. Only the US itself can recover the dollar's status as an international key currency. Therefore, in the long run, decreasing the budget deficit and enhancing productivity are vital steps. (Wakasugi, 1987)

Taking issue with each of these quotes, this section argues that the financial market globalization, IRP, and FSP processes as discussed in the previous section are new driving forces responsible for the large trade and investment imbalances that began in the 1980s and 1990s. *More autono- mous and controlling international financial flows are often causing changes in trade and economic growth, rather than vice versa.* Proper consideration of the structural changes from this chapter leads to some new conclusions about the international adjustment mechanisms and key variables that affect trade and investment flows. Increasingly, the nation should not be seen as a self-sufficient or 'balanced' economic region.

As discussed in the previous section, more lenders have been put in contact with more borrowers by financial market deregulation and the information revolution. Larger sums of money have been moving more quickly and profitably around the world. Those who tend to spend more than their current income, dissavers, have been more quickly accommodated with an appropriate interest rate by those who tend to spend less than their current income, savers. Inherent tendencies, whether toward dissaving or saving, have thus been encouraged for individuals, firms, and countries.

The establishment of saver and dissaver countries was especially noticeable during the initial 'boom years' for international financial markets in the early and mid-1980s. The biggest new saver country was Japan, where individuals were saving more than 15 percent of their disposable personal income. In addition to accommodating the borrowing needs of its business and government sectors, personal savings allowed Japan to increase its net long-term lending to the global financial markets from less than $20 billion in 1983 to $50 billion in 1984 to $62 billion in 1985.[45]

The biggest new dissaver country was the US, where individuals reduced their personal savings rates from 9 percent in the early 1980s to an average of only 4 to 5 percent after the mid-1980s. In late 1998, US savings rates actually reached zero. Over the 1980s and into the 1990s, European personal savings rates were midway between the Japanese and US rates in the 7–13 percent range. (Chapter 4 elaborates the quite different environment for savings since the recent economic crisis, whereby US household savings rates have now risen back to 5 percent and Japanese rates are instead approaching zero.)

No matter how US personal savings was measured, beginning in the early 1980s it was not nearly enough to meet the borrowing needs of the US business and government sectors. For example, without the benefit of foreign lending and investment in 1985, US personal savings would have provided only $58 billion for the business sector after financing the $200 billion federal budget deficit—not enough to keep the economy running at its 1985 output rate of $4 trillion.

It was the increase in the net inflow of foreign lending and investment into the US from $9 billion in 1982 to $118 billion in 1985 which allowed the US business sector to maintain a high level of output and employment in the mid-1980s, while at the same time the US government was running record deficits. Since the mid-1980s, the US economy has continued to dissave or 'absorb' a large share of the rest of the world's savings. As discussed throughout the remainder of the book, this continuing absorption and use of world savings in the US economy has been one of the most significant structural changes associated with the new global economy, and it affects just about everything including economic growth, government budgets, trade patterns and various financial crises and recession. For example, as discussed in Chapter 3, the 1997 Asian financial crisis and the 1997 unexpectedly strong US economy were (not coincidentally) associated with a sudden jump in net financial flows out of Asia and into the US, where the net inflows exceeded $200 billion per year.

Why, in the 1980s, was the US personal savings rate exceptionally low compared to, for instance, Japan? The generally accepted reasons are as follows.

1. Earnings on US savings (interest and dividends) are taxed, whereas interest expense on borrowing (for home ownership and business-related purposes) is tax deductible. The incentive is therefore to borrow and spend, not to save. In Japan, most savings have been completely exempt from taxes, that is, until 1 April 1988, when many of 'the world's largest tax loopholes' were closed.[46]
2. The US baby boom, that is, people born from 1946 to 1958, were in their key spending years for housing, cars, and so on. The savings years and the earnings power were just arriving in the 1980s as the baby boomers entered their fifties and sixties.
3. The US social security system covers a broader base of people than does Japan's system, which reduces the anxiety to save. A more developed corporate pension plan in the US also reduces concern for the future. The Japanese must generally save as individuals for their retirement. Social security contributions in the US, the largest income security program,[47] are not measured as personal savings; thus the commonly reported US personal savings rate understates the true level of savings.
4. Americans are home owners compared to the Japanese. By spending money on home ownership, Americans are building up equity and financial security for their future, but this 'residential investment' reduces rather than adds to the supply of loanable funds. The Japanese must save more money for future rental of housing, including furniture and appliances because they do not as commonly own these things. Also, when the Japanese buy a home they must save for a more substantial down-payment.
5. In the 1980s many credit accounts in Japan worked like the US system of decades ago—little black books at the corner store or post office. The credit card revolution in the US encouraged borrowing by making it easier and more socially acceptable. In 1980, the average unpaid balance per American cardholder was $375, in 1986 approximately $940, and by 1990 it exceeded $2,000.

6. A larger share of farm income has historically been saved in the US compared to other sources of income, and farm income has declined from 4 percent of all personal income in 1973 to less than 1 percent of all personal income after 1990.

7. An additional, rarely mentioned explanation of the low US savings rate, which applied especially since the 1980s, is that the new global economy has provided the US with new, low interest rate borrowing opportunities. The US savings rate declined from over 8 percent in the early 1980s to 4 percent in the mid-1980s, which was the same period of time during which the US financial markets were integrated with the financial markets of Japan and other lower interest rate, saver countries. US interest rates declined by approximately 4 percentage points from the early 1980s to the mid-1980s, largely due to the inflow of newly deregulated profit-seeking foreign funds. Consequently, the US incentive to save was reduced, and the incentive to borrow and spend was increased, both of which reduced the US personal savings rate.

Most likely, it was (7), the globalization of financial markets, which reduced the US personal savings rate to post-World War II lows by the mid-1980s. Most of the other (1)–(6) commonly accepted reasons for the low US savings rate were in place in the 1970s as well as the 1980s, and it is unlikely that they caused the dramatic drop in the US savings rate right after 1981. But many of the financial market deregulations mentioned in this chapter occurred right at the beginning of the 1980s, including UK and Japanese liberalization of foreign capital controls. Profit-seeking foreign capital, which allowed for lower US interest rates and lower US savings, was also attracted to the US by the big Reagan tax cuts of 1981–83 which enhanced returns on US investment. The Reagan tax cuts also led to the large federal budget deficits and government dissaving and attractive returns on Treasury securities (see Chapter 2, Section VI).

Removal of the US withholding tax on interest payments to foreigners in 1984 further encouraged foreign purchases of US Treasuries in 1984–85. There was no increase in foreign purchases of US corporate bonds in 1984–85 due to removal of the withholding tax, because corporate bonds had been available in the Eurodollar market for some time without being subject to withholding.

Lower US interest rates and lower US savings after 1981 were also allowed when US banks reduced their exposure to LDC debt and repatriated funds back to the US. Virtually all new private loans to the LDCs stopped when the world debt crisis hit in 1982.

The low US personal savings rate together with record federal government budget deficits caused the US to become a 'debtor' country in 1985; the first time since 1914. In just four years, from 1982 to 1986, the US reversed its position as the world's biggest 'creditor' nation and became the world's biggest debtor nation. Japan became the biggest creditor nation. By the mid-1990s, Japan had accumulated $800 billion net ownership of foreign assets, and the US found that foreign ownership of US-based assets exceeded US ownership of foreign-based assets by more than $1 trillion.

Commonly reported as the annual increase in US 'debt' to foreign countries, actually much of it indicated that foreigners were purchasing more US real estate, business assets, and other property compared to US claims on foreign property. The Commerce Department estimated that more than 10 percent of the $4.5 trillion in US business assets were foreign owned by 1988, 1.3 percent of the $7.5 trillion in US real estate, and 5 percent of the $8.4 trillion in debt owed by all US sources.

The author's position is that US federal budgets with deficits over $150 billion would not have been passed between the mid-1980s and the mid-1990s without the ready availability of foreign savings. A (hypothetically) financially self-sufficient US economy in this period with $100–$150 billion of household savings 'left over' for the business sector assuming a $150 billion federal deficit would have been severely recessionary.

National policymakers, whose electiveness and careers frequently require them to maintain economic growth, thus began encouraging the inflow of foreign funds in the 1980s. In a surprising turnaround from previous speeches, US President Reagan argued on 11 January 1987 that 'inflows of foreign capital are not necessarily a sign of an economy's weakness'.[48] Comparing the national debt to California's external debt to other states, Reagan said 'does this augur bad days ahead for California? On the contrary, one might argue it's a sign of strength'.

NOTES

1. 'Capital Markets Survey', *The Economist*, 21 July 1990, p. 7.
2. 'Central Banks Issue Warning on Trading', *The New York Times*, 28 March 1996, C1.
3. 'Japanese Firms Make Controversial Bid in the US Government Securities Market', *The Wall Street Journal*, 7 January 1986, p. 32.
4. 'The Globalization of the Industrialized Economies', *Barron's*, 4 May 1987, p. 45.
5. 'New Guidelines for Derivatives Are Delayed', *The Wall Street Journal*, 9 May 1997, p. A4.
6. 'Harbours of Resentment', *Financial Times*, 1 December 2008, p. 11.
7. 'Down and Out on Trillionaire's Row', *Financial Times*, 11 October 1993, p. 14.
8. 'Storm Survivors', *The Economist*, 16 February 2013, http://www.economist.com/news/special-report/21571549-offshore-financial-centres-have-taken-battering-recently-they-have-shown-remarkable.
9. 'Tax Havens, the Mission $20 Trillion', *The Economist*, 16 February 2013, http://www.

economist.com/news/leaders/21571873-how-stop-companies-and-people-dodging-tax-delaware-well-grand-cayman-missing-20/print.

10. 'Banks and Information Technology', *The Economist*, 5 December 2009, p. 83.
11. 'The New American Challenge', *The Wall Street Journal*, 3 November 1986.
12. 'The Global Money Market', *The New York Times*, 4 May 1986, p. 10 F.
13. 'Your Future in Telecommunications', *Business Week Careers*, November 1986, p. 59.
14. Ibid.
15. 'Business Bulletin', *The Wall Street Journal*, 10 March 1988, p. 1.
16. 'Business Goes Body Shopping', *Newsweek*, 10 July 1989, pp. 46–7.
17. 'Foreign Issues Flood London OTC Trade', *The Wall Street Journal*, 18 April 1986, p. 22.
18. Data from Spencer Nilson and *The Nilson Report*, Oxnard, California, mid-1996.
19. 'Central Banks and Digital Currencies: Redistributed Ledger', *The Economist*, 19 March 2016, p. 75.
20. This case study, as it affected the US balance of payments, is analyzed in Cooper (1965).
21. 'Three Big Japanese Firms Enter Ranks of Primary Dealers Despite Opposition', *The Wall Street Journal*, 12 December 1986, p. D-1.
22. 'Stakes High for Britain's Financial Firms in Freer Markets', *The New York Times*, 6 October 1986, p. 34.
23. 'London's Exchange Braces for Big Bang Set to Occur Monday', *The Wall Street Journal*, 24 October 1986, p. 1.
24. 'Common Market Seeks New Rules on Limiting Exposure of Lenders', *The Wall Street Journal*, 1 December 1986.
25. 'Ontario Will Open Securities Industry to Foreigners, Domestic Finance Firms', *The Wall Street Journal*, 5 December 1986, p. 38.
26. 'Global Finance: Tale of 3 Cities', *The New York Times*, 31 October 1986.
27. 'French Denationalization Lures US Firms', *The Wall Street Journal*, 24 October 1986, p. 28.
28. 'China's Embryonic Stock Market Expands', *The Wall Street Journal*, 12 November 1986, p. 38.
29. 'School at China's People's Bank Trains New Generation of Financial Whiz Kids', *The Wall Street Journal*, 18 November 1986, p. 39.
30. 'China's Initial Offering of Eurodollar Bonds Is Set', *The Wall Street Journal*, 21 August 1987, p. 21.
31. 'Confronting the Soviet Financial Offensive', *The Wall Street Journal*, 22 March 1988, p. 34.
32. 'East Europe's Sale of the Century', *The New York Times,* 22 May 1990, p. C1.
33. Source: Bank for International Settlements, based on information from banks in the Bank for International Settlements reporting area, comprising 18 industrialized countries and seven offshore banking centers.
34. 'Capital Unchecked', *The Economist*, 19 October 1985.
35. 'US Business Should Take On More Debt', *The Wall Street Journal*, 1 December 1986.
36. Ibid.
37. Ibid.
38. 'Japan's Tax Policy—A System that Works', *San Francisco Chronicle*, 21 November 1985.
39. Source: IMF.
40. 'Finance Officers' Wider Role', *The New York Times*, 20 October 1986.
41. 'Escape from Debt', *The Economist*, 21 July 1990, p. 84.
42. The replacement of equity with healthy debt-financing in the US did seem to minimize the disruptive, uninsured, junk-bond financing techniques of corporate raiders. In 1990, shortly after the indictment of its junk-bond king Michael Milken, Drexel Burnham Lambert declared bankruptcy. Drexel Burnham Lambert had accounted for 40 percent

($10 billion) of junk-bond trading in 1989, and in the late 1990s this market had smaller volumes than its levels of the late 1980s.

43. 'Soaring Shares of Japan's NTT Worry Analysts, Delight Holders', *The Wall Street Journal*, 24 April 1987, p. 17.

44. 'All the World's a Ratio', *The Economist*, 22 February 1992, p. 72.

45. 'Japan's Foreign Fundings', *The New York Times*, 13 April 1986.

46. 'Japan to End One of the World's Largest Tax Loopholes', *The Wall Street Journal*, 23 March 1988, p. 22.

47. In 1986, according to the US Census Bureau, the value of US poverty programs was equal to $48.2 billion, while social security benefits amounted to $196.1 billion ('Benefits Beat Taxes as Income Equalizer', *The Wall Street Journal*, 28 December 1988, p. A2).

48. 'Reagan Says October Crash Resulted from Markets, Not Deficits and Dollar', *The Wall Street Journal*, 12 January 1988, p. 3.

2.   Financial instabilities and trends in the 1980s

Structural changes in the global economy provoke other structural changes, as is true of most evolving systems. In Chapter 1 it was argued that advances in information-processing technology and government deregulation provoked the rapid expansion and globalization of financial markets. Because of their 'marriage' with the communications revolution, financial markets have more quickly expanded and become globalized than markets for merchandise and non-financial services. Analysts including Peter Drucker were emphasizing as early as the mid-1980s that the evolving financial markets had taken on a profit-seeking life of their own, quite independently of the markets for merchandise and services (Drucker, 1985–86). For example, by the mid-1980s the value of trading on the London Eurodollar market was 25 times the value of world trade in merchandise and services. Eurodollar deposits and trading were non-existent two decades earlier.

Continuing advances in technology and international payment systems allowed even more exotic new money forms:

> Today's money: the synthesis. [Bank] reserves perch atop the money pyramid. Conventional money (the measured m's) is next [as the pyramid widens]. The e-transfers, or EFT as earlier known, follow. One level below is the newest kind of e-money: the smart card and computer cybermoney forms slowly taking shape. Free money, by definition without specific formal backing, and e-barter collect at the base of the pyramid . . . As you get further away from the reserve base and the money that passes through banks, it becomes harder to track 'money'. This is especially true with bundling a lot of different corporate information or settlement in some kind of commodity account (e.g., oil or futures). The value of an aggregate-flows gross becomes supported by a dwindling reserve and money base relative to the expanded electronic blob as a whole. (Solomon, 1997, pp. 91, 95)

The creation and use of these new money forms have allowed an explosion of financial transactions. In the US payments systems alone, the Federal Reserve estimated electronic transactions value at more than $500 trillion per year by the mid-1990s, and globally this number was certainly an order of magnitude higher—nobody knows for sure because of the speed with which money can recycle between accounting measurements, and because of the flows through offshore financial markets that are not measured.

Revolutionary changes require us to rethink how the system works. In Schumpeter's terms, clusters of new innovations can destroy the old ways of doing things, and create new ways—a process of 'creative destruction'. This chapter identifies one such phenomenon that is not consistent with traditional economic thinking; namely, in Sections I–IV, it is demonstrated that more of the 'money pyramid' has recently been used to accommodate the fast growth of financial markets, and proportionally less of the money supply is *simultaneously* available for non-financial or GDP purposes. In terms of the famous 'quantity equation', this phenomenon shows up as a decline in the income velocity of money.

In turn, as discussed in Sections V–VIII, this structural decline and increased variability of the income velocity of money in the 1980s was behind many of the large-scale financial crises and recessions during the 1980s, including the 1982 global recession and 1982 world debt crisis, and the 1987 world stock market crash. An understanding of money supply and demand, monetary velocity, and related statistics is thus crucial for the purposes of this book.

I.   NEW TRANSACTIONS AND ASSET DEMANDS FOR MONEY, AND MONETARY VELOCITY

In the US, from 1960 to 1980, the income velocity of money (v), measured as the ratio of nominal GDP to a narrow measure of the money supply (m1), grew predictably at 2 to 4 percent per year (Figure 2.1). (m1) includes coins, currency, and checkable demand deposits in the banking system. This predictability allowed for the use of (m1) money supply targets by central banks to guide movements in income and inflation, as specified by the 'quantity equation':

$$(m1) \times (v) = (p) \times (q) \qquad (2.1)$$

where (p) is the GDP price level, (q) is real GDP, and (p × q) is nominal GDP.

Before 1980, US monetary policy could therefore be based upon the following cause-and-effect relationships: due to the relative stability of (v), an increase in real money balances (m1/p) will increase (q) by a predictable amount; the increase in (q) occurs because the increase in (m1/p) causes interest rates to decline, which in turn stimulates borrowing and

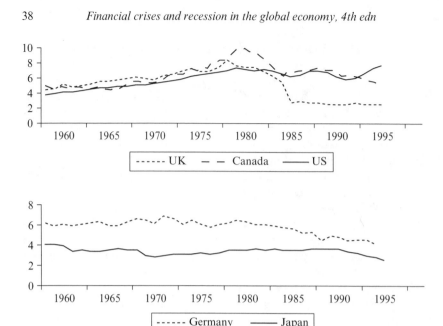

Source: IMF.

Figure 2.1   Worldwide instability and weakness in the growth of the income velocity of money after 1980

purchasing across the economy. Thus, aggregate demand for GDP rises, and producers respond to meet that demand. Because central banks can directly control (m1) but not (m1/p), they may stress the importance of interest rate targets rather than money supply targets.

The expansion of narrow money supplies (m1) is usually successful in increasing economic growth (q), because (m1) usually rises faster than inflation (p), and because nominal interest rates usually fall relative to inflation, that is, real interest rates fall. However, if there is not much capacity in the system to expand production, or if there is not much incentive or ability to expand loans and purchases, then the expansion of (m1) may be ineffective—inflation rather than economic growth may be the result. Also, excessive inflation may hurt growth and lead to other undesirable instabilities in the system.

Typically, a successful expansion of (m1), which lowers real interest rates and stimulates borrowing and spending and economic growth, will be associated with a proportionate expansion of broader monetary aggregates, such as (m2) and (m3). In the US, (m2) equals (m1) plus retail money market fund (MMF) balances, savings deposits, and small time deposits. (m3) equals (m2) plus large time deposits, and various institutional accounts such as repurchase agreements, Eurodollars, and institution-only MMF balances. (m3) was discontinued as an officially reported data series by the Federal Reserve after February 2006, but private estimates are available (Chapter 4). When the central bank expands (m1) and generates a borrowing and lending expansion and lower real interest rates on these narrow money accounts, then the expansion will usually 'spill over' into broad money accounts. Growth of broad money accounts also encourages economic growth, because some of the accounts which are included in (m2) and (m3) are held for GDP-participation purposes, although they may not be so 'liquid' as (m1) accounts. The complicated relationships between (m1), (m2), and (m3), for example when they do not change together, are elaborated in Chapter 3 as part of 'Japan's Crisis, 1989–'. For the purposes of this chapter, and its case studies, it is sufficient to frame the analysis in terms of (m1) and assume that the various monetary aggregates move together, except where indicated otherwise.

Since 1980, the (m1) income velocity of money has become quite unstable, and has declined (or broken downwards) from its historic trend in many of the money centers (Figure 2.1). In Japan's case, a significant decline began in 1993. Hence, the historic cause-and-effect linkage from (m1/p), to interest rates, to real GDP has become unpredictable, and monetary policies have reacted haphazardly to economic conditions instead of finding a sound base in economic theory. The use of monetary aggregates which are broader than (m1) has been less than satisfactory, leading *The Wall Street Journal* to comment in 1988 with regard to the US situation:

> Money-supply growth targets have been dethroned, and Fed officials are desperately seeking a substitute. Chairman Alan Greenspan dissects the monthly employment data; Vice Chairman Manuel Johnson eyes the credit markets, Governor Wayne Angell watches gold and soybean prices. And the financial markets look on in confusion. The Fed, they fear, is adrift.[1]

And, as echoed in the economics literature:

> Including data from the 1980's sharply weakens the postwar time-series evidence indicating significant relationships between money (however defined) and nominal income or between money and either real income or prices separately. Focusing on data from 1970 onward destroys this evidence altogether. (Friedman and Kuttner, 1992, p. 472)

This section argues that the structural changes in globalizing financial markets as discussed in Chapter 1 are the root cause of the instabilities and declines in income velocity since 1980. A careful consideration of these structural changes in the context of monetary theory helps regain the relationship between narrow monetary aggregates and GDP. A more optimistic outlook for the rationalization of monetary policies is thus possible. Justifications are provided for the following two hypotheses:

1. The profitability and value of financial transactions compared to non-financial transactions are important missing variables in most monetary policy research. Their consideration allows for better predictions of the income velocity of money. For example, in globalizing money centers in the 1980s, the money supply was used less frequently for GDP transactions, because more of it was used instead to accommodate the fast growth of financial markets.
2. During a dramatic financial upheaval or structural change as per the UK's Big Bang deregulation in 1986 or Germany's reunification in 1990 or Japan's financial crisis in the 1990s, the income velocity of money also declines as the new opportunities are figured out and reacted to. Temporarily, there is not sufficient information for investors to pursue rational strategies, and the price of money-liquidity rises sharply. An increase in money demand occurs to reduce the risk of loss and in order to regain an optimal investment portfolio quickly once the information environment improves. In the author's view, this options demand for money can divert money-liquidity away from GDP and other markets during chaotic times; however, it is not generally recognized in monetary theory.

Neither the economics profession nor monetary policymakers fully considered these structural changes beginning in the 1980s, as indicated by a recurring bias in macroeconomic forecasts, and the recurring use of overly restrictive monetary policies. Incorporating these structural changes into more conventional monetary theory is the objective at hand.

The quantity equation (2.1) is frequently rearranged as:

$$(m1) = (1/v) \times (p \times q) \qquad (2.2)$$

Here, the equation better represents the income version of the quantity theory of money, which originally assumed that people want to hold a constant fraction $(1/v)$ of nominal GDP $(p \times q)$ in the form of money. Research predicts that the fraction $(1/v)$ will decrease (increase) when there is an increase (decrease) in the interest rate (Goldfeld, 1973, 1976), an increase (decrease) in real GDP (Goldfeld, 1973, 1976), an increase (decrease) in the expected rate of inflation (Judd, 1983), and an increase (decrease) in the state of financial market innovations (Dotsey, 1985).

The empirical evidence for these theories and others is contained in Judd and Scadding (1982), Laidler (1985), Stone and Thornton (1987), and Friedman (1988).

Historically, changes in interest rates have been found to be the most important reason why (1/v) changes. If interest rates increase, then the asset demand for money declines relative to the asset demand for high interest rate financial securities, money is used more efficiently to accommodate GDP transactions (as people take advantage of the high interest rates in non-money accounts), and (1/v) declines. The asset demand for money might also decline with higher inflation, because money is more quickly spent rather than held as people try to maximize purchasing power over time. Also, at higher levels of real GDP and with improved financial market innovations, there are economies in the use of money for transactions purposes, and (1/v) declines due to a proportionate decline in the transactions demand for money.

In the 1960s and 1970s, the income version of the quantity theory of money was generally preferred instead of the transactions version. The transactions version replaces nominal GDP in equation (2.2) with the value of all transactions in the economy, including not only GDP transactions, but also transactions involving second-hand and intermediate sales of merchandise and services, and transactions involving non-money financial assets. The transactions version implies that people want to hold money in proportion to all of the transactions which they make, rather than just the GDP transactions. A discussion of the quantity theory of money and the limitations of the transactions version is contained in Friedman (1970).

The transactions version drew increased attention in the 1980s, however, because of widespread failure to predict (1/v) as it is defined in the income version. For example, between 1973 and 1980, US households and businesses were holding much less money than predicted by Goldfeld's equations, which were based upon the income version. As estimated by Porter et al. (1979), this shortfall amounted to approximately \$30 billion in mid-1976 and \$55 billion in early 1979. Then, after 1981, the 'case of the missing money' was replaced by the 'case of the reappearing money' as more money was held than predicted.

The unexpected rise in (1/v), that is decline in (v), beginning in the early 1980s, as it is defined by the income version, was especially troublesome. For example, as per equations (2.1) and (2.2), it meant that the 1982 US recession was not foreseen. From 1981:Q3 to 1982:Q4, the growth rate of US nominal GDP declined by 9.7 percentage points. But, forecasters missed the collapse of velocity and predicted a decline of only 3.3 percentage points (Section VI).

Spindt (1985) attempted to explain this collapse of velocity by identifying the uses of money directly, from data on the debits to various money accounts. However, his direct measurement of (v), when used in the quantity equation, has not 'demonstrated any apparent gain over (m1) for policy purposes [of predicting nominal GDP], and is more difficult to calculate' (Batten and Thornton, 1985, p. 29).

The direct measurement of (v) has not proved to be practical because, for each type of money account, one must decide how much of the turnover is for the purchase of a final product (GDP) instead of for check cashing or other movements of money between money accounts; non-final product purchasing, including raw materials purchases, wholesale purchases by a retailer, and second-hand sales; and the purchasing of non-money financial assets. However, the alternatives to direct measurement are also not practical because, in Spindt's words, they are not 'equipped to deal with a changing payments mechanism or menu of financial assets'.

II.   FINANCIAL GLOBALIZATION AND MONETARY VELOCITY

The author's research since the late 1980s (Allen, 1989) indicates that the structural changes in financial markets discussed in Chapter 1—advances in information technology, deregulation, and internationalization—are of crucial importance in understanding the recent decline and increased variability of the income velocity of money. The following examples, labeled (1)–(3) were especially important in the 1980s.

1. Advances in information technology: technological advances continue to reduce the costs of transferring money and paper documentation and therefore the costs of financial transactions. In this regard important advances have been made in electronic and regular mail services, telephones, computers, modems and fax machines, image processing devices, communication satellites, fiber optics, ATMs, electronic points of sale, telephone banking, interactive screen communications between financial intermediaries and their wholesale and retail customers, debit and credit and smart cards, electronic money and transfer systems, the World Wide Web, and so on.

2. Deregulation: policymakers have removed ceilings on interest rates, reduced taxes and brokerage commissions on financial transactions, given foreign financial firms greater access to the home financial markets, allowed increased privatization and securitization of assets, and allowed increased competition between banks, securities firms,

insurance firms and other financial institutions. These deregulations and many others have increased the profitability of domestic finance and blurred the differences between money and non-money financial assets. For example, the US created negotiable order of withdrawal (NOW) accounts after 1981, which allowed interest to be earned on checkable, (m1) accounts for the first time. NOW accounts thus accumulated funds that would otherwise be put into non-money financial assets such as MMFs.

3. Internationalization: advances in information technology and government deregulation have in turn allowed funds to move more freely and profitably between international and national markets. As documented in Chapter 1, virtually every type of international financial asset has experienced a dramatic increase in trading since the early 1980s. Financial globalization is supported by increased globalization of all economic activity.

In the new global economy these structural changes allowed financial transactions to become comparatively more profitable than merchandise and services transactions during the early 1980s. Consequently, the demand for money for financial market participation increased. Deregulation as per new interest-earning NOW accounts increased the asset demand for money, as did new opportunities to shop globally for the best money-asset accounts. Improved technologies and new international opportunities increased the transactions demand for money for financial market participation—opportunities for financial speculation, hedging, and arbitrage were created as never before.

Transactions costs associated with financial market participation were lower and new opportunities for favorable interest rates and portfolio composition were created. A threshold was reached whereby increasingly significant amounts of labor and capital services were devoted to the transfer of money and documentation. Financial market activity expanded rapidly.

Most researchers have not found defensible relationships between the expanded trading volumes of finance and the income velocity of money. Wenninger and Radecki (1986) made a noteworthy early attempt, but their approach was subject to several limitations.

They treat (m1) or (m1/p) as the variables to be predicted with a one-equation econometric model when financial market volumes are included as alternate independent variables, rather than (v) or (1/v) as the variables to be predicted. (m1) and to some extent (m1/p) have been controlled as important target variables by the central bank, and thus Wenninger and Radecki have the simultaneity problem of trying to explain money supply and money demand with the same variables. Alternatively, (v) has not been significantly controlled by the central bank, and (v) can be predicted with the one-equation approach without a significant simultaneity problem.

Changes in (v) are more directly related to changes in money demand than to changes in money supply, and it is changes in (v) and money demand which forecasters have failed to predict since 1980, not changes in money supply. Wenninger and Radecki's simultaneity problem limited their ability to contribute to previous research in this regard. For example, they concluded that when GDP and financial market volumes 'are included together in the . . . equation at most one performs well' because both 'are alternative proxies for total transactions in the economy . . . and one of the two is redundant' (p. 30). However, GDP and financial market volumes might not be redundant in an equation which explains (v)—if, for instance, financial market volumes are a more important demand variable and GDP is a more important supply variable, that is, central bank monetary policy reacts more to GDP trends than financial market trends. These problems should be considered more explicitly before they conclude that 'the more rapid growth of financial transactions is not having a very large effect on (m1) growth' (p. 29).

And, they used data only through 1985, just when financial markets began expanding the most dramatically, and began reaching a high profitability relative to the non-financial markets. It was the last few years of their data set, especially 1985 itself in which 'it seems that financial transactions played a major role, adding roughly two percentage points to (m1) growth' (p. 28). However, they dismissed the volume of financial transactions as a variable which is likely to be significant, even in the mid-1980s, because the 'rapid growth of financial transactions over the longer run (1959–1985) has not been associated with an acceleration of (m1) growth. For financial transactions to explain the rapid growth of (m1) in 1985, it would be necessary to find reasons why the historical relationship between financial transactions and (m1) might have changed' (p. 30). In the author's view, the missed historical changes are advances in information-processing technology, deregulation, and internationalization.

Perhaps Milton Friedman (1988) provided the most noteworthy attempt to relate the expansion of financial markets in the 1980s to the income velocity of money. He put forth the first direct 'econometric attempt to relate the level of stock prices to the demand for money' and also considered the estimates of financial and non-financial transactions debits compiled by Spindt (1985).

Friedman rationalized an inverse relationship between stock prices and monetary velocity (or direct relation between stock prices and the level of real cash balances per unit of income) in three different ways:

(1) A rise in stock prices means an increase in nominal wealth and generally, given the wider fluctuation in stock prices than in income, also in the ratio of wealth to income. The higher wealth to income ratio can be expected to be reflected in a higher money to income ratio or a lower velocity. (2) A rise in stock prices reflects an increase in the expected return from risky assets relative to safe assets. Such a change in relative valuation need not be accompanied by a lower degree of risk aversion or a greater risk preference. The resulting increase in risk could be offset by increasing the weight of relatively safe assets in an aggregate portfolio, for example, by reducing the weight of long-term bonds and increasing the weight of short-term fixed-income securities plus money. (3) A rise in stock prices may be taken to imply a rise in the dollar volume of financial transactions, increasing the quantity of money demanded to facilitate transactions. (Friedman, 1988)

Offsetting the inverse effect of items (1)–(3) is the positive effect of what Friedman describes as a (4) substitution effect: 'the higher the real stock price, the more attractive are equities as a component of the portfolio.' Using quarterly data from 1961 to 1986, he concludes that items (1)–(3), especially the wealth effect, 'appear stronger than the substitution effect . . . [however] annual data for a century suggest that the apparent dominance of the wealth effect is the exception, not the rule'.

Friedman's use of Spindt's data leads him to conclude that 'the volume of [both financial and non-financial] transactions has an appreciable effect on (m1) velocity but not on (m2) velocity'.[2] In his (m1) velocity equations, he is unable to conclude whether it is non-financial transactions debits or financial transactions debits, as a ratio to GDP, which is the more significant variable. These results do not allow him to accept the hypothesis that financial transactions 'would "absorb" money, hence reducing income velocity'. Instead, Friedman seems to side with 'the received view [of Wenninger and Radecki and others] that financial transactions are so highly money-efficient that they do not absorb any appreciable quantity of media of exchange and have little if any effect on velocity'.

Since Friedman's work, mainstream literature has sided with the income version of the quantity theory of money rather than the transactions version. People are believed to hold money in proportion to the level of GDP rather than in proportion to all of the transactions which they make. However, as the author argues next, there is strong evidence from case studies of the US, the UK, Germany, and others that just the opposite is true.

III. THE INSTABILITY OF THE INCOME VELOCITY OF MONEY IN THE US

The decline from trend, and increased variability of US (m1) income veloc-ity, occurred at the end of 1981. As documented by Stone and Thornton (1987), replacing nominal GDP in the income velocity formula with any other measure of non-financial transactions does not significantly change the basic rise and fall of the velocity chart; other measures include gross domestic final demand, Spindt's broad measure of non-financial transac-tions debits, and permanent income. Also, replacing (m1) with most other measures of money is concluded to make very little difference with regard to this decline of velocity, including the Fed's (m2), (msi), and Spindt's (mq).

However, replacing nominal GDP in the income velocity formula with various measures of the volume of financial transactions, such as Spindt's financial transactions debits, produces a 'financial transactions monetary velocity' which does not decline in the 1980s. The annual growth rate of Spindt's financial transactions debits velocity averaged about 10 percent over the 1980s, compared to 12 percent from 1970 to 1981. From the late 1970s to the late 1980s, this financial market velocity ratio increased at a remarkably regular rate of about 20 points each year. Money was thus used more efficiently in the 1980s to accommodate financial transactions, and this increase in efficiency was fairly steady and predictable.

In the author's view, the growth in the volume of financial transactions beginning in the early 1980s outpaced the supportive efficiency with which money was used to accommodate these transactions. These transactions thus absorbed money taken away from other markets. When data is con-sidered that shows a rapid, geometric growth beginning in the early 1980s in the total volume of those types of financial transactions which are espe-cially likely to absorb money away from other uses (Figure 2.2), then the following hypothesis become obvious: the rapid expansion of US financial transactions beginning in the early 1980s may be a dominant, exogenous factor which caused the simultaneous break in the US income velocity of money. Furthermore, because technological change, deregulation, and internationalization are the root causes of the increased profitability and rapid expansion of US financial transactions, this hypothesis implies that they would be the root cause of the break in the US income velocity of money.

The author's regression analysis which verifies this hypothesis and identifies the pre-1982 and (1982–) causality between US financial market expansion, interest rates, income velocity, and other variables appears in the Appendix to this chapter.

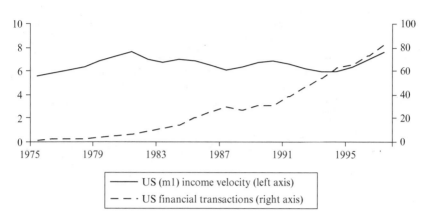

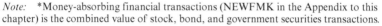

Note: *Money-absorbing financial transactions (NEWFMK in the Appendix to this chapter) is the combined value of stock, bond, and government securities transactions.

Sources: US Department of Commerce, Federal Reserve Bank.

Figure 2.2 *Expanding volumes of money-absorbing financial transactions* in the US ($trillion/year), and the US (m1) income velocity of money, 1975–97*

Several types of financial transaction included in Spindt's aggregate cannot be expected to make money unavailable for alternate uses for a significant period of time; some not even as the debit itself is entered. These include, especially, the movement of funds between money accounts, such as check cashing, and the movement of funds between money and near-money accounts, such as when certificates of deposit are redeemed. The types of financial transaction which are more likely to absorb money are purchases and sales of stocks, bonds, government securities, and other longer-term investments, such as, in the 1980s and early 1990s, when five working days were required before securities sales could be cashed.

In June 1995 the US Securities and Exchange Commission (SEC) short-ened the settlement time for corporate and municipal securities from five to three days, and in February 1996 the securities industry converted to a 'same-day funds settlement system'. Therefore, money-absorption in these markets was reduced, which can be seen in Figures 2.1 and 2.2 as an increase in US (m1) velocity after 1995.

International transactions especially tied up funds in financial markets in the 1980s and early 1990s, until international transfers began to move as efficiently as national transfers, and until the same margin-holding require-ments and quick settlements were applied. Furthermore, chaotic financial globalization ties up funds in financial accounts due to an increase in the options demand for money-liquidity. The chaos prevents investors from pursuing rational strategies, and the demand for flexible and secure money-liquidity rises sharply. An increase in money demand occurs to reduce the risk of loss and in order to regain an optimal investment portfolio quickly once the information environment improves.

Stone and Thornton (1987) recognize that 'the financial transactions velocity measure does not show the downturn in the 1980s that character-izes the non-financial and GDP-based velocity measures'. However, they incorrectly state that the financial transactions velocity measure does not 'show substantial increases during the 1980s which would be required if the rise in financial transactions is to account for the decline in (m1) velocity'—an incorrect statement because regardless of the quantity of money which people use to facilitate a given volume of financial trans-actions (and how fast that quantity is changing), and regardless of how much of that money is at the same time unavailable for GDP transactions, the total volume of financial transactions could expand sufficiently to absorb money away from GDP markets, thus reducing income velocity. In fact, the ratio of Spindt's financial transactions debits to non-financial transactions debits increased from 7/1 in early 1982 to 16/1 in early 1987, suggesting that financial transactions could have absorbed enough money to significantly reduce income velocity over this period.

If the money-absorption hypothesis is rejected, how do people explain the relation between US financial market activity, GDP, (m1), interest rates, and velocity over this important period? The explosion in US stock market activity and capital transactions which began in the early 1980s and accelerated in subsequent years, shown in Figure 2.2, is widely believed to be a result of declining interest rates and an economy coming out of recession. The received scenario proceeds as follows: the reduction in real money balances of 6 percent in 1981 raised interest rates by approximately 2 percent; the high interest rates caused the growth rate of nominal GDP to decline by 9.7 percentage points from 1981:Q3 to 1982:Q4, and a major-ity of this decline was a decline in the inflation component; the 15 percent drop in world crude oil prices in early 1983 further broke the expectations-fed inflationary spiral; by the mid-1980s the disinflationary trend allowed expansionary monetary policy, which began in late 1982, to bring interest rates down to their levels of the early 1970s; and the expectations of and eventual realization of low interest rates, low inflation, and strong eco-nomic recovery all fueled a boom in stock and bond markets. The lower interest rates, lower inflation, and higher real GDP are seen as the cause of the decline in income velocity.

This common view, that US interest rates were determined largely by US monetary policy in this period, and that interest rates were a dominant, exogenous factor in the expansion of non-financial and financial markets, largely ignores technological change, deregulation, and internationalization. The author believes that low interest rates and a non-inflationary expansion of GDP in the US would not have been possible by the mid-1980s without these structural changes. The US savings rate began declining in 1981 until it hit a post-World War II low of 3.7 percent in 1985, and without the benefit of the new, more efficient international financial markets the US would have had a woefully inadequate $60 billion of domestic savings in 1985 after financing the $200 billion federal budget deficit to keep nominal GDP running at an annual rate of $4 trillion. As elaborated in Chapter 1, it was technological change, deregulation, and internationalization which encouraged a net capital inflow into the US of close to $100 billion per year by 1985 compared to a net capital outflow of $6 billion in 1981. The new profit-seeking US capital inflow in the mid-1980s in turn allowed for the continuing expansion of financial markets, low US interest rates, and the longest post-World War II expansion of US GDP.

The results shown in the Appendix allow the following conclusions: (1) the demand for money for financial market transactions became an important source of money demand which absorbed money away from other uses; (2) the expansion of financial markets in the context of other variables caused the decline and increased variability in US income velocity after the end of 1981; (3) because improved technology, deregulation, and internationalization are the root causes of the expansion of financial markets, they are also the root causes of the decline and increased variability in income velocity. Aside from the author's publications (Allen, 1989, and previous editions of this book), these results (1)–(3) cannot be found in the economics literature.

IV. THE INSTABILITY OF THE INCOME VELOCITY OF MONEY IN OTHER COUNTRIES

The UK and Germany experienced recent declines and increased variability in the income velocity of money in the 1980s, and for the same structural reasons as the US. Although a thorough econometric analysis for these two countries and others is beyond the scope of this book, the correlations between (m1) velocity, deregulation, internationalization, and financial market activity seem obvious enough that the reader will hopefully tolerate the author's conclusions. However, the author encourages others more familiar with the unique financial history of these and other countries to pursue a thorough econometric analysis of velocity as per his US equations. French and Italian financial deregulation and interna-tionalization did not occur as suddenly and as forcefully as in the other G7 countries, and the author would especially rely on other researchers to test his US equations for these countries. The drop in Canadian (m1) velocity paralleled the US drop, and is especially correlated with the major Canadian financial deregulations and increased financial turnover in 1986 (Figure 2.1). The decline in (m1) velocity in Japan in the early 1990s is elaborated in Chapter 3 as part of 'Japan's Crisis, 1989–'.

A.   The UK Case

Figure 2.1 shows a decline in UK (m1) velocity beginning after 1980 and then a big drop after 1986. The collapse after 1986 is partly due to the inclusion of building society money deposits as part of the narrow money supply beginning in 1987. Beginning January 1987, as defined by the Building Societies Act of 1986, the International Monetary Fund (IMF) began including these deposits in its series 34 definition of (m1) that the author uses for the purposes of this chapter. Given that build-ing society deposits increasingly served the purpose of narrow money, the author would rely on others to figure them precisely into monetary aggregates. The UK's money definitions, unlike the IMF's, do not include the private and official sector foreign currency deposits, and thus have this limitation—foreign currency deposits became especially important to the UK economy after 1986.

Whichever reasonable definitions are used for money in the UK, a decline in income velocity does occur contemporaneously with deregu-lation, internationalization, and increased financial market activity. In October 1979 the UK removed all inward and outward barriers to capital flows. Consequently, Britain experienced an annual portfolio investment outflow for the 1980–83 period that was 1,800 times higher than in the 1975–78 period (Taylor and Tonks, 1989), and the initial break in velocity did occur in 1980.

The even more significant deregulation, internationalization, and increased financial market activity within Britain was the 26 October 1986 'Big Bang' which scrapped 85 years of fixed commissions for brokers as well as separation of powers between brokers. And, as stated by John M. Hennessy, chairman of Crédit Suisse First Boston Ltd., a leading interna-tional investment bank based in London, 'Big Bang is an attempt to gener-ate a few global competitors among the British institutions'.[3] Competition increased immediately. Forty-nine firms, including American, European, and Far Eastern financial giants had signed up before 26 October to market British stocks and government bonds; only 19 companies had been

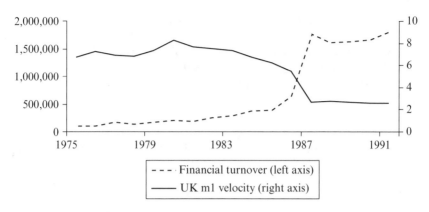

Sources: IMF, Bank of England.

Figure 2.3   *The relation between financial market growth (£million) and (m1) velocity in the UK during the Big Bang deregulation period*

doing this trading previously.[4] After 26 October, commissions charged by financial intermediaries dropped as much as 50 percent.

Figure 2.3 shows how the turnover of financial transactions in the UK, due to this new profitability and internationalization, increased after 1980 and then exploded upward during the Big Bang period. The turnover variable, which aggregates government securities, other fixed-interest securities, and equities, does mirror the (possibly exaggerated due to the building society issue) decline in (m1) velocity. The leveling off of financial turnover and (m1) velocity since 1987 in the UK suggests that the impacts of deregulation and internationalization had been mostly realized a year after Big Bang.

The author's hypothesis, that the new financial markets absorbed money taken away from non-financial markets and caused a collapse in (m1) velocity, thus appears to be confirmed for the UK. In addition to the direct absorption of (m1) as financial transactions turn over, the author would suggest that a related form of absorption occurred in the UK case due to uncertainty or information failure experienced by holders of money, that is, during a dramatic upheaval or structural change as per Big Bang, financial portfolios must be reallocated dramatically as the new opportunities are figured out and reacted to. For a time, there is not sufficient information for investors to pursue rational strategies, and the price of money-liquidity rises sharply. An increase in money demand occurs to reduce the risk of loss and in order to regain an optimal portfolio quickly once the information environment improves.

In the author's view, this 'options demand' for money can divert money-liquidity away from GDP and other markets during chaotic times, but it is not generally recognized by the economics profession. However, many securities market professionals swear by it. For example, Joseph Grundfest, former commissioner of the US SEC, explains the 1987 stock market crash as follows:

> Simply put, I suggest that a large component of recent market volatility is the rational result of an 'information failure' in the market for liquidity rather than the consequence of rapid and irrational changes in the market assessment of the value of securities . . . The lack of information about either fundamental business prospects or about the magnitude and composition of an atypically large demand for immediate trading can be sufficient to induce substantial market volatility . . . [A] sharp increase in the price of liquidity is reflected in a simultaneous widening of spreads and in a general price decline in the equities and futures market alike . . . Once sufficient information comes to the market describing expected short-term trading flows, and once the returns to providing liquidity become high enough, the peak-load nature of the demand subsides, the risk involved in trading is reduced, the price of liquidity declines, spreads narrow, and equity prices recover a large portion of their losses. (Grundfest, 1991, pp. 67–8)

The economics profession has trouble with this options demand for money because it is not very separable from other sources of money demand, because it is not measurable, and because it stands in opposition to the popular 'efficient market hypothesis' (EMH). The EMH, like most economic theory, assumes away the likelihood of significant information failure or transactions costs.

Yet given 'the lack of information about either fundamental business prospects or about the magnitude and composition of an atypically large demand for immediate trading' during Big Bang, Grundfest's scenario might explain the behavior of the UK financial markets during the 1986–88 world stock market crash period. The drop in velocity of certain monetary aggregates during this period, the rise in UK short-term interest rates by 1 percentage point shortly before the crash as money-liquidity demand was not accommodated by an increase in money supply, the subsequent crash, and the subsequent recovery and ultimate stability of financial markets as the money supply was increased—all fit into Grundfest's scenario.

As elaborated in Section VIII, similar scenarios in the other G7 countries during 1986–88, especially the US, might well account for the worldwide nature of the 1987 stock market crash. Yet it was the UK Big Bang which provided the most obvious, sharpest money-liquidity demand due to information failure shortly before the 1987 crash. Therefore, the UK financial markets may have been the most culpable.

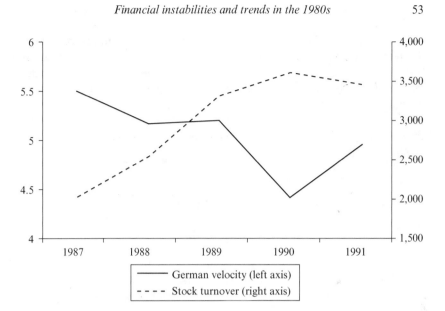

Sources: IMF, Bundesbank.

Figure 2.4 *The relation between financial market growth (marks billion) and (m1) velocity in Germany during the chaotic 1989–90 period*

B. The German Case

Figure 2.1 shows how Germany's (m1) velocity began declining from its historic trend after 1981. This break coincided with the major German liberalization of exchange controls in March 1981, and the one-year 1989–90 collapse corresponded with German reunification and the revolutions in Eastern Europe. Germany's case study thus also seems to support the author's thesis that deregulation, internationalization, and increased financial activity have driven declines in income velocity.

Figure 2.4 shows the inverse relationship between German financial activity as measured by stock market turnover versus income velocity over the chaotic 1989–90 period. The 1989 revolutions in Eastern Europe and the full German monetary reunification on 1 July 1990 both resulted in information failure and confusion about fundamental business prospects. An atypically larger demand for financial asset trading occurred as the new opportunities were figured out and reacted to, and this demand subsided in 1991 as the information environment improved. Initially, money demand increased in order to reduce the risk of loss and in order to regain an optimal portfolio quickly once the information environment improved. Therefore, income velocity collapsed before reversing its fall in 1991.

The increased German money demand and collapse in velocity from 1989 to 1990 were not accommodated by the Bundesbank with an expanded money supply; therefore, a money-liquidity shortage occurred and interest rates rose rapidly. The German money market rate rose from 4.0 percent in 1988 to 8.8 percent in 1991 whereas the government bond yield climbed from 6.1 to 8.6 percent—indicating a liquidity crisis especially in the more money-related side of the financial markets.

These high German interest rates in the context of the European Exchange Rate Mechanism (ERM) required overly restrictive monetary policies throughout Europe to stabilize exchange rates, which in turn led to the recessionary 1990s and the problems within the ERM. Germany's European partners could not tolerate such restrictive monetary policies for more than two years, and after 1991 most of them chose to lower interest rates and restore economic growth at the expense of the ERM. The recessionary early 1990s period is elaborated in Chapter 3.

V. CASE STUDY OF US–FOREIGN TRADE, 1981–

The US, a country especially exposed to the globalization of financial markets since the 1980s, was, consequently, especially exposed to new patterns of merchandise and services trade. The US economy, therefore, provides a good case study for the arguments of this chapter. For example, it is argued next that the continuing large US trade deficit is a result of the continuing large net inflow of foreign savings into the US. Contrary to conventional wisdom, the inflow of foreign savings is argued to be the more initiating, autonomous development, and the US trade deficit is argued to be the more accommodating development.

Before the 1980s, the major purpose of most international financial transactions was to accommodate merchandise and services trade. Growth in trade produced a nearly equal growth in international financial markets, especially the amount of foreign currency that was swapped. In contrast, by the early 1980s the expansion of international financial markets had taken on a profit-seeking life of its own. As discussed in Chapter 1, the deregulation of financial markets and the global information revolution made international borrowing and lending and other investment very efficient and profitable by the mid-1980s. Consequently, most of the money which was moving between countries by the mid-1980s had little to do with merchandise and services trade, but instead was accommodating 'pure' financial transactions—those which involve only the exchange of money

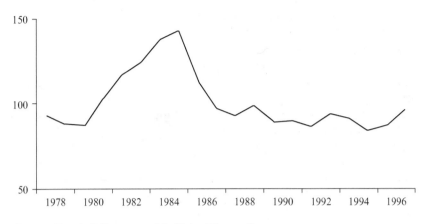

Source: Board of Governors of the Federal Reserve System.

*Figure 2.5   The trade-weighted exchange value of the US dollar, 1978–97
(March 1973 = 100)*

and documentation. For example, between 1980 and 1986 the volume of
foreign currency trading doubled, so that by 1986 this volume was roughly
12 times the volume of worldwide trade in merchandise and services.

Whether the international businessperson is engaged in financial or
non-financial transactions, often the currency exchange rate is the key
determinant of his/her profit rate in the 1980s. No other production or
sales condition was likely to have such a large impact on the gap between
costs and revenues from one year to the next. For example, from January
1981 to January 1985 the trade-weighted exchange value of the US dollar
increased 65 percent, meaning that the side of a US-foreign transaction
which made the currency conversion could have lost or gained a similar
change in revenue depending upon when they chose to make the conversion. Also, between January 1985 and January 1987, the trade-weighted
exchange value of the dollar reversed its upward trend and fell back to its
1981 level (Figure 2.5).

Due to the increased volatility of exchange rates, and the increased
importance of international commerce to the US economy, by the late
1980s one out of four US companies surveyed were trading foreign
currencies as a hedge against foreign exchange losses.[5]

As discussed in Chapter 1, interest rate parity (IRP) became the dominant equilibrium in international commerce during the 1970s and 1980s,
and participants were paying increasing attention to interest rate differentials. Increasingly, any shock to the system which pushed interest rates
up in one country encouraged the international community to lend money

there, and discouraged the international community from borrowing money there.

Two such shocks were occurring in the US in 1981 that eventually pushed US interest rates up to record highs: the administration of newly elected President Reagan began pursuing policies which increased the size of the federal budget deficit; and the US Federal Reserve Board was restricting the growth of the US money supply. The increased federal budget deficit increased the borrowing needs of the US government and the slower growth of the US money supply reduced the ability of US financial institutions to make money available for lending. In order to ration the scarce funds of lenders among competing borrowers, interest rates were raised to very high levels compared with what the economy would otherwise have produced.

For example, the US prime interest rate moved in 1981 to 5 or 6 percentage points above the rate of inflation as measured by the US consumer price index, and stayed there until 1984. In contrast, through the mid and late 1970s, the US prime interest rate had stayed within 2 percentage points (above and below) the rate of consumer price inflation.

If the US financial markets had been closed to foreign investors in the early 1980s, then the extra US government borrowing and reduced US money growth might or might not have increased the total loan volume in the US—despite more government borrowing, some borrowing by US businesses and individuals would have been 'crowded out' by the higher interest rates.

However, given the rapid deregulation and globalization of financial markets that was occurring, high US interest rates in the early 1980s created a strong incentive for the world's lenders: find a way in the new global markets to gain access to these rates! For example, Japanese lenders saw US money market interest rates jump 9 percentage points higher than Japanese money market interest rates in 1981, compared to an average US advantage of only 0.2 percentage points from 1971 to 1980. Many US lenders also suddenly found themselves with money tied up abroad at equally disadvantageous interest rates; their portfolios were thus over-exposed to foreign borrowers in the early 1980s even without considering the new risks of default that began to surface on US loans to developing countries.

Accordingly, in the early 1980s, US and foreign lenders began to favor the US market. As shown in Table 2.1, which is a summary of US international financial transactions from 1980 to 1985, US lenders were able to direct their funds into the US faster than foreign lenders, certainly because US lenders already had more unregulated connections to US borrowers. The 'capital outflow' from the US made its significant drop from 1982 to

Table 2.1   The turnaround in the US capital account, 1980–85 ($billion)

	1980	1981	1982	1983	1984	1985
Capital inflow to US	58	83	94	83	103	127
Less capital outflow	86	111	121	50	24	32
Equals net identified inflow	−28	−28	−27	35	79	95
Plus statistical discrepancy	26	21	36	11	27	23
Equals net capital inflow	−2	−6	9	47	107	118

Note: Components may not add due to rounding.

Source: US Commerce Department.

1983, a drop of $71 billion. However, it took foreign lenders some time in the rapidly globalizing financial markets to take advantage of the high US interest rates. The 'capital inflow' to the US actually declined from 1982 to 1983 before increasing $20 billion from 1983 to 1984 and $24 billion from 1984 to 1985.

The statistical discrepancy account in Table 2.1 is used to reconcile measured flows of commerce and payments for those flows. This account became very large in the late 1970s and 1980s—it assumed a debit balance averaging less than $1 billion from 1960 to 1977, then a credit balance averaging $21 billion during 1978–86, then large debit and credit balances since 1987 including a credit of $64 billion in 1990 and a debit of $53 billion in 1996.

The statistical discrepancy is generally considered part of this capital account balance, that is, its large credit position shown in Table 2.1 is assumed to reflect an unmeasured part of the international flow of funds coming into the US. However, there is no way to verify exactly how much of the statistical discrepancy reflects actual flows of capital.

For example, what if much of the $64 billion credit position of the statistical discrepancy account in 1990, its largest imbalance ever, did not reflect an actual inflow of capital to the US? Then one could more easily conclude that the US recession of 1990–91 has its explanation. Without some of this inflow, especially given the simultaneous drop in the net identified inflow, US investment and consumption growth could not be sustained. In the author's case study of the early 1990s US recession in Chapter 3, he documents that the economics profession is unable to explain the recession, and also that the profession ignores this possibility. Similarly, the author argues in 'Asia's Crisis, 1997' in Chapter 3 that unmeasured as well as measured capital flows coming into the US from Asia and elsewhere made for an unexpectedly strong US economy.

The bottom line in Table 2.1 sums up yearly changes in the international financial position of the US over the 1980–85 period. This bottom line is called the net balance on the US capital account (now called 'financial account'), which went from a deficit (or debit) to a surplus (or credit) in 1982. After sending more investment funds to other countries than were received from other countries by $2 billion in 1980 and $6 billion in 1981, the net flow reversed direction and the US began receiving foreign investment on balance. In 1982, 1983, 1984, and 1985 the US received more funds from the rest of the world than it sent to the rest of the world by $9 billion, $47 billion, $107 billion and $118 billion, respectively.

What was happening in the foreign exchange market to the value of the dollar as approximately $157 billion, net, of international investment flowed into the US in the important reversal period 1981–84? Because US investment is conducted in dollars, and because foreign investors have other currencies to invest with, the demand for dollars from the foreign exchange market increased by $157 billion, and the supply of other currencies to the foreign exchange market increased by an equivalent amount. In other words, $157 billion moved out of the inventories of foreign exchange traders into the US economy and an equivalent amount of other currencies moved out of the global economy into the inventories of foreign exchange traders.

However, merchandise and services trade as well as international investment require currency swaps and therefore also exert pressure on exchange rates. From 1981 to 1984, the US bought $155 billion more of merchandise and services from the rest of the world than the US sold to the rest of the world. This excess of US imports over exports (including government grants and private remittances abroad) is called a $155 billion deficit or debit in the current account of the US.[6] The current account summarizes all non-financial transactions between the US and the rest of the world, just as the US capital account (now called financial account) summarizes all financial transactions.

The $155 billion deficit in the US current account from 1981 to 1984 affected the foreign exchange market as follows: foreign exporters to the US generally want to receive their own currency as payment and US importers generally have dollars to spend, therefore one side of a US importing transaction must buy the foreign currency from the foreign exchange market with the unwanted dollars. The opposite happens in a US exporting transaction. Therefore, because US importing exceeded US exporting by $155 billion in 1981–84, $155 billion, net, were sold to the foreign exchange market from the rest of the global economy and an equivalent amount of other currencies was bought from the foreign exchange market. To accommodate the US current account deficit, global foreign exchange trading thus exerted downward pressure on the value of the dollar from 1981 to 1984.

At first glance the downward pressure on the exchange value of the dollar exerted by the deficit in the US current account seems to be approximately equal in magnitude to the upward pressure exerted by the surplus in the US capital account, that is, $155 billion of downward pressure compared to $157 billion of upward pressure. One might naively conclude that the value of the dollar probably stayed constant between 1981 and 1984.

Nothing could be farther from the truth, however, as the trade-weighted exchange value of the dollar increased 50 percent from 1981 to 1984. A less naive understanding is necessary, which results in the following scenario:

- deregulation and globalization of financial markets in the 1980s led to:
- a large net flow of international funds into the US (US capital account surplus), a dissaver country due to its high interest rates and productive, safe-haven environment, which led to:
- a higher valued foreign exchange price for the dollar as international investors on balance demanded more dollars from the foreign exchange markets to gain access to the new investment opportunities and high interest rates in the US, which inevitably led to:
- more US imports and less US exports, because the higher valued dollar made US products less competitive in international trade, and the net inflow of international investment into the US increased US economic growth and imports relative to other countries; and
- this US trade deficit (US current account deficit) had to widen until it was large enough to supply foreign exchange traders with the amount of dollars that they needed to accommodate the increased flow of international funds into the US.

Figure 2.6 illustrates this scenario. The current accounts of the US, Japan, and (West) Germany were balanced in 1980–82. Then, the deregulation and globalization of financial markets resulted in substantial flows of investment funds from West Germany and Japan into the US, which in turn resulted in the high-valued dollar, US current account deficit, and the Japanese and German current account surpluses. These changes in the direction of merchandise and services trade between the world's three largest economies, largely caused by the deregulation and globalization of financial markets, were the most significant directional changes in world trade since World War II.

These trade imbalances shrank during the early 1990s due to unique circumstances, such as the Persian Gulf crisis, German reunification, and

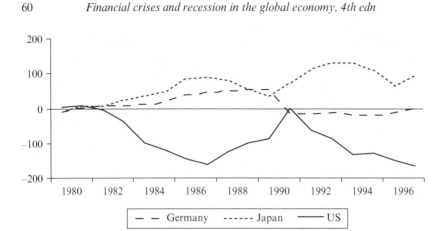

Source: IMF.

Figure 2.6   *Changes in the direction of merchandise and services trade*
              between the world's three largest economies, 1980–97 (current
              account balances, $billion)

a money-liquidity crisis in Japan, but they soon returned to historically
high levels because of the continuing flow of investment funds into the US.

VI.   THE 1982 RECESSIONARY PERIOD

Historically, national political leaders have entered office with a grand
design for the economic future of their country. Significant changes in
monetary and fiscal policies may be made in order to fight inflation, unemployment, and other ills in the national economy. In addition, the new
administration generally has an ideological slant in the way that it regulates
business and labor.

   In the early 1980s, just as the international financial markets began
to expand rapidly and create the new global economy, French President
François Mitterrand embarked upon an experiment in economic social-
ism. At the same time, newly elected leaders Margaret Thatcher in England
and Ronald Reagan in the US were pursuing conservative policies aimed at
restoring a more capitalist tradition. Each of these one-country economic
experiments failed to recognize the new structure of the global economy,
and as a consequence each experiment created severe economic hardships
within one or two years.

Table 2.2   US monetary and fiscal policy and the 1982 recession

Year: quarter	Ratio of personal tax payments to personal income	Ratios to natural GDP				
		Gov. spending	Federal budget deficit	Money supply	Actual GDP	Long-term interest rate
1981:Q1	15.9	18.6	1.3	14.4	97.1	14.4
1981:Q2	16.1	18.3	1.3	14.3	96.0	15.2
1981:Q3	16.2	18.3	1.8	14.0	95.8	16.3
1981:Q4	15.8	18.4	3.2	13.7	93.8	16.0
1982:Q1	15.8	18.1	3.3	13.8	92.8	16.1
1982:Q2	15.8	17.7	3.4	13.7	92.4	15.7
1982:Q3	15.4	18.0	4.7	13.6	91.5	14.7
1982:Q4	15.4	18.3	6.1	13.8	90.5	12.2
1982:Q1	15.1	17.8	5.2	14.0	90.4	12.0
1982:Q4	15.4	17.6	4.7	14.1	91.6	11.6

Sources: Economic Report of the President (February 1983), and *Survey of Current Business* (July 1983).

A.   The US Situation

The Reagan administration came to Washington in January 1981, determined to stimulate the US economy with a 'supply-side' policy of large tax cuts, and a substantial increase in government defense spending which was to be more than offset by a cut in government non-defense spending. To reduce inflation, which was then 10 percent, the Federal Reserve Bank accelerated its recently enacted policy of restricting the growth rate of the US money supply.

As Table 2.2 shows, the Reagan administration was successful in restraining government spending in its first few years. Government purchases of merchandise and services as a percentage of the economy's total, long-term trend purchases, called natural gross domestic product (natural GDP), declined from 18.6 percent in the first quarter of 1981 to 17.6 percent in the second quarter of 1983. It was actually state and local spending that accounted for this decline, as federal spending remained approximately constant—both are included in 'government spending'.

In its first few years the Reagan administration was also successful in reducing tax rates. Although the administration did not achieve its proposed 30 percent cut in total personal income tax rates, Congress did approve a 25 percent reduction—a 5 percent reduction on 1 October 1981 and two successive 10 percent reductions on 1 July 1982 and 1 July 1983. The first two of these three tax cuts are reflected in the first column of Table 2.2.

If everything else except these changes in government taxing and spending had remained the same in 1981–82, then the US economy might have expanded a little bit faster. The contractionary effect of the government spending restraints would have been more than offset by the expansionary effect of the tax cuts, particularly in late 1982 as the first of the two 10 percent tax cuts began to have its effect. However, everything else did not remain the same: between early and late 1981, as shown in Table 2.2, the Federal Reserve Bank reduced the money supply by approximately 6 percent relative to natural GDP.

This dramatic reduction in the money supply cut the supply of loanable funds in the US economy, so much so that interest rates rose to historically high levels. As shown in Table 2.2, long-term interest rates increased from an already high level of 14.4 percent in the first quarter of 1981 to more than 16 percent in late 1981 and early 1982. It was these historically high interest rates that triggered the recession which began in late 1981 and lasted through 1982. The recession was characterized by a rapid slowdown in nominal GDP. The annual growth rate of this statistic slowed by 9.7 percent, from almost 13 percent in the third quarter of 1981 to just over 3 percent in the fourth quarter of 1982. Of this 9.7 percent decline, slightly more than half can be attributed to a reduction in inflation and slightly less than half to a reduction in real GDP. Real GDP, which had been increasing steadily since 1975 at an average annual rate of 3.5 percent, declined 2.1 percent from 1981 to 1982 before recovering to increase by 3.7 percent from 1982 to 1983 and 6.8 percent from 1983 to 1984.

Table 2.3 shows the components of real GDP from 1981 to 1984, and it is clear that the components which are historically discouraged by high interest rates declined significantly from 1981 to 1982, namely, household purchases of durable products such as automobiles; non-residential fixed investment (business purchases of factories, machines, and equipment); residential investment (housing purchases), and inventory investment (the change in inventories of final products that businesses keep on hand). Together, these purchases declined by $37 billion from 1981 to 1982 (1972 dollars). Likewise, these components of real GDP experienced a significant recovery from 1982 to 1983 and from 1983 to 1984 as interest rates changed course and declined dramatically, increasing by annual amounts of $43.7 billion and $89.1 billion.

Because US tax rates had been reduced dramatically in the early 1980s, and because the recession reduced economic growth and the tax base, the

Table 2.3   *US GDP components and the 1982 recession (real GDP, 1981–84 in billions of 1972 dollars)*

	1981	1982	1983	1984
GDP	1515.2	1480.0	1543.7	1639.0
Consumption	950.5	963.3	1009.2	1062.6
Durables	140.9	140.5	157.5	177.9
Nondurables	360.8	363.1	376.3	394.2
Services	448.8	459.8	475.4	490.6
Investment	230.9	194.3	221.0	289.7
Fixed inv.	219.6	204.7	224.6	265.5
Residential inv.	175.0	166.9	171.0	205.2
Non-residential inv.	44.5	37.9	53.7	60.3
Inventory inv.	11.3	−10.4	−3.6	24.2
Gov. purchases	287.0	292.7	291.9	302.2
Net exports	43.8	29.7	12.6	−15.5
Exports	160.2	147.6	139.5	145.8
Imports	116.4	118.0	126.9	161.3

Source: *Economic Report of the President* (1985).

US government collected less in taxes. The Reagan administration in 1981 had forecast more balanced budgets, but in 1982 the federal budget showed a deficit of more than $100 billion (actual dollars—not 1972 dollars as in Table 2.3) for the first time in history, and in 1983 the deficit exceeded $200 billion. US fiscal policy thus required record amounts of government borrowing to cover these deficits, and it put upward pressure on US and world interest rates at a time when these were already high and the world was struggling to overcome the recession.

Historically, US net exports, defined as US exports minus US imports, have not declined significantly during a period of high US interest rates and recession. In fact, during a recession, US residents generally purchase fewer imports, and net exports may therefore increase. However, as shown in Table 2.3, US imports actually increased from 1981 to 1982. Also, because there was a simultaneous drop in US exports, US net exports fell, by 32 percent, from 1981 to 1982. A fall in US net exports reduces GDP because it reflects sales lost by US exporting firms as well as sales lost by US firms which produce import-competing products.

Why did US imports rise and US exports fall from 1981 to 1982 and therefore contribute to the recession? Most importantly, because the high US interest rates and restrictive US monetary policies, at a time when financial markets were globalizing, caused the exchange value of the US

Table 2.4   Actual versus predicted declines in the growth rates of US GDP and inflation, 1981:Q3 to 1982:Q4 (percentage points)

	Nominal GDP	Real GDP	Inflation*
Actual decline	9.7	3.8	4.7
Predicted decline	3.3	0.8	1.9
Forecast error	6.4	3.0	2.8

Note: *As measured by the GDP deflator.

Source: Gordon (1984, p.408). The predicted decline is the average of predictions made by Data Resources, Inc., Chase Econometric Associates, Inc., the MAPCAST group at the General Electric Company, Wharton Econometric Forecasting Associates, Inc., and the median forecast from a survey conducted by the American Statistical Association and the National Bureau of Economic Research.

dollar to increase by 30 percent against major foreign currencies over these two years. Foreign exchange traders were accommodating new demand for US dollars by deregulated international investors who were attracted to the high US interest rates. Based upon the new IRP conditions (Chapter 1), the 'net capital inflow' into the US from the rest of the world began to increase and the demand for dollars exceeded the supply.

The 30 percent increase in the value of the dollar over 1981 and 1982 caused US imports to be cheaper, in dollars, and US importers increased their total dollar purchases. Similarly, US exports became more expensive to foreign purchasers, in terms of foreign currency, so fewer US items were purchased by foreigners and the dollar value of US exports decreased. The decline in US exports can also be attributed to increased international competition from Japan and other newly developed countries such as South Korea and Taiwan, as well as to a reduction in US exports to many less developed countries (LDCs) that began using more of their dollar reserves to pay off their escalating international debts.[7]

How well did the leading economic forecasters predict the declines in US nominal GDP, real GDP, and inflation? Table 2.4 shows the forecast errors computed as the difference between the actual declines and the declines which were predicted one year in advance.

It is clear from Table 2.4 that forecasters were too optimistic about the US economy. They predicted a fairly straight course—the growth rate of real GDP over this 15-month period was predicted to decline by only 0.8 percent from then-current levels rather than the actual decline of 3.8 percent from then-current levels. In other words, forecasters predicted that the economy would produce 3 percent more merchandise and services, $95 billion at 1982 prices, than actually was produced. From a workers' perspective, this error meant that approximately two million more US jobs were lost than economists predicted, and expected US wages, salaries, and profits amounting to $95 billion were not attained.

To understand why forecasters failed to predict the 1982 US recession one should first understand that econometric forecasting models generally require 20–30 years of data to identify the underlying structure of the economic system. Recent structural changes, including the increased international transfers of investment based upon interest rate and financial strategy parities and the subsequent adjustments in international trade (Chapter 1), and the decline of monetary velocity due to deregulation, internationalization, and technological change as discussed earlier in this chapter, were thus only marginally included in the forecasting models, and the models therefore failed.

First, the increasing international transfers of investment allowed the increased US interest rates to have an unexpectedly strong negative impact on US net exports and therefore GDP via the trade effect discussed above. This trade effect, whereby high interest rates in a country cause that country's currency to increase in value, which in turn hurts its net exports, was not significant before 1971 when currency exchange rates were fixed administratively. Before 1971, national central banks kept exchange rates fixed by buying and selling currencies as well as redeeming currencies for gold at accepted prices.

After 1971, when fixed exchange rates and the gold standard were no longer maintained by the US and many other countries, economists had to begin including the trade effect of interest rate changes in their economic models. The trade effect was difficult for economists to estimate not only because of their limited experience with it, but also because interest rate changes affected currency values and, therefore, merchandise and services trade more strongly and unpredictably every year.

Every year, investors had better access to profitable opportunities in the world's major money centers, and there was an increased volume of money that was 'washing back and forth' in search of the best interest rates. A country which, for example, raised its interest rates as the US did in 1981–82 thus discovered an increased demand for its currency compared to historical periods; therefore a greater increase in the value of its currency; and therefore a greater reduction in its net exports. Econometric models which must use decades of historical data underestimated the significance of this trade effect.

Second, deregulation, internationalization, and technological change were behind the US recession of 1982 when policymakers underestimated the degree to which these structural changes would produce new financial market opportunities and absorb dollars away from the non-financial markets, as discussed earlier. More dollars were suddenly kept on hand in the form of currency and checking deposits to accommodate these invisible transactions compared to the volume of dollars that were kept on hand to accommodate GDP transactions. Both types of transactions borrow dollars for a short period of time and then recycle them back into the economy to be used again.

The significance of this dollar-absorption by financial markets beginning in the early 1980s escaped most analysts. Therefore, they did not recognize the following fact: restricting the supply of US currency and checking deposits (m1) at a time when income velocity (v) was dropping because more of this spendable money was being used for financial transactions would more than proportionately reduce the amount of money which was being used for GDP transactions. Therefore, based upon the quantity equation (m1 $\times$ v = p $\times$ q), nominal GDP (p $\times$ q) would decrease more than expected following restrictive monetary policies. The decline in value of nominal GDP is usually split between a decline in the physical volumes of merchandise and services production, that is, real GDP (q), and a decline in the GDP price level (p). As shown in Table 2.4, during the 1982 recession real GDP declined by 3.8 percent and the GDP price level by 4.7 percent.

Clearly, the forecasters who predicted that US nominal GDP would decline by 3.3 percent from the third quarter of 1981 to the fourth quarter of 1982 in the US due to restrictive monetary policies did not fully anticipate what was happening to the velocity of money. The actual decline in nominal GDP was a severe 9.7 percent. 'Forecasters missed the collapse of velocity almost entirely' (Gordon, 1984, p. 406).

B.   The UK Situation

The British economic experiment of the early 1980s, like the American experiment just discussed, placed major emphasis on reducing the growth rate of the money supply in order to reduce inflation and, ultimately, interest rates. And, as in the US, these goals were achieved: between 1980 and 1983 inflation had been lowered from 18 percent to 3 percent and short-term interest rates had dropped from 16 percent to 10 percent. However, also as in the US, these goals were achieved at a tremendous, unexpected cost to the economy in terms of unemployment and lost output. During 1980, the first year of Thatcher's administration, the growth rate of the British economy plunged to −2.0 percent and continued to fall through 1981. In 1982, the unemployment rate had increased to 12.3 percent, the highest among the major industrialized countries.

Both Thatcher and Reagan made overly optimistic promises of economic performance which were not achieved due to widespread ignorance of just how powerful restrictive monetary policy had become. In the early 1980s, the financial side of the new global economy began absorbing an unexpectedly large supply of national currencies away from GDP markets. Therefore, GDP markets would have been faced with an unexpected liquidity crisis even without governmental moves to tighten credit. So destructive were the short-run effects of the UK's monetary experiment, that 364 university economists and nearly all of the retired senior economic advisors to past British governments issued an unprecedented public statement condemning the experiment:

> First, there is no basis in economic theory or supporting evidence for the Government's belief that by deflating demand [with restrictive monetary policy] they will bring inflation permanently under control and thereby induce an automatic recovery in output and employment; Secondly, present policies will deepen the depression, erode the industrial base of our economy and threaten its social and political stability; Third, the time has come to reject monetarist policies and consider urgently which alternative offers the best hope of sustained economic recovery.[8]

Fortunately for the British policymakers, they did not highlight their ignorance of the new global economy, as did the Reagan economists, by setting specific targets for economic performance. The British promises were for the most part only generalized commitments for change, but even these were not attained. Large reductions in central government spending were not realized, and, as in the US, there was ultimately an increase in the central government's share of the economy—just the opposite of what both Thatcher and Reagan had promised their constituents. Thatcher's conservative mandate from the voters soon lost some of its momentum, and in a key power struggle with the National Union of Mineworkers the government halted its attempt to close down operations at redundant coal pits. Industry was not freed from 'the shackles of labour and government'; instead, large loans and subsidies were given to British Steel, British Leyland, Rolls-Royce, British Shipbuilders, and British Airways.

C. The French Situation

While the American and British monetary experiments were combining with austere economic policies in West Germany to create a global recession in the early 1980s, François Mitterrand began implementing policies which were designed to stimulate the French economy. Increased government spending, as mandated by Mitterrand's socialist revolution, allowed the French economy to grow by 1.7 percent in 1982, a year when economic growth in the US and West Germany declined by 2.1 percent and 1.1 percent, respectively. Of the major industrial countries besides France, only Japan realized a moderate economic growth rate in this recessionary year.

Instead of ushering in a period of economic prosperity or stability relative to its trading partners, France's attempt to buck the recessionary trend of the global economy soon ran into serious difficulties. The strong French economy sucked in more imports while the weaker economies of other nations purchased fewer French products. As a result, the French trade deficit almost doubled, from Fr 50 billion in 1981 to Fr 92 billion in 1982. This deterioration in the trade balance was unexpected, largely because policymakers were unaware of just how much the French economy had become integrated into the new global economy.

The ballooning French trade deficit soon meant a loss of international investor confidence in the French franc and low levels of investment in French manufacturing firms. Ultimately, profit levels declined and jobs were lost. In mid-1982, Mitterrand was forced to abandon his stimulative economic policies, and instead adopt the 'most deflationary postwar austerity package'.[9] Government spending was cut and taxes were raised to reduce the growing government budget deficit. French travelers were allowed only $275 per year of foreign travel expenditures, and the foreign use of credit cards was banned. Public utility rates were raised by 8 percent, and the money supply was tightened as in the US and Great Britain. These reforms prompted Andre Bergeron, head of the moderate *Force Ouvrière* labor union, to announce: 'today we have had a cold shower, and I assure you that our militants and members will not accept it'.[10]

The French austerity programs began to have their desired effect, in that they cut the trade deficit in half, from Fr 92 billion in 1982 to Fr 44 billion in 1983. The French franc finally stabilized against the US dollar and the German mark, but at a very low rate. However, the growth of the French economy slowed to zero in 1983, and Mitterrand's rating in the public opinion polls sank to a low of 30–35 percent by late 1983. Opposition parties began winning more local elections and seats in the French senate, and Mitterrand's main opponent, Jacques Chirac, substantially increased his political influence.

By 1986, Chirac had been elected Prime Minister, and his center-right coalition began remolding the economy somewhat in America's free-market image. An unexpectedly popular $40 billion sell-off of government corporations to the private sector seemed to mark the end of the socialist revolution, a revolution which might have continued through the late 1980s and spread elsewhere if Mitterrand had not made his early mistakes.

France's failed attempt to act independently of the new global economy weakened its alliance with other members of the European Community (EC), who thought that France had more of a commitment to stability and moderation. As a member of the European Monetary System (EMS), France was expected to keep the value of its currency stable in relation to other EMS currencies, especially the German mark. However, when the franc began devaluing in the early 1980s, France did not immediately take corrective action with domestic monetary and fiscal policies as suggested by the EC. Instead, France attempted to maintain its one-country economic experiment, which meant blaming some of the currency problem on the Germans and threatening to pull out of the EMS. The integrity of the EMS was not restored until the mid-1980s when Mitterrand's socialist revolution became more moderate and 'middle-of-the-road'.

In the early 1980s, Mitterrand's socialist revolution had helped to define the 'left wing' of the political-economic spectrum within the developed Western world. At the same time, Reagan's and Thatcher's capitalist revolutions had helped to define the 'right wing' of electable political-economic philosophies. But as the decade progressed, the more fervent ideological dogma faded from each of these revolutions; instead, more globally pragmatic politics prevailed. These revolutions failed to maintain their original, more extreme, 'grandstanding' forms because these forms required monetary and fiscal policies which were not sufficiently compatible with average global trends.

The new global economy may thus have narrowed the political-economic spectrum of workable ideologies within the developed Western world. It has become less practical for these major trading nations to pursue significantly different monetary and fiscal policies, and therefore it has become less practical for them to adopt significantly different monetary and fiscal philosophies. Where significantly different political-economic ideologies still exist, they are instead based more narrowly upon different types of business–labor relations, but even these contrasts are becoming less common due to the internationalization of corporations. As discussed, the increased number of international joint business ventures and overseas production activities, as well as the increased international ownership of once-national corporations, are exposing business and labor everywhere to a more global blend of regulations and incentives.

VII. THE WORLD DEBT CRISIS, 1982–

The economic integration of nations has been underestimated. As argued in the previous section, the recession of the early 1980s could largely have been avoided if economic policies had reflected a greater understanding of the rapidly evolving one-world financial market. Overly restrictive, separately enacted, national monetary policies led to high interest rates, money-liquidity crises, and ultimately the 1982 recession. US and UK monetary policies were especially responsible; the US and UK financial markets were dominant and required the greatest liquidity; and the recession began in the US and UK and rapidly spread to the rest of the global economy.

In this section, a further examination of economic policies in the US, UK, and elsewhere places even more responsibility for global economic welfare at the feet of policymakers. It is argued here that these economic policies were also the single most important cause of the 1980s world debt crisis.

The story starts in the early 1980s when the Reagan administration cut US income tax rates by 25 percent to stimulate economic growth. Unfortunately, restrictive monetary policies in the US and UK due to the unexpected absorption of money by globalizing financial markets pushed up US, UK, and therefore world interest rates to historically high levels. These high interest rates created the 1982 world recession, and the Reagan and Thatcher administrations did not achieve the supply-side economic growth that had been predicted.

The prime interest rate charged by US banks discounted by (i.e. over and above the rate of) US inflation increased from an average of 0.4 percent in 1975–79 to an average of 6.5 percent in 1980–86. In the UK, the equivalent rate was negative every year from 1975 to 1980, and then positive every year from 1981 to 1986 with an average value of 5.0 percent. The initial, 1979–81 increases in these real costs of borrowing were due to the restrictive US and UK monetary policies; after 1981, and especially by 1983, the large US federal budget deficit was more to blame, as monetary policies were loosened somewhat.

How did these monetary and fiscal policies affect the world debt situation? Between 1972 and 1979, when interest rates charged on US dollars were only slightly above the rate of US inflation (as was typical in the developed world), the international indebtedness of the LDCs had increased at an annual average rate of 21.7 percent (Bogdanowicz-Bindert, 1985–86, p. 261). In this period price improvements in the LDCs (as on LDC exports) were higher than in the US, meaning that inflation-adjusted interest rates in the LDCs on US dollar loans were frequently negative, and considerable borrowing from the US could be justified. Also, the increasingly international, IRP nature of financial markets implied that considerable borrowing from London, Frankfurt, Tokyo, and other money centers was similarly justified.

Then, in 1980 the money-liquidity crisis began to hit as the US, UK, and other developed countries pursued restrictive monetary policies. By

1982 the continuing liquidity crisis had created recessions in the developed countries, which in turn meant a collapse in the export markets for many of the products supplied by the LDCs. For example, 60 percent of Mexico's merchandise exports go to the US, and when the US economy 'caught a cold' in the early 1980s, many Mexican industries 'caught pneumonia' for this reason alone.

Higher US dollar interest rates and lower prices for LDC exports, both of which were largely due to the liquidity crisis and recession that began in the US, soon made it impossible for many LDCs to continue paying back their loans. The US prime interest rate discounted by the price on non-fuel exports of the LDCs increased from 5.7 percent in 1975–79 to 19.5 percent in 1986 (United Nations, 1986). This 13.8 percent increase in the real cost of financing non-fuel production and exports was devastating to the LDCs. Many of the old loans were variable and soon reflected the higher US prime rate and London Interbank Offered Rate. New loans, even when needed only to service the old debt, could rarely be justified in the private marketplace. Virtually all new private lending to the LDCs stopped.

Before long, the 13.8 percent increase in the real cost of financing non-fuel production and exports in the LDCs meant that (approximately) a 13.8 percent increase in the growth of these export industries would have been necessary to maintain the same ability to service foreign debt. Such growth would not have been possible even without the global recession. The world debt crisis had been created, primarily by US and UK economic policies.

The situation for major fuel exporters, such as Mexico, was the most devastating. By the time world oil prices had fallen by $18 a barrel from 1981 to 1986, oil-dependent Mexico had lost tens of billions of dollars of export revenues. A one-dollar drop in the world oil price reduces Mexico's export earnings by a half billion dollars per year. The LDC debt crisis cannot be blamed upon an independent collapse of OPEC (Organization of the Petroleum Exporting Countries) and oil prices, however. Brazil's economy is not so significantly affected by changes in oil prices, and Brazil became the biggest and perhaps the most heavily burdened LDC debtor. Also, the inability of OPEC to maintain high US dollar-denominated oil prices was significantly influenced by the drop in US dollar-demand for oil due to the restrictive dollar monetary policies and world recession.

The story continues in the mid-1980s. The US federal budget deficits continued to exceed $100 billion and even $200 billion per year after 1983 and there was still a bias toward restrictive monetary policy in the US and elsewhere. Consequently, US interest rates remained high, and in the rapidly integrating world financial markets these high interest rates began to pull international funds into the US at an unprecedented rate. The net flow of international funds into the US exceeded $100 billion per year by 1984 and, directly or indirectly, began financing about half of the US federal budget deficit.

By the mid-1980s, US government borrowing in and of itself was no longer significantly adding to the liquidity crises in the US nor exerting significant upward pressure on US interest rates—fortunately for US fiscal policy, the net inflow of foreign funds both responded to and exceeded the volumes of new US government borrowing. Unfortunately for many LDC debtors, however, some of the more than $100 billion per year, net, that was being pulled into the US came from their already cash-short economies. Therefore, some of the liquidity crisis was effectively transferred from the US and other developed economies to the LDCs in the mid-1980s, thus compounding the LDC debt crisis.

For example, despite attempts to channel Mexican loans into productive investments for the Mexican economy, it has been estimated that one-half of Mexico's foreign borrowings in the late 1970s and early 1980s instead left Mexico as capital flight, with the US and Switzerland as the primary safe havens for this cash. Sizable capital flight has also been a significant problem for Brazil, Venezuela, Argentina, and others (Figure 2.7). In the more globalized financial markets, capital controls used by the LDCs could not prevent the ultimate transfer of wealth to the most attractive international investment opportunities, which increasingly were in the US.

Back to US economic policies: US Treasury Secretary James Baker, who presided over US economic policies in the early and mid-1980s, proposed

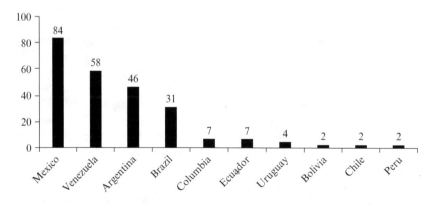

Source: Morgan Guaranty Trust Co.

Figure 2.7   Capital flight from Latin America, 1977–87 ($billion)

Table 2.5 *Money flows into the US financial markets in the 1980s and saves US banks from bad foreign debts*

	End-1982	End-1986	End-1988
Nine major US banks			
% of bank capital in:			
Developing countries	287.7%	153.9%	108.0%
Latin America	176.5%	110.2%	83.6%
All other US banks			
% of bank capital in:			
Developing countries	116.0%	55.0%	32.2%
Latin America	78.6%	39.7%	21.8%
Total bank capital			
(billions of dollars)			
Nine major US banks	$29.0	$46.7	$55.8
All other US banks	$41.6	$69.4	$79.8

Source: Federal Financial Institutions Examination Council, 'Country Exposure Lending Survey', 25 April 1983, 24 April 1987, and 12 April 1989.

the Baker Plan for dealing with the debt crisis in 1985. The primary emphasis of this plan was to protect the short-run solvency of US banks. There was no call for debt reduction or any other effective means of ultimately reducing the debt burden in the LDCs; instead Baker called for new loans to service existing LDC debt so that US banks could continue to receive normal payments and not have to classify a significant portion of their LDC debt as bad debt. As reigning Federal Reserve Board Chairman Paul Volcker stated years later about this period, 'we make a choice as to what to protect and what not to, and the strategic element to protect is essentially the banking system' (Feldstein, 1991, p. 178).

Indeed, the solvency of many US banks was at stake when the debt crisis hit in the early 1980s. For example, as shown in Table 2.5, the nine major US banks had 176.5 percent of their capital in heavily debt-burdened Latin American countries at the end of 1982. This ratio means that 176.5 percent of the entire stock market value of these banks had been loaned to Latin America as of year-end 1982. Having to write off a majority of this debt might therefore have left the major US banks with insufficient capital to remain in business.

Protecting the solvency of the major US banks during the 1980s required one or both of the following: either significant write-offs in LDC debt had to be avoided, or the stock market (capital) value of the banks had to significantly increase. As it turned out, the Baker Plan insured the former in the short run, until the rapidly globalizing financial markets and US monetary and fiscal policy had insured the latter.

As shown in Table 2.5, the total stock market capital value of the nine major US banks increased from $29.0 billion to $46.7 billion to $55.8 billion at year-end 1982, 1986, and 1988, respectively, thus lowering the percentage of their total capital in Latin America to 110.2 percent at year-end 1986 and 83.6 percent at year-end 1988. By the late 1980s, therefore, the major US banks were no longer in danger of being insolvent if major write-offs of Latin American debt occurred, and US policymakers could turn their attention to broader issues, such as the ultimate resolution of the debt crisis, and the overall health of the US and international financial markets. For example, the (new Treasury Secretary) Brady Plan in 1989 finally formalized and encouraged several ways in which private markets were already writing off LDC debt including resale discounts of this debt in the secondary markets.

Question: what accounted for the increased stock market capital value and, therefore, the return to secure solvency of the major US banks from 1982 to 1988, despite the obviously negative effect that the debt crisis must have had upon their stock market values over this period? Answer: the net flow of foreign funds into the US financial markets of more than $100 billion per year by 1984. As discussed previously, these funds allowed for a non-inflationary expansion of the US bank money supply, the longest post-World War II expansion in US economic growth, and the tripling of US stock market values from 1982 to 1988 even considering the stock market crash of 1987.

The story now takes an ironic turn. As elaborated in the next section, the 15 percent increase in the US money supply during 1986 was perfectly reasonable given the inflow of foreign funds and increased absorption of money by financial markets. However, excessive concern about inflation and lack of cooperation between the developed countries in 1987 led to restrictive monetary policies in the US and elsewhere, which in turn caused the stock market crash of October 1987. It was truly a world stock market crash in that the value of assets in the LDCs declined in proportion to developed country losses.

Table 2.6 shows the discount rates at which banks were able to sell off the debt of various developing countries before and after the October 1987 world stock market crash. These discount prices represent private market perceptions of the ability of countries to repay debt and thus indirectly the prices represent the income potential of country assets. As an example, Brazil's foreign debt sold for 62–65 cents per dollar of face value in May, 1987, indicating that 35–38 cents on the dollar of Brazilian debt could be written-off during debt-equity swaps in that month. In November, 1987,

Table 2.6   *Foreign debt prices, before and after the 1987 stock market crash (in cents per dollar of face value)*

	May 1987	November 1987
Argentina	58–60	33–37
Brazil	62–65	37–41
Chile	67–70	50–53
Colombia	85–88	72–76
Ecuador	52–55	31–34
Mexico	57–60	48–52
Peru	14–18	2–7
Philippines	70–72	55–60
Venezuela	72–74	49–53

Source: Shearson Lehman Brothers Inc.

one month after the crash in world stock markets, Brazil's debt sold for 37–41 cents on the dollar, indicating write-offs of 59–63 cents.

Reduced selling prices from May to November, 1987, for the debt of all of these developing countries verifies the truly global impact of the stock market crash. The crash reduced the average market value of developing-country investments as per Table 2.6 just as much as it reduced the value of investments within the richer nations as shown later in Table 2.7.

As discussed in the next section, stock market losses in the developed countries, which added up to more than the entire $900 billion debt of the LDCs, might largely have been avoided if central bankers, especially in the US and UK, had cooperatively maintained looser monetary policies in order to accommodate the natural expansion of the money centers.

Now for the whole, ironical, sequence of events: high interest rates in the developed world in the early 1980s, especially caused by US and UK monetary policies, created a global recession and the LDC debt crisis. Continuing high interest rates during the mid-1980s in the developed world, still primarily due to monetary policies, but then also because of the US federal deficits, pulled newly loaned global funds out of the LDCs as capital flight. This capital flight did not reduce the official LDC debt, but instead made it harder for LDC countries to generate the economic growth that would allow debt to be serviced.

Then, capital flight funds (actually, larger amounts of monetary wealth) were destroyed by the world stock market crash, itself caused primarily by US and European monetary policies. There was then much less channeling of funds into Latin American LDCs in the late 1980s and early 1990s, but instead, poorer developed as well as developing countries continued to send more than $100 billion per year, net, into the US (an amount approximately equal to either Mexico's or Brazil's total foreign debt).

These global funds maintained the capital strength of the major US banks, allowed the US government to maintain large budgets through the 1990s for national defense, social welfare, and other purposes, and paved the way for a continuing non-inflationary expansion of the US economy.

VIII.   THE STOCK MARKET CRASH OF 1987

As documented earlier, deregulation, internationalization, and technological change created the following trend which began in the early 1980s: more money-liquidity has been required by the US, UK, and other economies in order to support the simultaneous growth of nominal GDP and the new financial markets. How much more money-liquidity has been required? Despite the research of the author and others, the financial side of the new global economy expanded too rapidly and unpredictably compared to GDP to allow for accurate estimates.

For example, in an unprecedented demonstration of how fast money can be channeled into the financial markets, so much money flowed into the US stock markets in January, 1987 that US household wealth locked up in these financial investments increased by more than $250 billion in just this one month.[11] Then, when the US stock market crashed 22.6 percent on 19 October 1987, $500 billion was lost in one day.

As another example, commercial lending by foreign banks, which captured 9 percent of the US market in the late 1970s, increased its share to 16 percent by the mid-1980s.[12] This foreign lending added to the volume of US financial transactions, and, because it can quickly move in and out of the US money supply, it is very difficult to quantify its effect on the economy. The same thing can be said about foreign lending to the US government, that is, foreign purchases of US government securities, which totaled $14.3 billion in just the first six months of 1986, compared to $10 billion in all of 1980.[13]

International financial transactions denominated in US dollars expanded to the point where dollar holdings by foreign investors reached $1 trillion by 1990, approximately 20 percent of the expected nominal GDP for that year. Predicting how these holdings were being used in the US economy was difficult.

Similarly, in the UK the 1986 Big Bang deregulation period allowed dramatic increases in both the profitability and turnover of financial markets. As shown in Figure 2.3, UK financial market turnover doubled from 1985 to 1986 and then doubled again from 1986 to 1987.

As the velocity of money continued its decline in the mid-1980s, most notably in the US and UK but also in other globalizing financial centers (Figure 2.1), expansionary monetary policies pursued by the major industrial nations had only weak positive effects on nominal GDP compared with historical periods. More of the expanding money was absorbed by the new, more international financial markets and less was used by people to boost their purchases of merchandise and services. Despite the mistakes of forecasters in 1981–82, this new structural environment for monetary policy was not yet fully understood. For example, scores of articles appeared in reaction to the expansionary monetary policy that was started in the US in late 1982, each expressing confusion at the minimal resulting increases in real GDP and inflation.

Analysts can hardly be chastised for their confusion, because the structural environment for monetary policy changed very fast in the 1980s. Econometric forecasting models which must use decades of data could not be expected to fully incorporate these structural changes. Also, direct measurement of the share of (m1) which is absorbed in the turnover of financial transactions and simultaneously unavailable for non-financial, GDP transactions is next to impossible, despite the well-respected work of Spindt (1985) and others. For example, how do we know the degree to which people see their NOW accounts as interest-earning investments rather than as checking accounts for monthly shopping requirements?

In light of this new, misunderstood environment for monetary policy, the unprecedented world stock market crash of 1987 can now be explained. On 19 October 1987, the Dow Jones Industrial Average fell an astonishing 508 points, or 22.6 percent, its biggest one-day percentage decline ever. This unexpected crash in the US market triggered panic selling in all of the world's major stock markets, which had become inextricably linked in the 1980s.

As shown in Table 2.7, from 25 August 1987, the record high for the US stock market, to 11 November 1987, the world markets declined anywhere from 43.4 percent (Australia) to 18.7 percent (Italy). After mid-November, the markets began a gradual recovery as fear-driven selling moderated, and as central banks dramatically (and finally!) increased national money supplies.

Why did the world's stock markets crash? The most commonly mentioned and commonly agreed-upon explanations seemed to be the following:

1. Speculation had driven stock market valuations too high relative to stock earnings, so that a major shift of funds out of stocks into bonds, other investments, and cash was overdue.
2. Investors lost confidence in the economic policies of the US

Table 2.7   World stock market decline, 1987

Percentage change in each market between 25 August 1987, the record high for the US market, and 11 November 1987:

US	−27.8
Japan	−19.8
UK	−27.2
West Germany	−38.4
Canada	−28.4
France	−34.7
Switzerland	−30.5
Australia	−43.4
Italy	−18.7
Netherlands	−33.6

Source: Morgan Stanley Capital International Perspective.

government, especially its attempts to reduce the federal budget deficit and to maintain the foreign exchange value of the US dollar. Both of these conditions were felt to be necessary in order to insure healthy international financial markets.

3.   Sudden fear that the US dollar would lose much of its value, especially after the announcement of an unexpectedly large US trade deficit, caused international investors to move much of their money out of the US stock market. As the US stock market crashed, fear spread through the other markets and they crashed as well.[14]

4.   Less mentioned, less agreed-upon, but more fundamental explanations attributed the world stock market crash to monetary policies. For example, on 22 October 1987, the editorial page of *The Wall Street Journal* carried two articles by prominent economists, one claiming that the crash occurred because monetary policy was too restrictive, and one claiming that the crash occurred because monetary policy was too loose.[15]

Although there are valid points in both of these *The Wall Street Journal* articles, neither mentions the new structural environment for monetary policy that has been created by the deregulation, expansion, and globalization of financial markets. As discussed previously, in the 1980s an increasingly larger money supply has been needed to support the rapid growth of financial markets as well as the normal growth of GDP. Recognition of this trend, combined with an examination of the relevant economic data, should make it clear that the world stock market crash occurred because monetary policy was too restrictive—not only US monetary policy, but also monetary policy in the UK and other countries which have participated in the expansion of international financial markets.

US monetary policy in fact became quite restrictive in 1987 in the time period leading up to the stock market crash. The annual growth rate of the US money supply, whether measured by (m1) or the broader measures (m2) or (m3), declined by approximately 4 percentage points in the first five months of 1987, compared to its growth rate in 1986. For example, US (m1) grew by 15 percent in 1986, a rate which allowed the globalizing US financial markets to expand and at the same time allowed US inflation and real GDP to expand at historically low rates close to 2 percent. Then, in the first five months of 1987, the US Federal Reserve Bank reduced the annual growth rate of (m1) to just over 10 percent.

After May, 1987, the US Federal Reserve Bank slowed the annual growth rate of (m1) even further, to 3.0 percent growth in June, 5.3 percent contraction in July, 2.1 percent growth in August, and 3.9 percent growth in September, the last month before the stock market crash. The Federal Reserve Bank was reacting to the rising, but incorrect, expectation that inflation was just around the corner, as well as a mounting fear that the foreign exchange value of the dollar would fall precipitously, thus causing capital flight out of the US currency, further declines in its value, and the erosion of investor confidence. Restrictive monetary policy was implemented to fend off these risks, and it was felt to be justified because the probability of a recession within the near future was slim.

Leading up to the October crash, contractionary monetary policies were being pursued in Japan, West Germany, and England, as well as in the US. From July to October, interest rates on three-month Eurodeposits denominated in yen, marks, and pounds increased by 1 percent, while those denominated in US dollars increased by 2 percent. Somewhat tighter monetary policy was pursued in the US to defend the dollar, and to 'reassure financial markets by demonstrating that the Fed was on guard against inflation'.[16]

The short-term result of restricted money and higher interest rates was a very costly reversal in the expansion of the international money centers. This expansion had continued steadily through the mid-1980s thanks to deregulation, internationalization, and advances in information-processing technology, all of which had given the world's borrowers and lenders increased ability to make profitable investments. Higher interest rates despite continued sluggish real GDP growth around the world squeezed the new-found profitability and shattered investor confidence. Nervousness spread until the markets finally sold off.

World stock market losses, which added up to more than the entire

$900 billion debt of the LDCs, might have been largely avoided if central bankers had cooperatively maintained looser monetary policies in order to accommodate the natural expansion of the money centers. Instead, just when international monetary expansion was most needed shortly before the crash, West Germany raised its interest rates. The increase in West German interest rates created fear that the US Federal Reserve Bank would have to raise interest rates even further to prevent a withdrawal of foreign investment from the US and a decline in the foreign exchange value of the dollar. Just when the US and other countries needed to lower interest rates and increase money supplies, Germany stubbornly encouraged the confused central bankers to make their move in the opposite direction, to achieve what ultimately was a trivial and unsustainable goal: exchange rate stability.

Germany's overly restrictive monetary policy, relative to the other major industrial countries, resulted in a 43 percent decline in the German stock market, measured from the beginning of 1987 to the end of 1987. While the other stock markets began recovering at the end of 1987 as central banks injected more money into their economies, the German market was less able to recover, making it the big loser of the world's major stock markets in 1987.

Interestingly, shortly after the crash, the US stock market was valued at roughly the same level as it was at the end of 1986. Also, the monetary reserves of the US banking system, an alternate measure of the amount of money-liquidity in the US financial markets, was at the same level shortly before the crash as it was at the end of 1986. With no extra money-liquidity available for the US financial markets over the first nine months of 1987, it is not surprising that the US financial markets ultimately maintained approximately the same valuation over this period.

As indicated by this case study of the crash in world stock markets, as of 1987 economists had not learned the important lessons from their forecasting errors of the early and mid-1980s (Table 2.4). Sufficient attention was still not being paid to the continuing deregulation, expansion, and globalization of the money centers. Therefore, the continuing drop in the velocity of money in early 1987 was not expected, and monetary policy was made much too restrictive. The result was the destruction of hundreds of billions of dollars of wealth and the erosion of investor confidence.

Unlike the money-liquidity crisis of the early 1980s, which primarily deflated the then relatively less profitable non-financial markets, the unaccommodated drop in velocity in the late 1980s deflated the then relatively less profitable financial markets.

NOTES

1. 'Reserve's Policy Drifts as Its Officials Heed Different Indicators', *The Wall Street Journal*, 22 April 1988, p.1.
2. The author's research corroborates the work of others, that 'since (m1) comes closer than (m2) to approximating a medium-of-exchange concept of money, there is reason to expect that the demand for (m1) would be affected more by the volume of transactions than the demand for (m2), and that has turned out to be the case' (Friedman, 1988).
3. 'Stakes High for Britain's Financial Firms in Freer Markets', *The New York Times*, 6 October 1986, p.34.
4. 'London's Exchange Braces for Big Bang Set to Occur Monday', *The Wall Street Journal*, 24 October 1986, p.1.
5. 'Business Bulletin', *The Wall Street Journal*, 14 January 1988, p.1.
6. Without including government grants and private remittances abroad, the value of exports minus imports would equal the more commonly mentioned 'Trade Balance'.
7. The 'Case Study of US–Foreign Trade, 1981–' is discussed in Section V of this chapter.
8. 'The 364 Economists' Attack on Government Policy', *Barclays Review* 56, May 1981, p.27.
9. *Business Week*, 4 April 1983, p.67.
10. Ibid.
11. 'While Investors Are Acting on Their "Wishful Thinking . . . "', *Business Week*, 2 March 1987, p.24.
12. 'Banking's Balance of Power Is Tilting Toward the Regionals', *Business Week*, 7 April 1986, p.56.
13. 'Financing US Deficit Abroad', *The New York Times*, 7 November 1985.
14. An excellent summary of various potential causes of the crash, especially the trade deficit announcement, is contained in Mullins (1989).
15. 'Monetary Policy Caused the Crash . . . Not Tight Enough . . . Too Tight Already', *The Wall Street Journal*, 22 October 1987, p.34.
16. Ibid.

APPENDIX   REGRESSIONS OF US (M1) INCOME VELOCITY OF MONEY AND RELATED VARIABLES

The author's analysis of the pre-1982 and (1982–) causality between US financial market expansion (NEWFMK), interest rates (r), income velocity (v), and other groups of variables (t,w,x,y,z), is represented by the following equations. Before 1982 financial market expansion is seen as a domestic variable which is more dependent on other domestic macroeconomic variables; after 1982—as financial globalization proceeds—it is a more exogenous, internationalized driver of domestic macroeconomic variables such as interest rates and income velocity:

Pre-1982: $(r) = f_1(t)$ (2A.1)

$(NEWFMK) = f_2(w)$ (2A.2)

$(v) = f_3(r,x)$ (2A.3)

(1982–): $(NEWFMK) = f_4$(tech. change, , deregulation internationalization)   (2A.4)

$(r) = f_5(NEWFMK,y)$ (2A.5)
$(v) = f_6(NEWFMK,r,z)$ (2A.6)

Technological change, deregulation, and internationalization in the author's view are thus the root cause of much of (a) the rapid expansion of financial markets beginning in the early 1980s and the massive new capital flow into the US; (b) the subsequent rapid decline in US interest rates; and therefore (c) the sustained expansion of US GDP beginning in 1983. Each of (a)–(c) increases money demand, *ceteris paribus*. (a) and (c) increase the transactions demand for money, and (a) and (b) increase the asset demand for money. (a) and (b) decrease the income velocity of money; the effect of (c) upon income velocity is less certain, although some economies of scale in the use of money when GDP increases might cause it to increase velocity.

The first consequence of technological change, deregulation, and internationalization is the expansion of financial markets, and it is largely the expansion of financial markets from which the author believes that the other changes flow. Yet research, and notably the work of Friedman (1988), has not conclusively identified a linkage between financial market expansion and income velocity. The author believes that the econometric work of Friedman and others falls short on this score, first because of a failure to identify the exact time at which the structural changes began to have their strong impact; and, second, because structural changes within a very dynamic, evolving marketplace are difficult to model (Chapter 4, Section IV).

Friedman (1988) tests for a structural shift in his (m1) velocity equation by running the same regressions over two sub-periods: (1970:Q1–1979:Q4) and (1980:Q1–1986:Q2). He chooses 1980:Q1 to begin the second sub-period because of the shift from accelerating inflation to disinflation, and because it so happens that total transactions accelerated sharply after 1980.

In contrast to Friedman, the author argues that the second sub-period should begin in 1982:Q1, when the money-absorbing financial transactions accelerated and when the US began receiving the massive net inflow of foreign investment. The initial, rapid expansion of Spindt's financial transactions debits variable in 1980, as used by Friedman to date the structural shift, was due to the early deregulation reshuffling of money between money and near-money accounts. These transactions are less likely to contemporaneously absorb money away from other uses compared to stock, bond, and government securities trading, especially when international trading is involved.

The author has used regression analysis to estimate equations (2A.1)–(2A.6) for the US, and his key results appear below.[1]

The author's regression analysis of the pre-1982 period corroborates the research of Friedman (1988) and others who, because of the date or methodology of their research, have not let the (1982–) period add significant 'noise' to their equations (2A.1)–(2A.3). Yet to the author's knowledge, no one else has estimated equations (2A.4)–(2A.6) specifically for the (1982–) period. Because (f_4), in the opinion of the author, is unquantifiable, he has taken (NEWFMK) as given, where (NEWFMK) is the combined volumes of US stock, bond, and government securities transactions. The US government three-month Treasury bill yield is used for (r), and (v) is the (m1) income velocity of money.

As shown below, regressions over the period (1982:Q1–1998:Q2) highlight the strong negative relationship that existed between financial market expansion and both interest rates and (m1) income velocity after the beginning of 1982 (Equations A, B). These regressions thus confirm the causality of equations (2A.4)–(2A.6) above, whereby financial markets absorb money away from GDP markets. Indeed, a majority (approximately 80 percent as measured by the R^2 statistic) of the fluctuations in interest rates and income velocity (the dependent variables) can be explained simply by the fluctuations in financial market transactions (the independent variable) in a simple linear equation. In this simple equation, a 0–1 dummy variable was included (D96Q1) to account for the reduced absorption of money by financial market transactions beginning in early 1996 when, instead of a three-day settlement period for transaction funds to be released, the SEC allowed a same-day settlement period. The regression results, as well as Figure 2.2, show a sudden increase in income velocity since 1995 due to this deregulation. Actually, the SEC moved from five-day settlement to three-day settlement in 1995, but the author's research indicates that the move from three-day to same-day was more significant for the (m1) income velocity.

When the pre-1982 and (1982–) periods are combined, then econometric equations are unable to explain changes in velocity. The author concludes that if the periods prior to and following the initial strong impact of technological change, deregulation, and internationalization upon financial market expansion are combined, then their impact upon interest rates and income velocity cannot be properly identified. Friedman's failure to identify a strong negative relationship between financial transactions and velocity can thus be attributed to his use of the period (1980:Q1–1986:Q2), which includes two years before the rapid expansion of money-absorbing financial transactions. The Appendix shows that two financial market expansion variables, NEWFMK and NYSE (New York Stock Exchange Composite Index),[2] have a statistically indefensible coefficient (as measured by the t-statistic) over Friedman's period when, as per equation (2A.3) and Friedman's equations, the interest rate is also included (Equations C, D).

Additional income velocity equations over the period (1982:Q1–1995:Q3) are shown below, which was a period stopping right before the SEC went from five-day to three-day and then same-day funds settlement. For the (1982:Q1–1995:Q3) period, when real GDP (q) is included in addition to the financial transactions variable, then a positive coefficient is estimated for real GDP (Equation F). The positive coefficient indicates that there are economies in the use of money for transaction purposes at higher levels of real GDP, *ceteris paribus*, as suggested by the literature. The author also considered the inflation rate as an additional explanatory variable in his income velocity equations. Inflation (INF) is measured by the GDP deflator, and the results of Equation F confirm that, when inflation rises, money is more quickly spent rather than held as people try to maximize purchasing power over time. The interest rate (r), as measured by the three-month Treasury bill rate, is also included in Equation F, and the results confirm that people do hold less money (velocity increases) when they are able to take advantage of increased interest rates on non-money interest-earning accounts. Of course, as documented by Equation A, most of the changes in interest rates over this period can be explained by the financial transactions variable, and including both terms as independent variables is somewhat redundant and biases the results—Equation G excludes the interest rate and is thus theoretically the best equation.

Equation H in the Appendix extends the regression period to 1998:Q2 and thus covers the recent SEC funds-settlement changes—once again the 0–1 dummy variable is included to capture the funds-settlement change.

The estimated dummy variable coefficient indicates that with more efficient quick settlement the rate at which financial transactions absorb money has decreased.

Regarding Friedman's (1988) suggestion of an inverse relation between income velocity and financial market expansion three quarters earlier (the wealth effect), and a positive relation between velocity and contemporaneous financial market expansion, no such effects were found. Lagging the financial market expansion variable reduces its level of significance in proportion to the length of the lag, and the negative coefficients are maintained.

Quarterly Data, 1982:Q1–1998:Q2

(Equation A): $(r) = (9.42) - (3.41 \times 10^{-7}) \times (NEWFMK) + (2.36) \times (D96Q1)$
t-stat: (20.66)   (−7.35)   (3.29)

One-Period Moving Average: MA(1) coefficient = 0.76, t-stat = 10.08
Adj.R^2: 0.81
Durbin–Watson statistic: 1.20

(Equation B): $(v) = (6.78) - (3.67 \times 10^{-8}) \times (NEWFMK) + (1.20) \times (D96Q1)$
t-stat: (61.73)   (−3.23)   (6.71)

MA(1) coefficient = 0.70, t-stat = 7.34
Adj.R^2: 0.78
Durbin–Watson statistic: 1.20

Quarterly Data, 1980:Q1–1986:Q2

(Equation C): $(v) = (6.14) - (2.22 \times 10^{-7}) \times (NEWFMK) + (0.090) \times (r)$
t-stat: (10.78)   (−0.34)   (2.25)

MA(1) coefficient = 0.42, t-stat = 2.13
Adj.R^2: 0.56
Durbin–Watson statistic: 2.09

(Equation D): $(v) = (6.15) - (0.127 \times 10^{-2}) \times (NYSE) + (0.093) \times (r)$
t-stat: (7.98)   (−0.25)   (2.45)

MA(1) coefficient = 0.42, t-stat = 2.14
Adj.R^2: 0.56
Durbin–Watson statistic: 2.09

Quarterly Data, 1982:Q1–1995:Q3

(Equation E): $(v) = (6.91) - (5.68 \times 10^{-8}) \times (NEWFMK)$
t-stat: (77.1)   (−5.91)

MA(1) coefficient = 0.64, t-stat = 5.74
Adj.R^2: 0.74
Durbin–Watson statistic: 1.17

(Equation F): $(v) = (3.94) - (5.03 \times 10^{-8}) \times (NEWFMK) + (0.062) \times (r)$
t-stat: (4.85)   (−2.45)   (2.17)

$+ (0.028) \times (INF) + (0.00136) \times (q)$
t-stat: (1.28)   (2.45)

MA(1) coefficient = 0.70, t-stat = 5.67
Adj.R^2: 0.83
Durbin–Watson statistic: 1.12

(Equation G): $(v) = (3.23) - (5.63 \times 10^{-8}) \times (NEWFMK) + (0.077) \times (INF)$
t-stat: (4.24)   (−4.73)   (6.16)

$+ (0.0189) \times (q)$
t-stat: (4.08)

MA(1) coefficient = 0.91, t-stat = 13.38
Adj.R^2: 0.82
Durbin–Watson statistic: 1.08

Quarterly Data, 1982:Q1–1998:Q2

(Equation H): $(v) = (1.54) - (6.95 \times 10^{-8}) \times (NEWFMK) + (0.069) \times (INF)$
t-stat: (2.22)   (−6.70)   (5.19)

$+ (0.0030) \times (q) + (0.48) \times (D96Q1)$
t-stat: (7.48)   (3.33)

MA(1) coefficient = 0.96, t-stat = 57.68
Adj.R^2: 0.86
Durbin–Watson statistic: 1.04

NOTES

1. Much of the theory and statistical analysis of this chapter is elaborated in the author's 1989 publication (Allen, 1989).
2. Friedman considered the Dow Jones stock market index, a narrower aggregate but of course highly correlated.

3. Financial instabilities and trends in the 1990s

I. THE EARLY 1990s RECESSIONARY PERIOD

Recessionary conditions in the early 1990s can, as in 1982, be blamed on overly strict monetary policies given the continually increasing money-liquidity and capital needs of the global economy. For example, Japan's 8.0 percent average yearly money growth from 1986 to 1988 was slowed to 2.4 percent in 1989 and 4.4 percent in 1990. This reduction contributed to the destruction of Japan's financial surplus and long-term capital outflows that had helped sustain economic growth in Europe and the US. The wealth lost domestically in Japan as its stock market fell 60 percent from 1989 to 1991 temporarily slowed growth there. But, unlike the US, Germany, and others, Japan had the fiscal means in the early 1990s, including a $120 billion fiscal stimulus package in mid-1993, to avoid recession (at least until 1998). As elaborated below, restrictive monetary policies in Europe and the US, together with Japan's 'turning inward' contributed heavily to the early 1990s global recessionary conditions.

The global regions hit especially hard by recessions in the early 1990s were those that lost international capital. The timing of recessions in the US and Europe demonstrates this fact. Also, the probability of early 1990s recessions in the developed countries increased due to the return of international investment to the less developed countries (LDCs). Net inflows of foreign direct investment (FDI) into LDCs averaged $13 billion per year from 1985 to 1989, then jumped to $18 billion in 1990 and $31 billion in 1991.[1] Unlike in the 1970s, Asian LDCs rather than Latin American LDCs were receiving the major part of this direct investment. As direct investment to the LDCs soared in 1991, developed countries saw their average inflows shrink by one-fifth.

A. The European Situation

The late 1980s was a time of strong economic growth for Germany and others within the European Community (EC). The Single European Act signed in 1987 to 'complete the internal EC market by 1992' began abolishing border controls and other technical barriers to trade including inconsistent health, safety, and environmental regulations; it commenced opening up public procurement, most significantly in energy, telecommunications, transportation, and water supply; and began creating a unified market for financial services.

The perceived efficiencies of 'Europe 1992' led to a cross-border European investment boom beginning in 1987, not only in the internal European market, but also from the European affiliates of US, Japanese, and other foreign firms. For example, majority-owned foreign affiliates of US companies increased capital spending in Europe from $15.4 billion in 1987 to $18.8 billion in 1988 to $21.1 billion in 1989. And by 1989, 411 Japanese manufacturers had opened or made plans to start production in Europe, thus tripling the number of Japanese plants since the early 1980s; the Toyota plant constructed in Great Britain in 1990 was the largest foreign investment ever in Britain. The French, who had long been one of the most protectionist countries against Japanese trade and investment, reversed their stance in April, 1989, when Industry Minister Roger Fauroux said that the French government has decided that 'it is better to have Japanese [factories] than to have unemployment' (Prudential-Bache Securities, 1989, p. 14).

Aided by international capital and internal efficiencies, economic growth for all of Western Europe averaged over 3 percent per year from 1987 to 1990. As the biggest exporter of capital goods within Europe, West Germany gained the most from Europe 1992, achieving economic growth rates of 4 percent in both 1989 and 1990. Able to export more easily to its strengthened neighbors, West Germany's trade surplus within the EC widened from DM32 billion in 1985 to DM94 billion in 1989. Thus, 60 percent of West Germany's trade surplus was with the rest of Europe by 1989.

German reunification was forwarded in the hope that the late 1980s EC economic growth rates would continue through the 1990s. Under this assumption the German economy would have been able to absorb the estimated cost of successful reunification without severe hardship. The DM94 billion ($55 billion) West German trade surplus with the EC in 1989 equaled 4.6 percent of its total economic output. Therefore, if growth rates had continued and all of this trade surplus with the EC was instead directed toward East German investment without any immediate return, the West German economy would have been in a minor recession, and East Germany would have had the $350–$400 billion necessary for modernization before the year 2000.

Unfortunately, not only was the initial forecast of $350–$400 billion required for the modernization of East Germany too low, but also the EC growth rate slowed. Foreign firm-to-firm investment into East Germany after reunification was slower than expected, given legal tangles over ownership of real estate and business assets, dilapidated transportation and communication systems, and the general uncompetitiveness of East German industry compared to international standards. Only 30 percent of East German companies were capable of competing in the EC market, 50 percent needed overhauling to survive, and 20 percent were doomed to bankruptcy.[2]

The inability to compete within the EC led to substantially increased unemployment within East Germany after the full monetary union of 1 July 1990. Obliged to conduct all business in newly issued West German marks after that date,[3] East German firms were thrown into many of the rigors the EC labor and product markets could stand, but how to compete when the output per worker in East Germany was 40 percent of the output per worker in West Germany, approximately equivalent to West Germany in the late 1960s?[4] Unemployment doubled in July to 270,000 workers, and three times as many East Germans were placed on reduced work time.[5]

Closing this productivity gap between the two Germanys required a continuing $70–$80 billion per year transfer to East Germany from the global economy through the turn of the century rather than the $50 billion per year originally estimated. DM200 billion ($118 billion at $1 to DM1.7) was necessary to restore the roads and railways, link the canals to West Germany's, and build a new international airport in East Berlin.[6] On 20 June 1990, a DM55 billion ($32 billion) plan to modernize the East German telephone system was unveiled, DM30 billion of which West Germany's state-run telecommunications group, Bundespost Telekom, expected to raise from the capital markets by 1998.[7] Further governmental expenditures were required for postal and telecommunications systems, and other public works, and even greater rates of private investment were necessary.

Attracting enough international capital to Germany to help support the $70–$80 billion per year necessary for successful reunification, especially given initial pledges not to raise taxes, required high German interest rates. The German 'identified capital flow' with the rest of the world (direct investment plus portfolio investment plus other capital), which had been a net outflow of $70 billion in 1988 and 1989, began turning inward to a net outflow of $50 billion in 1990 and a net inflow of $11 billion in 1991.

The high German interest rates and capital inflows in the early 1990s led to a temporary break-up of the European Monetary System (EMS) and the delay of other economic efficiencies of Europe 1992. In addition, the restrictive monetary policies of the other EMS countries through mid-1992 as they tried to maintain EMS interest rate and exchange rate parities with Germany led to recessionary conditions.

Economic output of the EC's 12 member states declined slightly in 1993, the first shrinkage since 1975, and the EC unemployment rate rose to 11 percent. Clearly, Germany's restrictive monetary policies and fiscal requirements put it at the center of the European Exchange Rate Mechanism (ERM) crisis in September 1992. Declining competitiveness and confidence in Germany due to the appreciating mark and, still, high interest rates, escalating costs of reunification, and widespread Eastern European problems scared some international capital away from Germany. Pre-reunification German capital outflows returned, and the German economy contracted 1.2 percent in 1993. In mid-1993 German unemployment rates reached 7.5 percent in the West and 15.3 percent in the East.

During this period of instability in exchange rates and high German interest rates, in September 1992 the UK and Italy were forced to leave the ERM when their exchange rates reached the lower limits of their required currency bands, the Finnish markka started floating, and attempts by others to maintain their exchange rates led to high interest rates and recession. For example, Sweden's crisis as discussed next was exacerbated by increases in interest rates to defend the Swedish krona.

B. Sweden's Crisis, 1991

Sweden's banking crisis in 1991, including the swift government response to 'nationalize' the affected banks, or at least issue a general guarantee of bank obligations and create a 'bad bank' (Securum) to handle toxic assets, is frequently cited as a good policymaking response relevant to more recent crises. The direct cost to the government of Sweden of intervention, estimated at 2.1 percent of GDP (Jennergren and Näslund, 1997), was a smaller percentage of GDP than was expended even just one year after recognition of the 2007– crisis by many affected countries, and although in Sweden it responded to a more local and likely containable crisis, it may be a good example of the benefits of swift 'lender-of-last-resort' intervention.

Based upon the common patterns of large-scale financial crisis as elaborated in Chapters 4 and 5, Sweden (along with Japan discussed later in this chapter) provides a very instructive case among the developed countries, and is thus chosen for the purposes of this book, although similar episodes were experienced in Norway and Finland in the late 1980s and early 1990s.

Sweden's crisis, like many others, occurred after a 'boom phase' of deregulation and liberalization (1983–85) and leveraged credit expansion (1986–90) that was typical of the 1980s financial globalization in developed countries as discussed in Chapter 1. Deregulation included abolition of required liquidity ratios of banks in 1983, and removal of interest rate ceilings and lending ceilings for banks in 1985. As in the US in the

1980s, rising national government budget deficits encouraged a rapidly growing market for Treasury bills and related certificates of deposits and other money market instruments. In 1989 Swedish residents' foreign currency investments and foreigners' investments in domestic securities were also freed from currency regulations. Further sustaining a commercial real estate boom (275 percent price appreciation from 1980 to 1985 and 140 percent from 1985 to 1990), the maximum loan-to-value ratio for mortgage loans was increased from 75 percent to 90 percent in 1988. And, increased household borrowing allowed for a 4 percent per year consumption growth boom in 1986 and 1987. Like the US subprime mortgage expansion in 2000–06 preceding the recent crisis, in this rapidly liberalizing 'boom phase' for Sweden, lax standards and the inability of banks to monitor loan portfolios increased systemic risk:

> the banks did not have information systems capable of handling the new situation with rapidly expanding credit portfolios. In many cases, banks lacked an overview over their credit portfolios, and did not have a clear picture, for example, of the fraction of the total stock going to a single borrower. The large share of lending to finance companies added to the information problem, since borrowers denied credits over a certain limit in banks often had loans with the finance company. Second, the rate of expansion and the apparent profitability of new lending created a difficult problem in allocating scarce human resources between credit evaluation and credit expansion. (Englund, 1999, p. 96)

And, like the initial subprime mortgage market failures in the US that launched the recent crisis in early 2007, Swedish finance companies with heavy exposure to real estate began having trouble rolling over their real-estate related loans in September 1990 (the market for *marknadsbevis* totally dried up within a few days as bankruptcies loomed), and the crisis quickly spread to other parts of the money markets as measured by rapidly increasing interest rate margins between Treasury bills and bank certificates. During 1990–93, accumulated banking losses equaled 17 percent of lending, and the impact on the real economy led to an accumulated 35 percent decline in private investment and 5 percent decline in GDP over 1991–93.

And, just as the subprime mortgage crisis in the US was allowed to become, in the view of the author, more of a systemic economy-wide liquidity crisis in July–September 2007 than necessary, given 'too-little-too-late' money-liquidity expansion, Sweden exacerbated its crisis in the summer of 1992 with *increases* in interest rates. Overnight interest rates were raised by the Riksbank from 12 percent in July 1992 to 16 percent in August in an ultimately unsuccessful attempt to defend the value of the krona in the context of the European ERM climate and exaggerated concerns of inflation. German mark interest rates had been high due to the financing costs of reunification, and interest rate parity (IRP) considerations were channeling funds out of the krona and other European currencies into the mark. On 19 November 1992 the krona was finally allowed to float, which led to a 9 percent devaluation the next day and a 20 percent devaluation by the end of 1992.

The creation of the 100 percent government-owned Securum on 1 January 1993 to take over bad collateral assets of banks, and then dispose of them, is a good policy response for countries to consider in future crises, and for research into the nature and function of banks in general. Securum owned approximately 2,500 properties corresponding to perhaps 2 percent of all commercial real estate in Sweden, and these were disposed of, mostly over 1995 and 1996 as the market began to recover, through initial public offerings on the Stockholm stock exchange, corporate sales aside from the stock exchange, and through a variety of other deals on individual properties. The cost to the taxpayer was thus held to SEK35 billion or 2.1 percent of GDP, and the banking system outside of Nordbanken and Gota quickly recovered in the mid-1990s as assisted by the government's general guarantee of bank obligations.

C.   The US Situation

The official US recession, as dated by the National Bureau of Economic Research (NBER), occurred during the last two quarters of 1990 and the first quarter of 1991. More generally, US economic growth averaged less than 1 percent from the beginning of 1989 to 1993, as compared to 2.3 percent from 1973 to 1989. Compared to a hypothetical 2.3 percent growth rate continuing (the 'natural potential rate of growth'), during 1989–91 there was a $225 billion loss in potential GDP, approximately half of which was a decline in consumption and half a decline in fixed investment. Aside from these figures, a small increase in net exports was balanced by a small decrease in inventory investment and a small decrease in net government spending.

At the American Economic Association (AEA) meetings in January 1993, the main conclusion seemed to be that established models have been unhelpful in understanding this US recession. In papers given by Robert Hall of Stanford and the NBER (1993), and Olivier Blanchard of the Massachusetts Institute of Technology (MIT, 1993), there was only the general consensus that consumers may have lost confidence about the future. From Hall:

A spontaneous decline in consumption would probably result in unusual behavior of consumption during the recession relative to its pre-recession values and relative to real disposable income . . . There was a considerable swing in consumption at much lower than a recession frequency from 1987 to 1991. At the same time, survey measures of consumer confidence fell from record high to somewhat subnormal levels. Although a sharp spontaneous contraction of consumption was not part of the story of the recession, changes in consumption not associated with changes in disposable income may be an important part of a bigger story about the late 1980s and early 1990s.

And from Blanchard:

By far, the main proximate cause of the recession was a 'consumption shock', a decrease in consumption in relation to its normal determinants. Because the effects of such shocks are long lasting, this also explains why, in contrast to previous recoveries, the last recovery was a slow and weak one . . .

What was especially revealing about assessments of this US recession was the scant attention paid to global conditions including increased international transfers of investment based upon interest rate and financial strategy parities, and the subsequent adjustments in international trade (Chapter 1), and the structural decline and increased variability of the income velocity of money (Chapter 2). Presumably reflecting the research of the NBER as it advises the US government, Hall's (1993) paper devotes only a few sentences to the rest of the world:

It appears unlikely that events in the rest of the world contributed to the recession . . . net exports grew a little during the recession. It would be almost impossible to tell a story in which events in world markets caused a US recession but US net exports rose . . . There was no outside force that concentrated its effects over a few months in the late summer and fall of 1990 . . .

In fact, one only needs to look at Figure 3.1 to find an international force that adversely affected the US economy beginning in 1990. As shown in Figure 3.1, the identified capital inflows to the US for direct investment, portfolio investment, and other investment (monetary authorities plus general government plus banks plus other sectors) collapsed in 1990. Aggregating these categories shows a net identified capital inflow to the US of close to $100 billion per year until the sudden drop to $13 billion in 1990 and $30 billion in 1991. After 1991, the net inflow rose again to average over $100 billion.

The net identified capital inflow shown in Figure 3.1 excludes the very suspect 'statistical discrepancy' account which reconciles differences between measured commerce and payments for that commerce. The

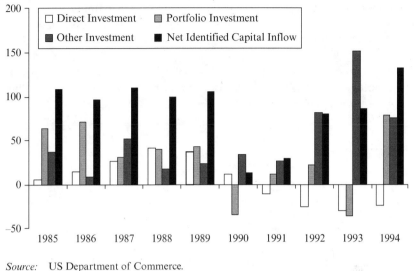

Source: US Department of Commerce.

Figure 3.1 *Explaining the 1990–91 US recession: the decline in net
identified capital inflows (by category, $billion)*

statistical discrepancy is generally considered part of the capital account
(now financial account) balance; however, there is no way to verify exactly
how much of the statistical discrepancy reflects actual flows of capital. In
1990, the statistical discrepancy account had a $64 billion credit position,
its largest imbalance ever. The author's view is that some of this $64 billion
did not actually flow into the US, which thus contributed even more to the
US credit crunch and recessionary conditions.

From 1989, the last pre-recession year, to the depth of the US recession in 1990–91, the US economy was thus receiving approximately
$100 billion/year less net foreign investment, and the NBER and others
claim that there was no outside force that concentrated its negative effects
on the US economy in 1990–91! Certainly the $225 billion loss in potential
GDP during 1989–91 could be completely accounted for by this decline in
net foreign investment once one figures out the reduced US income, monetary wealth, and therefore reduced consumption that would occur combined with the immediate loss of fixed and inventory investment. Based
upon the timing lags and cause–effect material discussed in Chapter 2, the
author's position is that the collapse in foreign investment inflow initiated
the recession, rather than vice versa.

German reunification was pulling international funds into Germany, and Japan's money-liquidity crisis was pulling international funds into Japan—independently of US domestic economic conditions. Also, the approximately $100 billion/year reduction in net foreign investment into the US could certainly account for the depreciation of the dollar during the recession against, especially, the Japanese yen—Japanese foreign investment especially dried up during 1990. In turn, the depreciating dollar and reduced US income (therefore more competitive US exports and less US demand for imports) could certainly account for the small rise in US net exports during the recession. Yet, in direct contrast to this scenario, Hall (1993) claims that:

> Any force that decreased the volume of resources going to capital formation would raise the volume going to other purposes, especially consumption ... it would be almost impossible to tell a story in which events in world markets caused a US recession but US net exports rose.

Obviously, Hall among others did not acknowledge the possibility that international flows of finance based upon interest rate and financial strategy parities can be an initiating, profit-seeking force that drives changes in trade and GDP growth among affected countries.

Hall's (1993) regression models, which are based largely on domestic income trends, do not explain the drop in US consumption during the recession period when foreign investment into the US collapsed, nor do they explain the surge in US consumption during 1987 and 1988 when international investment into the US reached record inflows: 'it is worth mentioning, however, that consumption exceeded its predicted value by a large margin ($41 billion) in 1987 and by over $20 billion in 1988'. This under-prediction of consumption during 1987–88 provides further evidence that the international flow of investment is a missing variable.

The US economy went into its 1990–91 slump at the same time that the identified capital inflow collapsed, and the US dollar subsequently depreciated to its lowest level. Then, these trends began to reverse themselves somewhat in 1991 and 1992 as the identified capital inflow began to improve. Also, in the first two quarters of 1991 the US received 'official unrequited transfer' net inflows of $17.45 and $7.61 billion respectively—a current account line item reflecting in this period payments from allies due to the US Persian Gulf actions. The official unrequited transfers balance of the US is generally negative. Its annual balance over 1987–92 was −$12.49, −$13.01, −$13.28, −$20.25, $20.98 (in 1991), and −$17.56 billion, respectively.

The $35–$40 billion improvement (more payment inflow) in this one current account category in 1991 plus the $50 billion increase in identified capital account inflow to the US in 1992 (Figure 3.1) initiated the weak US economic recovery and dollar appreciation in 1991–92. Once again financial flows were driving changes in GDP and trade. The US current account balance, which had dropped close to zero in 1991 due to the Persian Gulf contributions from other countries to the US, weak US economy import demand, and low US dollar, began to deteriorate again in 1992 (Figure 2.6) as the capital inflow resumed.

Thus, a stronger US economy, as in the 1980s, remained associated with a larger US trade deficit. This result is contrary to most economic adjustment literature in situations wherein international factors (rather than internal factors and changes in domestic demand) are driving the changes in the trade balance. Also, it helps explain why the economics profession had trouble modeling the early 1990s US recessionary period.

Economic models also failed to explain the early 1990s US recession because, as with 1980s financial crises and recession, insufficient attention was paid to the income velocity of money. US (m1) velocity fell 3 percent from 1990 to 1991 at the same time as the Federal Reserve Bank was restricting the growth rate of monetary aggregates. The result, as in 1982, was a contraction of nominal GDP from its growth path, and this was split between its two components, real GDP and inflation.

Instead of adjusting the money supply to maintain nominal GDP along its growth path, which would have appropriately been 6.5 percent as in 1988–90, the Fed seemingly returned to money-supply targeting and over-concern with inflation in late 1990. While Hall (1993), among others, discussed the collapse of nominal GDP below its 6.5 percent growth path, velocity was not discussed, nor did the collapse in nominal GDP seem to worry him. He excuses Fed policy as a source of the recession because he does not find that the Fed consciously adopted a lower nominal GDP target and because US interest rates remained low and even fell during the recession.

US interest rates did decline during the recession, but not until the fourth quarter of 1990 when the Fed began reducing the discount and federal funds rates. Also, the cut in these short-term rates midway into the recession was not followed by a significant fall in long-term rates, such as the 30-year Treasury bond, until a year or two later. The yield gap between the discount rate and the 30-year government bond thus approached 4 percent at the end of 1991, a gap seen before only during the 1982–84 LDC debt crisis period when US bank solvency was threatened.

Such a gap, twice as large as normal, helps re-capitalize banks and restores their profitability, because banks can borrow at the discount rate and lend at the 30-year bond rate. A joke going around in the early 1990s was of a 10–2–4 club. Bankers would take in short-term 3 percent deposits or draw-downs at the Fed discount window at 10:00 a.m., invest these funds in long-term 7 percent Treasury bonds at 2:00 p.m., and then hit their private clubs at 4:00 p.m. Presumably they had not managed to loan money to businesses or households in the process.

When domestic yield-gap re-capitalization is occurring, domestic borrowing may suffer, which was the case during the early 1990s US recessionary period. In effect, banks were subsidized as intermediaries between domestic monetary and fiscal policy, and the rest of the economy felt a money-liquidity crisis from being 'left out of the loop' despite rapidly declining short-term rates.

Longer-term US interest rates are more subject to the international IRP conditions than the shorter-term interest rates. The shorter-term interest rates can be set more directly by the Fed via changes in the discount and federal funds rates. The high international interest rates in 1991 in Germany and elsewhere kept US longer-term rates high, and the Fed's move to reduce short-term US rates in 1990–91 probably encouraged the US capital outflow and dollar depreciation.

In contrast, at the end of the 1982 recession the US began receiving big increases in net foreign investment due to the structural changes associated with globalization (Chapters 1 and 2). Unlike the early 1990s recessionary period, the 1982–84 capital inflow soon made up for the shortfall in domestic investment. The US in 1983 and 1984 was thus able to have strong economic growth while at the same time capitalizing its banks. Coming out of the 1990–91 recessionary period, recovery was slower; not until 1994 did the net capital inflow rise above the pre-1990 levels (Figure 3.1).

II.   THE 1994–95 MEXICAN CRISIS

The 1980s Latin American debt crisis appeared to have been resolved by the late 1980s, and economic growth in Mexico and elsewhere had returned. Financial liberalization and globalization in Mexico, and less uncertainty regarding its economic and political prospects, led to rapid credit and quasi-money expansion and inflows of foreign investment. From 1990 to 1993, Mexico received $91 billion in net capital inflows, which was approximately one-fifth of all net inflows to developing countries. Bank credit extended to the private non-financial sector increased from 10 percent of GDP in 1988 to more than 40 percent in 1994. Oversight by the National Banking Commission in this period was weak, partly due to the rise of offshore finance (Chapter 1) and other complicated international monetary channels that directed funds into Mexico. Dollar-denominated bonds (*tesobonos*), which were guaranteed by the Mexican government based on its dollar reserves, expanded rapidly and were classified by the Mexican government as domestic debt. By late 1994, there was $18 billion in *tesobonos* held by foreigners, and $11 billion in *tesobonos* held by Mexicans—all of which were short term and coming due in 1995.

Unfortunately for Mexico, contractionary monetary policies began in the US in February 1994, which were reciprocated in the other hard-currency money centers. From 1 February to 1 August 1994, interest rates on ten-year government bonds increased by the following percentage point amounts: 1.4 percent in the US, 0.9 percent in Japan, 1.4 percent in Germany, 1.6 percent in France, and 2.4 percent in the UK—severe increases given the absence of any general rise in inflation or economic growth rates.

Given these increases in interest rates in the money centers, flows of international investment into Mexico could not be sustained. Furthermore, Mexican investment was discouraged by increased political and economic uncertainty in Mexico following the Chiapas uprising (which began in January 1994 to coincide with the North American Free Trade Agreement), the assassination of presidential candidate Colosio, and the corruption charges against President Salinas and his family. Subjective perceptions can be extremely important in the marginal decision-making of inter-national investors, who flirt with small deviations in expected rates of return on investment between countries. An internal memo issued to the Emerging Markets Group of a major US bank, dated 13 February 1995, read, in part:

> While Chiapas, in our opinion, does not pose a fundamental threat to Mexican political stability, it is perceived to be so by many in the investment community. The government will need to eliminate the Zapatistas to demonstrate their effective control of the national territory and of security policy. (Hawkes, 1996, p. 189)

National and international investors also knew that the Mexican economy had been slowing and that inflation had outstripped productivity growth, yet the Salinas administration had not allowed a devaluation of the peso to reflect these trends. As of early December 1994, a majority of investors did not believe that these trends required a devaluation. Capital inflows into Mexico had been mostly curtailed six months earlier, yet the Bank of Mexico had pledged to support the peso with expenditure of its dollar reserves. Dollar reserves had thus been declining, yet the Bank of Mexico had been slow to admit the extent of the decline. However, in December, when the Mexican government released data indicating that a major devaluation was likely, traders rushed to get out of the peso. Furthermore, they removed their US dollar holdings out of Mexican institutions. These dollar holdings were very liquid, because debtors had issued short-term dollar bonds that promised redemption at face value. On 21 December 1994, $29 billion of *tesobono* short-term liabilities were for sale, $18 billion of which were the responsibility of the Mexican government, and this news made the front page of *The Wall Street Journal*.

Just like a run on a bank, investors ran on Mexico:

> Like small savers who see their neighbors lining up outside a bank and join the queue to withdraw their deposits before the bank's cash reserves are exhausted, investors in government bonds have an incentive to liquidate their holdings when others do likewise and they fear that the government's limited foreign exchange reserves will be exhausted . . . the magnitude of capital flows can leave a government facing a debt run, like a bank facing a run by its depositors, no choice but to suspend payments, regardless of the damage to its creditworthiness. On the eve of the crisis, the Mexican government was responsible for more than $18 billion of dollar-denominated and dollar-indexed liabilities, roughly triple its foreign exchange reserves. Once investors began to liquidate their holdings, the authorities were at their mercy. (Eichengreen and Portes, in Federal Reserve Bank of Kansas City, 1997, p. 195)

Unlike the Latin American debt crisis of the 1980s, which involved large loans from money-center banks, this time stocks and bonds were the vehicles for much of the foreign investment into Mexico. Selling of these liquid securities was thus immediate, and it could not be slowed by negotiations between government officials, the International Monetary Fund (IMF), and large financial institutions. When the Mexican finance minister presented his economic crisis management program at the Federal Reserve Bank of New York on 21 December 1994, various mutual fund and hedge fund managers were present, who represented only a subset of the exposed investors—if Mexican officials had wanted to renegotiate terms with its creditors, they would have had trouble even identifying them. As the peso and the Mexican stock and bond markets crashed in December, the market pushed short-term peso interest rates above 100 percent at an annual rate. Many Mexican banks and other firms, which had debt obligations in foreign currency, and which owned stocks and bonds, experienced a rapid decline in net worth and creditworthiness. In 1995, Mexico would have its worst recession in decades—real GDP would fall 6 percent, and the industrial output portion would fall more than 10 percent.

Much of the transfer of Mexican monetary wealth into dollars and out of the country went, initially, into offshore financial markets. This data is mostly not reported in balance of payments statistics, but Table 1.1 estimates what was happening at least with 'LDC fuel exporters' and offshore dollar markets—Mexico can be presumed to account for the major share of these flow changes between 1993 and 1994. As shown in Table 1.1, in

1992 and 1993 the LDC fuel exporters did not accumulate or lose dollar reserves, but in 1994 there was a $20 billion loss (this portion of the data is fairly reliable as reported to the IMF). This loss in reserves occurred despite $20 billion in 'net financing in dollars' by LDC fuel exporters in 1993 and $25 billion in 1994 (still reliable data). Where did these monetary reserves and credit supplies of dollars held by LDC fuel exporters go? Table 1.1 estimates that, from all sources (not just LDC fuel exporters) there was a flow of hidden dollar income into offshore centers and tax havens of $50 billion in 1993 and $55 billion in 1994, and additional 'capital flight' into the dollar is estimated at $40 billion in 1993 and $50 billion in 1994 (unreliable data now). Industrial countries (excluding the US) were accumulating dollar reserves in this period (an additional $40 billion in 1993 and $80 billion in 1994); therefore they were not likely to be contributing dollars to offshore financial markets. Likewise, the US was receiving a massive inflow of dollars in all investment categories. Therefore, the LDCs, especially Mexico, probably accounted for a majority of the dollar flows into offshore markets, which in turn were mostly transferred to the US and other industrial countries (see 'uses' of foreign savings in dollars in Table 1.1).

By early 1995, the only solution to avoid Mexican government insolvency, and bankruptcies across the Mexican economy, was to find an international lender of last resort. On 31 January, the rescue package was finalized when the IMF agreed to provide $10 billion in five-year loans on top of the $7.8 billion in credit it had already promised Mexico. Additionally, by executive order, US President Clinton approved $20 billion in loans with terms of as much as ten years by tapping the US Treasury's Exchange Stabilization Fund (normally used to support the dollar); major industrial nations contributed $10 billion in short-term credit through the Bank for International Settlements; Canada pledged $1 billion; and Latin American nations pledged $1 billion. The US and IMF conditions for these loans included strict targets for money supply, domestic credit, fiscal spending, and foreign borrowing. Furthermore, unprecedented international collateralization was obtained—Mexico's oil export revenues could be held by the Federal Reserve Bank of New York to guarantee US loans. The total rescue package thus amounted to approximately $50 billion, which was enough to stabilize the Mexican economy. Foreign investors, who had seen their Mexican holdings reduced 45 percent by the depreciation in the peso since December, drove the peso up 18 percent on 1 February and stock prices rose 5.2 percent.

III. JAPAN'S CRISIS, 1989–

The story of Asia's crisis in 1997 should begin with Japan's crisis, which hit in 1989. By the mid-1990s, most Japanese real estate as well as stock market prices had dropped 50 percent from 1989 levels, economic growth was stagnant, and the 'Japanese miracle' was over. The author's position is that the monetary contraction allowed by the Bank of Japan under Governor Mieno, beginning with interest rate increases in May and October of 1989, was a mistake which caused much of the crisis.

A reduced valuation of Japanese land and equity prices was coming anyway in the early 1990s given 'the law of one price' for real property that was quickly being established across the global economy due to integration and globalization of markets (see the discussion of 'interest rate parities' and 'financial strategy parities' in Chapter 1). For example, price/earnings ratios in the Japanese stock market would naturally drop closer to the 20/1 global averages from their historic levels of 50/1, as newly deregulated investment funds could leave Japan in search of more favorable price/earnings ratios elsewhere. In 1989, given this investment outflow which was required by the law of one price, a 'hollowing-out' of the Japanese money and investment base, and GDP-deflation, were more of a risk than inflation—restrictive monetary policy turned the risk into reality.

The Bank of Japan's restrictive monetary policies continued through the early 1990s, despite the asset deflation and the increasing consensus by international investors that Japan faced deflationary risks similar to what happened in the US during the Great Depression after the 1929 stock market crash. According to many influential foreign investors, 'Governor Mieno was a general fighting the last war [against inflation]' (Brown, 1996, p. 24). Taking account of the shift in private consumption toward discount outlets, the GDP price level in Japan was probably falling by 2 percent or more by 1995, yet Japanese money market interest rates were kept up at 2–3 percent—a historically high real rate of 4–5 percent. The high real interest rates deepened the recession, and Japanese banks began having troubles with non-performing loans. This recessionary deflationary-debt spiral continued through the late 1990s, and only a partial return to normal growth rates occurred over several years until the recent crisis hit Japan in 2008 (with an 8 percent annualized decline in real GDP during the fourth quarter of 2008).

The author's position is that the 1990s 'hollowing-out' of the Japanese economy could have been largely avoided with more accommodative monetary policies. Instead, Japan lost its financial surplus and therefore its means to maintain record rates of foreign investment. Its net outflow of direct investment plus portfolio investment plus other capital (the 'identified capital outflow') dropped to $22 billion in 1990 from an annual average of $58 billion over 1986–89. In 1991, temporarily, the Japanese narrow money supply (m1) was once again increased significantly, by 9.5 percent, and the identified capital outflow jumped back up, to $72 billion. However, monetary policy remained restrictive on balance through the 1990s (real short-term interest rates of 4–5 percent), and Japanese land and equity price deflation spread to GDP markets as the Bank of Japan continued to 'fight the last war against inflation'.

As elaborated in Chapter 2, 'absorption' of base money by financial markets and therefore a decline in its rate of circulation for GDP purposes (v), in times of financial distress, can also be measured by a weakness in the growth of broad money. Namely, expanded supplies of high-powered money may not be able to serve as a base for expanded supplies of broad money if the high-powered money supplies are instead consumed by financial institutions to resolve bankruptcies, increase reserves, and meet other capital requirements. In this case, a decline in broad money would correspond to a decline in the velocity of high-powered money as it is absorbed by distressed financial markets rather than being used to support growth in GDP. As shown in Figure 2.1, Japan's (m1) velocity began dropping significantly in the early 1990s.

Figure 3.2 also shows this scenario for Japan. A dramatic decline in the growth of Japan's broad money supply (m2 + CDs) was allowed in the 1990s which correlated with declines in the stock market, real estate values, and real GDP (in July 1998 a GDP recession began). Maintaining the growth of the narrow money supply (m1) did not prevent deflation and recession, because more of the (m1) was absorbed by distressed financial institutions. Elaborating this situation further, research in 1998 indicated that:

> A central bank *in a deflationary situation with troubled banks* must avoid interpreting low [nominal] interest rates as an indicator of an expansionary policy. When monetary growth is low and default risks are high as in Japan today, low interest rates reflect expectations of both low (or negative) inflation and rates of return. In such a situation, *the appropriate focus of monetary policy is on money and not interest rates* [broad money supplies should be expanded despite low interest rates]. (Federal Reserve Bank of St. Louis, 1998, p. 1)

Thus, what was initially seen in the literature as a reckless and speculative expansion of domestic credit in Japan in the 1980s, an unsustainable bubble, was instead increasingly seen as a more sustainable form of economic growth based upon monetary expansion. As shown in Figure 3.2, monetary expansion in the 1980s was not high compared to the 1970s. In the author's view, Japan in the 1980s printed the means to buy foreign

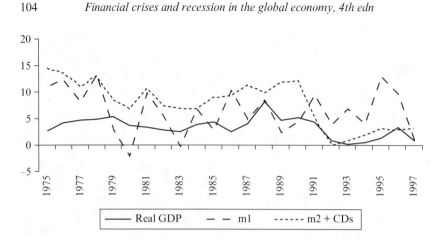

Note: The dramatic decline in Japan's broad money supply growth rate (m2 + CDs) in the 1990s was correlated with declines in the stock market, real estate values, and real GDP. Maintaining the growth of the narrow money supply, (m1), did not prevent deflation, because more of the (m1) was absorbed by distressed financial institutions. Japan's monetary contraction contributed to Asian and worldwide monetary deflation and recession.

Source: IMF.

Figure 3.2   Negative consequences of restrictive Japanese monetary policy after 1989 (annual percent rates of change, 1975–97)

assets and expand wealth domestically without accelerating GDP inflation. If overly restrictive monetary policies had not been used, the expansion could likely have continued but at a more moderate level in proportion to the new international investment opportunities that were being found by 'Japan Inc.' in the global economy.

IV.   ASIA'S CRISIS, 1997

The investment flows out of Japan in the mid-1990s found 'homes', primarily, in the rest of Asia as well as the US. Japan became the major source of bank loans to every major country in Asia except Taiwan and the Philippines. Japan's outstanding loans to South Korea, Taiwan, Thailand, Indonesia, Malaysia, and the Philippines, combined, rose 76 percent from the end of 1993 to the end of 1996, including a doubling of lending to South Korea and Thailand. Also, by 1996 Japan accounted for more than 40 percent of all bank loans to Hong Kong and more than 30 percent to Singapore. Japan's monetary outflow thus helped support what was essentially a monetary-investment expansion in the rest of Asia during the mid-1990s.

Global investment inflows into this region during this period were further encouraged by the deregulation and internationalization of capital accounts and foreign exchange transactions in all Asian countries, by privatization, and by government commitments to support Asian exchange rates against the dollar (Haggard and Maxfield, 1996). US and European companies were setting up factories in Asia (direct investment), and the portfolio investment inflows from the US and Europe exceeded those from Japan. The World Bank estimated that total international capital flows to 'emerging markets' increased from $50 billion in 1991 to $250 billion in 1996, with the majority going to Asia. Total capital formation (corporate, housing, and government investment) in Asia excluding Japan increased 300 percent from 1990 to 1996, which compared with much lower increases of approximately 40 percent in the US and Japan and 10 percent in Europe.

Perhaps Thailand was the most obvious home for international investment funds in this period. Technocrats had even manipulated interest rates and currency exchange rates with a formula designed to bring in international capital. This formula defied the covered IRP equilibrium (Chapter 1) by subsidizing holdings of Thai baht relative to the dollar:

> Since 1987 the Thai authorities have kept their currency locked to the US dollar in a band of baht 25–26 [to one dollar] while maintaining domestic rates 500–600 [basis] points higher than US rates and keeping their borders open to capital flows. Thai borrowers naturally gravitated towards US dollar borrowings and the commercial banks accommodated them, with the result that the Thai banks now have a net foreign liability position equivalent to 20 percent of GDP. The borrowers converted to baht with the Bank of Thailand the ultimate purchaser of their foreign currency. Fuelled by cheap easy money, the Thai economy grew rapidly, inflation rose, and the current account deficit ballooned. (HG Asia, 1996)

Because this Thai formula was so successful in attracting capital, it was soon copied by the central banks and finance ministers in the Philippines, Malaysia, and Indonesia. The IMF and the World Bank praised these policies, especially the elimination of barriers between domestic and global financial markets. As late as the second half of 1996, the IMF cited Thai policymakers for their 'consistent record of sound macroeconomic management policies'.[8]

In this optimistic financial liberalization phase, Thailand received large-scale international investment inflows mostly from private sources, including offshore financial markets. In 1994–96, offshore banks (Bangkok International Banking Facilities) were allowed to borrow funds internationally and lend them to Thai residents without limit. Unlike most banks, these banks were not required to disclose asset mixes (such as the extent of real estate loans) or non-performing loans, and they were allowed to purchase finance companies. In 1994–96, Thailand received a net inflow of approximately $25 billion in portfolio investment and another $50 billion in loans to Thai banks and enterprises. The latter mostly found its way into the stock market, consumer financing, and, especially, real estate. Commercial banks and finance companies were estimated to have 40 percent of their loans in real estate.

Thus, the mid-1990s was a financial liberalization phase for Asia as supported by the dollar, yen, and other hard currencies. Local currency and credit supplies were expanded dramatically based upon confident convertibility into the hard currencies, and the 'money-float' or 'money-pyramid' encouraged some reckless speculation. The IMF and other government agencies encouraged financial deregulation and free-market 'dollarization' of these economies (despite the rigged, unsustainable Thai interest rate–exchange rate regime discussed earlier), and the presence of these optimistic 'lenders of last resort' increased the moral-hazard problem whereby 'even if something goes wrong the agencies involved have an interest in bailing me out'.

Then came dollar-flight, dollar-contraction, and crisis, as discussed below.

At the core of the global financial economy is the dollar, which accounts for approximately 60 percent of the world's money supply, and at the core of this 'dollar-float' is the (m1) in US circulation, and at the core of this core is the money reserves of US depository institutions. The US Federal Reserve has significant control over the growth of these latter two statistics, and is thus a powerful driver of the high-powered money base of not only the US economy but also the world economy. Figure 3.3 shows the growth rate of both statistics from 1988 to a peak in 1992, and then a decline after 1992. Fears of inflation across the developed world were exaggerated after 1992 and translated into contractionary monetary policies and interest rate increases of 1–2 percentage points for the hard currencies. As discussed above in 'The 1994–95 Mexican Crisis', these increases in interest rates pulled money out of Mexico, which contributed to its crisis.

Viewed from the high-powered dollar core of the world economy, the mid-to-late 1990s period was thus characterized by extremely restrictive monetary policies and even 'dollar-destruction'. Further evidence for this view is provided by dollar currency appreciation and capital flight to the dollar relative to virtually all other world currencies, the historically high inflation-adjusted US dollar interest rates, and the dramatic decline in virtually all commodity prices measured in US dollars.

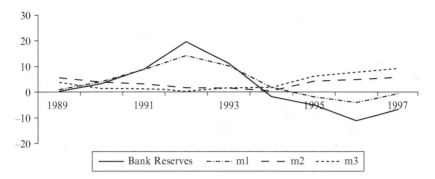

Note: Both US (m1) and bank reserves increased rapidly in 1992 and 1993, and thus contributed to a worldwide dollar-based monetary expansion; then, after 1993, both declined rapidly and contributed to restrictive worldwide monetary conditions and high US dollar real interest rates. High US dollar real interest rates attracted international investment into the US, especially as deposited in broad money accounts (m2 and m3). The US experienced a broad money expansion after 1993 and strong economic growth, but many other countries experienced a contraction in broad money supplies as investment flowed to the US. Financial crises in Mexico (1994–95) and Asia (1997–) were affected by this reversal from expansionary to contractionary dollar-based policies.

Source: Federal Reserve Bank.

Figure 3.3 Negative consequences of restrictive US monetary policy after 1993 (annual percent rates of change, 1989–97)

Regarding currency exchange rates, the dollar appreciated 20 percent against the German mark (and therefore most of the European currencies) and the Japanese yen, measured from the beginning of 1997 to the middle of 1998. Japan tried to maintain some stability between the yen and the dollar in mid-1997 to avoid further 'crises of confidence' in the Japanese economy, but these policies proved untenable by early 1998. This free-market appreciation of the dollar against the other hard currencies was required by supply–demand conditions as effected by the restrictive US monetary policies.

There was even more dramatic and sudden appreciation of the US dollar against the other Asian currencies over the same time period. As discussed above, Thailand and the others had a policy of keeping domestic exchange rates fixed against the dollar, and as part of this strategy they were expanding domestic currency supplies based upon a guaranteed convertibility into the dollar. In other words, small Asian countries were conducting a normal reserve-currency process of credit expansion with the dollar serving as 'real money' and the Thai baht and other local currencies serving as 'quasi-moneys' that are floated beyond an amount that could all be converted into dollars at once.

Unfortunately for Asia, by mid-1997 the restrictive US dollar monetary policies and supply–demand imbalance between the dollar and Asian currencies could no longer be denied. Asian monetary authorities no longer had enough reserves of US dollars to intervene with (by selling them to the private markets) in support of their fixed exchange rates (by buying local currencies off the private markets).

The crisis hit. The impossible rush to fully convert local quasi-moneys and credit into dollars happened first in Thailand with flight from the baht, and then the rush to convert was immediately copied in the Philippines, Malaysia, South Korea, and elsewhere. Ultimately, Indonesia was the hardest hit with the biggest decline in dollar value of its domestic currency, a decline that continued after the end of 1997 despite some recovery by the other Asian currencies as international bailouts were arranged. South Korea, for example, received $21 billion in credits from the IMF, and other international groups and nations provided the rest of a $57 billion package.

The currency devaluation process not only reduces the dollar value of domestic currencies, but it reduces real (dollar-measured) domestic wealth including the ability to maintain production and consumption. Recession, and even depression in the case of Indonesia, was immediate and devastating. Despite a $40 billion lender-of-last-resort plan led by the IMF for Indonesia, abject poverty rose to 40 percent and political instability led to the ousting of President Suharto.

Regarding capital flight to the dollar, not only Asia but also the rest of the world rapidly 'de-dollarized' their economies after the mid-1990s. US dollar short-term interest rates were maintained at approximately 5 percent by the US Federal Reserve from 1996 through 1998, despite declining inflation in the US economy. US GDP-inflation dropped from 2–3 percent in the mid-1990s to as low as 0–1 percent in 1998. Real interest rates, or the real rate-of-return from short-term investing in the US economy, thus climbed from 2–3 percent in the mid-1990s to 4–5 percent in 1998. The 4–5 percent rate is an extremely high real return, and it exceeded any other short-term safe return in the global economy. International investment thus poured into the US.

Official statistics identify key turning points in the late 1990s when worldwide financial flows began to favor the US. Foreign institutions and individuals increased the rate at which they were purchasing US financial assets from $563.4 billion in 1996 to $733.4 billion in 1997. This record inflow in 1997 came especially in the third and fourth quarters as US real interest rates increased and the Asian financial crisis hit—inflows of $182.5 billion and $219.5 billion, respectively. Then, in the first quarter of 1998, this inflow slowed to a more normal $90.5 billion, reflecting deteriorating Asian balance sheets and the subsequent need by Asian banks to repatriate foreign assets. For example, Japanese banks reduced their assets in the US from $358 billion in 1997 to $289 billion at the end of March, 1998, and there were similar percentage declines in all other Asian bank assets in the US except Taiwan, which had mostly escaped the crisis.

Similarly, in the late 1990s, US institutions and individuals reduced the rate at which they were purchasing foreign financial assets, but this reduction did not occur until the Asian financial crisis became widespread and threatened other regions of the world early in 1998. US purchase of foreign financial assets was $368.8 billion in 1996, $478.5 billion in 1997, and then only $47.4 billion in the first quarter of 1998. Combining foreign purchases of US financial assets, and US purchases of foreign financial assets, yields the 'net identified financial flow' between the US and the rest of the world, which was thus a net inflow into the US of $194.6 billion in 1996, $254.9 billion in 1997, and $43.1 billion in the first quarter of 1998. These net inflows into the US were much higher than in previous years, wherein transfers of $100 billion per year were normal.

As discussed in Chapter 1, the rise of offshore financial markets makes this data unreliable, because financial flows through offshore international banking facilities, 'spontaneous offshore sites', and 'tax havens' are difficult to measure. Aggregate worldwide data shows that monetary flows into official country accounts are systematically less than outflows, and economists believe that much of this difference adds to offshore financial markets. In the case of the US, what is called the 'statistical discrepancy' between monetary inflows and outflows (product trade as well as finance) amounted to $59.6 billion (an excess of measured outflows over inflows) in 1996, $99.7 billion in 1997, and only $5.2 billion in the first quarter of 1998. However, flows into offshore markets have as their major counterpart (often unmeasured) interbank transfers of dollars to the US economy.

These hidden dollar transfers to the US are most likely to show up in what the Federal Reserve measures as 'overnight and term Eurodollars (net)' held by US institutions. (A Eurodollar is a US dollar owned by a non-US citizen or institution.) Overnight and term Eurodollars (net) held in the US, which decreased steadily from $117.0 billion in 1988 (year-end) to $66.3 billion in 1993, then increased steadily to $80.8 billion in 1994, $88.6 billion in 1995, $109.2 billion in 1996, and $145.3 billion in 1997. In early 1998, these holdings began dropping once again, and stood at $136.3 billion in June. These changes in Eurodollar holdings in the US correspond to what would be expected based upon the rise in US dollar real interest rates after 1994, and the capital flight to dollar havens (first offshore markets and then the US) as Asia and other regions 'de-dollarized' their economies in 1997. It is thus likely that a certain amount of hidden net dollar transfers to the US should be added to the officially measured net inflows in recent years—a further sign that monetary policies, institutions, and perceived risk-adjusted return have favored the dollar and the US at the expense of other currencies and regions.

Further proof that US dollar monetary policies were quite restrictive, with worldwide consequences, was provided by the collapse in virtually all commodity prices as measured in dollars. Fewer dollars available for transactions in international markets means that fewer dollars are swapped for the same volume of commodities, that is, there is dollar-deflation in international commodity markets. According to the global commodity index published by *The Economist*, from end of July 1997 to end of July 1998 the decline in dollar prices of all commodities was 22.2 percent, the decline in dollar prices of food items was 20.6 percent, the decline in dollar prices of industrial commodities was 24.1 percent (including metals), and the decline in dollar price of crude oil was 34.8 percent.

These price declines mirror the percentage by which the dollar appreciated on currency markets against a trade-weighted basket of the world's other currencies over the same time period. Of course, country-by-country consequences of worldwide dollar price deflation and the related dollar-flight to dollar havens vary considerably based upon the degree to which countries export or import commodities, the degree to which they rely on domestic dollar supplies for monetary stability as discussed above, and so on.

What is clear to the author, then, is that restrictive US dollar monetary policies in the mid-1990s in the core of the global economy were an important cause of the 1997– Asian financial crisis, especially because these policies came so swiftly on the heels of the more accommodative monetary policies and liberal worldwide dollarization in the early 1990s. On 4 August 1998, US Federal Reserve Chairman Alan Greenspan stated: 'In the Spring of 1998 the Federal Open Market Committee was [still] convinced that a rise in inflation was the primary threat to the continued growth of the US economy.'

NOTES

1. 'Economic and Financial Indicators', *The Economist*, 20 June 1992, p. 108.
2. 'Spontaneous Union, a Survey of the New Germany', *The Economist*, 30 June 1990, p. 12.
3. In 10,000 booths and banks around the country, East Germans had one week to exchange 4,000 East German marks (more for the old, less for the young) at a rate of one-to-one into West German marks. Most of the remaining East German marks were traded in for only half as many West German marks. Most prices and wages were converted at one-to-one. This monetary union went smoothly in a macroeconomic sense in

that the increased supply of (West German) marks reflected the value of East German production. Therefore, West German inflation did not significantly increase, and the mark maintained its value on foreign exchange markets.

4. 'Spontaneous Union, a Survey of the New Germany', *The Economist*, 30 June 1990, p. 12.
5. 'Just a Question of Time', *The Economist*, 11 August 1990, p. 25.
6. 'Spontaneous Union, a Survey of the New Germany', *The Economist*, 30 June 1990, p. 12.
7. 'Bundespost to Raise DM30bn for E German Phone Network', *Financial Times*, 21 June 1990, p. 1.
8. 'Thai Crisis Highlights Lessons of Mexico', *Financial Times*, 19 September 1997.

4. The 2007– crisis: common patterns and new thinking

Especially as it played out in the US and Europe, the 2007– global financial crisis had many patterns in common with the other recent large-scale financial crises discussed in previous chapters, including in developed countries (e.g. Sweden 1991, Japan after 1989) and less developed countries (LDCs) (e.g. Latin America 1982, Mexico 1994–95, Asia 1997). Despite a huge historical literature on boom–bust processes, some of these more important patterns are only now being identified.

A good historical data set on severe financial crises has been developed only recently, by Carmen Reinhart and Kenneth Rogoff, which goes back in some ways eight centuries (Reinhart and Rogoff, 2007, 2008, 2009). Interestingly, since 1800, they find that the percentage of years that advanced economies have spent in banking crises is 7.2 percent, and emerging economies 8.3 percent; and those numbers only change to 7.0 percent and 10.8 percent in the time period since 1945. Their results indicate that the recent crisis was actually 'overdue' in terms of average historical frequency in advanced economies. Furthermore, since World War II there has not been any greater ability to avoid severe banking crises compared to the period since 1800.

Using their data set to include the Great Depression and 14 other, more recent severe banking crises, Reinhart and Rogoff also find that the average historical impact on major macroeconomic statistics is not unlike what resulted from the recent crisis. From peak of the boom to trough of the crisis the average historical results are (1) house prices decline 36 percent over 5.0 years; (2) equity prices decline 56 percent over 3.4 years; (3) unemployment rates increase 7.0 percent over 4.8 years; and (4) GDP per person declines 9.3 percent over 1.9 years (Reinhart and Rogoff, 2009). Of course, individual episodes vary widely around these averages, as in the Great Depression when the percentage point *increase* in the US unemployment rate was close to 20 percent rather than 7 percent. However, declines in house prices and equity prices in the US and Europe following the recent crisis were similar to the historical averages of 36 percent and 56 percent, respectively. And, there were similar impacts on unemployment and GDP, which generally follow in sequence the declines in asset prices—in the US case, for example, the official unemployment rate rose close to 10 percent in 2009, which was a 5–6 percent rise; including any measure of the massive spike in underemployment would certainly realize a 7.0 percentage point increase from levels of 4–5 percent in 2006.

This chapter presents some 'new thinking' on recent crises, based upon material from previous chapters. After describing the recent crisis in Section I with case studies of the US, Europe, and a comparison of China today with Japan's 1989– crisis, Section II summarizes the common patterns, and then some new thinking is presented: first, in Section III key financial variables are shown to be driven somewhat more by subjective, even transcendental ('transcendental' of observable GDP or 'real' processes) psychological and social constructs than is commonly understood. Since the 1980s, as discussed in Chapters 1 and 2, structural changes in evolving financial markets, especially advances in information-processing technology and government deregulation, have allowed a greater separation of financial market processes from GDP processes. Specifically, as per the author's econometric research summarized in Chapter 2, the demand for money-liquidity for financial market participation has become, especially during episodes of chaotic structural change, an important source of money demand which absorbs money-liquidity away from observable GDP uses. As a related process, monetary wealth can thus be created, transferred, and destroyed across time and space more powerfully and independently of observed GDP processes than is commonly understood.

Also relatively new to the literature, as elaborated in Section IV, expanding our understanding of the recent crisis can be assisted by evolutionary and complex systems approaches, especially ones that privilege the role of interactive knowledge and belief systems. The relative rise and fall of interactive institutional and technological systems, or 'meso' structures in the language of evolutionary economics, is seen to play a key role in driving boom–bust patterns. Transitions and imbalance between meso structures can account for long-run discontinuities or instabilities beyond what can be explained by normal business cycle theory.

As elaborated in Section V, these conclusions, along with an understanding of financial globalization from Chapter 1, direct us toward a new political economy of financial crisis. This new global economy of financial crisis, together with other material in this chapter, is used to draw various conclusions in Section VI, especially regarding how economists might rethink some basic assumptions about financial markets.

I.   SUMMARY OF THE RECENT CRISIS

The 'boom phase' of the recent crisis is dated by the author to be from the early 1980s to a peak in 2006. The initial 'drivers' of this boom phase were discussed at length in Chapters 1 and 2—in particular, advances in information-processing technology along with widespread deregulation of financial markets in the developed world, especially the Reagan administration reforms in the US and the Thatcher administration reforms in the UK. Financial liberalization and globalization in the 1980s was guided by ideologies and belief systems aimed at restoring a more market capitalist tradition, and they eventually prevailed across the global system. French President Mitterrand's attempt to advance a more socialist set of values and policies floundered by late 1982 and financial market deregulation and international integration spread not only in North America and Europe, but also Asia, Latin America, Africa, and Eastern Europe.

At the same time, newly unregulated financial products, entities, and markets came to play a larger role. Dramatic advances in information-processing technology (electronic banking systems, communication satellites, the computer revolution, etc.) facilitated international arbitrage. The commoditization and securitization of financial products by the private sector, including through virtually unregulated no-reserve-requirement 'offshore banking facilities', led to dramatic increases in international money-liquidity and credit, as documented earlier in this book.

This 1980–2006 boom phase of the recent crisis was thus driven by fundamental changes in the basic social and technical rules of the game, or meso structure of the global economy (as per the evolutionary economics language used later in Section IV of this chapter), which, among other characteristics, replaced more hierarchically organized, communitarian-disciplined, national-government-controlled rules with, instead, more free-market, technologically innovative, decentralized, and chaotically individualistic meso structures as financial globalism prevailed.

A.   The US Crisis

As elaborated in Chapters 1 and 2, these structural changes associated with financial globalization supported an increasing net financial inflow from the rest of the world into the US from near-balance in 1980 to approximately $800 billion/year or 6 percent of GDP as a net financial inflow in 2006—the peak of the long boom—which supported classic-pattern excesses in low interest rate debt-financing and spending, monetary-wealth creation processes, consumerism and financial asset inflation, and now-famous lax standards in mortgage financing and securitization

vehicles such as 'collateralized debt obligations' and 'structured investment vehicles' that passed the rights to the mortgage payments and related
credit/default risk to third-party investors. The US household personal
savings rate dropped from 8 percent of disposable income to 0 percent over
this 1980–2006 period, total private sector debt (households, non-financial
businesses, and financial concerns) increased from 120 percent of GDP to
300 percent of GDP, and 'net household worth' (the difference between
assets and liabilities of the household and non-profit sector) increased
from approximately $10 trillion in 1980 to $67 trillion in 2007 in nominal
terms.

The latter stage of the long boom in the US was concentrated especially in the housing market, and it was fueled by growth in 'subprime
mortgages'. Subprime mortgages are extended to borrowers with credit
quality below a qualifying threshold for conventional or 'prime' home
loans. That threshold is based on credit and payment histories provided as
part of the mortgage application. In the US market, one such threshold is
the Fair Isaac and Company (FICO) credit score from payment histories.
Subprime mortgages and other high interest rate mortgages were encouraged when the US Depository Institutions Deregulatory and Monetary
Control Act of 1980 began a process toward eliminating 'usury' protection and thus allowing whatever rates and terms the market would bear.
Subprime mortgages were non-existent until the mid-1990s, but then grew
rapidly, and originations reached $625 billion in the US at the height of the
boom in 2005. Similarly, the major boom in US housing prices was a 150
percent increase in the average US house price from $100,000 in the late
1990s to $250,000 at the peak in early 2006.

This US boom thus had the most common characteristics of major
financial crises in the modern era: a large net inflow of financial capital
from the rest of the world, which drove a run-up in housing and equity
prices:

> the run-up in US housing and equity prices that Kaminsky and Reinhart (1999)
> find to be the best leading indicators of crisis in countries experiencing large
> capital inflows closely tracks the average of the previous 18 post-World War II
> banking crises in industrial countries. (Reinhart and Rogoff, 2007, p. 339)

The end of this long boom from the early 1980s to 2006, and start of the
crisis or bust phase, began with the bursting of the US housing bubble and
a sharp rise in home foreclosure in the US during the fall of 2006, which
spread to become a more broad-based global financial crisis within a year.
The mortgage lenders that retained the risk of payment default, such as
Countrywide Financial, were the first financial institutions to be affected

as borrowers defaulted. By October 2007, 16 percent of subprime loans in the US with variable interest rate features were 90-days delinquent or in foreclosure proceedings, roughly triple the rate of 2005, and by January of 2008, this number increased to 21 percent. Major banks and other financial institutions reported losses of approximately $100 billion by the end of 2007.

Losses in the money-credit pyramid spread across the system including through the collapse in July 2007 of two hedge funds owned by Bear Stearns that were invested heavily in subprime mortgages. The lender-of-last-resort phase of the crisis began as the Federal Reserve took unprecedented steps to avoid a Bear Stearns bankruptcy by assuming $30 billion in its liabilities and engineering the sale of Bear Stearns to JPMorgan Chase. In August 2008 the US Treasury (and therefore US taxpayer) joined the lender-of-last-resort phase by taking over and guaranteeing the funding of Fannie Mae and Freddie Mac, the quasi government housing market entities. In September 2008 Lehman Brothers was allowed to fail, American International Group, with its exposure to credit default swaps, was bailed out by the Federal Reserve in an $85 billion deal, and then later that month the US taxpayer-sponsored $700 billion bailout bill (Troubled Asset Relief Program—TARP) was passed after Congress amended the plan to add more oversight, limits on executive pay, and the option for the government to gain equity in the companies that it bails out. As in Sweden's crisis in 1991 (Chapter 3), Europe and the US quickly moved to save most of the 'too big to fail' banks.

On 10 February 2009, the new US Treasury Secretary Tim Geithner revealed early details of an additional $2 trillion financial rescue plan that would leverage the remaining $250 billion in TARP along with Federal Reserve loans and private capital to create approximately $2 trillion in buying power to 'clean up and strengthen the nation's banks, bring in private capital to restart lending'. On 13 February, the US Congress agreed on a $787 billion economic stimulus plan, which included tax cuts and $150 billion in spending on infrastructure. And, on 18 March, the Federal Reserve announced plans to buy $300 billion in US government debt along with further purchases of securities issued by Fannie Mae and Freddie Mac up to a level of $1,450 billion—thus expanding the Fed's assets through money-creation toward 15 percent of US GDP, as compared to levels of 7–8 percent of GDP prior to the onset of the liquidity crisis in September of 2008. By comparison, central bank assets of the European Central Bank (ECB), Britain, and Switzerland also increased dramatically from the summer of 2008 to early 2009, from, respectively, 17 percent to 22 percent of GDP, 8 percent to 17 percent of GDP, and 23 percent to 38 percent of GDP.

The most significant intervention was the Federal Reserve's Large Scale Asset Purchase Program, which was popularly called 'Quantitative Easing (QE)' since funds were created by the Federal Reserve in unprecedented volumes to buy private as well as US government financial assets. QE ultimately involved, in stages 1, 2, and 3, an increase of the Federal Reserve's balance sheet from $0.9 billion at the start of 2008 to $4.5 trillion by 22 October 2014, when new purchases through this program ended—although reinvestment of the proceeds from longer-term Treasury securities, Fannie Mae and Freddie Mac (Agency) mortgage-backed securities and other long-term securities purchased through this program continues. Large-scale asset purchases of this magnitude have now become popular for other central banks, especially for the ECB, the Bank of England, and the Bank of Japan—regions where not only short-term interest rates, but also longer-term interest rates (through this program) have been driven down to record lows to avoid further recession and—especially in Japan's case—further deflation.

As of 2016, the US and others have thus moved back somewhat toward the 'social market capitalist' control of the financial system, that is, back toward the pre-1980 'meso' rule structures that were more hierarchically organized and communitarian-disciplined (by Treasuries and central banks and other official institutions) in place of the more free-market innovative, decentralized, and individualistic rule structures that dominated between 1980 and 2008. In testimony before the US Congress on 23 October 2008, former US Federal Reserve Chairman Alan Greenspan famously said that 'I made a mistake in presuming that the self-interest of organizations, specifically banks and others, was such that they were best capable of protecting their own shareholders'.

B. The European Crisis

As discussed in Chapter 1, most European and US financial markets had become integrated on 'interest rate parity' and 'financial strategy parity' bases by the 1990s, due to the common activities of shared financial services firms and joint markets for stocks, bonds, and government securities. The same was true for housing-related derivatives and the other risky assets that began to fail in the US in late 2007. In the 4 October 2007 summit meeting of European Union (EU) finance ministers, there was an estimate that 40 percent of all of the risky financial assets sold by American counterparts had ended up in Europe. However, like in the US—or even more so—the initial problems in these markets were felt to be contained. Jean-Claude Juncker, president of the Eurogroup of finance ministers, announced to the public in the run-up to this meeting on 2 October that 'European banks are healthy and Europe does not need plans to support them'.

In hindsight, of course, the unsustainable elements of Europe's financial boom prior to 2008 become more obvious, and share many elements of the US's '1980–2006 long boom'—as fueled by similar advances in information-processing technology, government deregulation of financial markets, and other forms of globalization. As documented in Chapter 2, the structural decline in the US income velocity of money (v)—as financial markets absorbed and created new money-liquidity independently of GDP markets—accelerated in 1982. The similar structural decline in the UK (v) occurred initially in 1980 (with removal of capital inflow and outflow restrictions) followed by a more dramatic decline in (v) in 1986 with its 'Big Bang' deregulation. Germany's (m1) income velocity of money began declining from its historic trend in 1981 with liberalization of exchange controls, and then collapsed in 1989–90 with German monetary reunification and revolutions and openness in Eastern Europe. These structural breaks in (v) in the core European financial centers represent inflows of money-liquidity (whether from Japan or elsewhere in the 1980s–90s) as well as an unprecedented increase of bank credits and reduced perceptions of risk. Financial markets began taking on a profit-seeking 'life of their own' as discussed earlier. Eventually, of course, as in the US, real estate and other asset bubbles in some European countries became unsustainable—in the last stage of the boom, from 2003 to 2007, total credit to the non-financial private sector from the then-18 Eurocurrency country financial institutions increased in real terms approximately 40 percent.

Also as in the US, this last run-up of credit was fueled by new financial inflows and easier lending conditions among cross-border banks. Even without taking into account intra-EU investment, at the time of the crisis, Europe had a 50 percent larger amount of foreign-owned assets than the US relative to GDP (Bastasin, 2012, p. 5). The combined assets of the three largest German banks in 2009 were equal to 118 percent of German GDP, up from 38 percent in 1990; the combined assets of the three largest French banks were 250 percent of French GDP in 2009 versus 70 percent in 1990; and the equivalent figures in the Netherlands were up from 154 percent in 1990 to 406 percent in 2009 (Bank for International Settlements, 2010). Also as in the US, there was an expansion of less-regulated shadow banks, especially in the real estate sector, which, as in Spain, supported a tripling of real estate prices from 1997 to 2007. And in Ireland, presaging its real estate crash, assets in the banking system were equal to 1.7 trillion euros in mid-2008, 70 percent of which were held by foreign banks—an amount equal to more than ten times Ireland's annual GDP. Low interest rates, a cut in the capital gains tax rate from 40 percent to 20 percent, and increased lending on collateral supported a 400 percent increase in average house prices in Ireland from 1996 to 2007.

The introduction of the euro as a single currency in most of the EU after 2000 led both to the creation of larger national banking groups, as governments braced for new cross-border competition, and to many private cross-border bank mergers and acquisitions. In what became known as the 'Mediterranean periphery' of this new currency union, these new banking groups expanded investment well beyond sustainable levels; for example, accumulated net inflows of capital into the combined group including Spain, Portugal, and Greece was equal to 70 percent of this group's GDP by 2008, which was the highest level reached of any small regional group of the 34 countries belonging to the Organisation for Economic Co-operation and Development (OECD). International investor confidence in this region was supported by the new use of the euro by these countries, which did not carry any significant market risk premium over uses of the euro elsewhere prior to 2007.

The creation of new saver–dissaver country imbalances in Europe became obvious: with their new inflows of foreign investment, Spain, Portugal, and Greece ran current account deficits averaging 7 percent of GDP from 2002 to 2007, while Finland, Germany, and the Netherlands (the dominant creditor countries) ran current account surpluses averaging more than 5 percent of their GDP. The unsustainable boom of investment in Ireland and Spain was mostly in real estate, but in Greece both government and private concerns, encouraged by the European Commission, had over-borrowed and over-spent on a wide array of infrastructure projects such as those supporting the 2004 Olympics in Athens. Thus, 'gross fixed capital formation' in Greece reached an all-time high of 16,615 million euros in the third quarter of 2007, having risen 60 percent in just four years.

Associated with these excesses and imbalances, prior to the turning point in 2008, confidence indexes in Germany and France and elsewhere of households and firms had reached their highest historical levels, and the European economy appeared to be thriving—especially in Germany which had recovered from the challenges of reunification in the 1990s. Concerns only surfaced with 'contagion' of bad debts from the US. For example, on 28 July 2007, IKB Deutsche Industriebank was rescued from investments in US subprime assets. And then, following the 15 September 2008 Lehman Brothers bankruptcy in the US, European banks dealing with Lehman saw the collapse of their assets.

The lender-of-last-resort phase of the European crisis was marked in late September 2008 by an agreement that would eventually transfer 100 billion euros into Hypo Real Estate Holding AG (HRE) by the German government along with a 90 billion euro loan from the ECB to

HRE; that bank had an official total asset balance of 400 billion euros, but it also had risky off-balance sheet activity of 1 trillion euros, and it was 'too big to fail'.

Europe-wide contractions in GDP and reduced tax revenues made Greece the first government in Europe to have problems servicing its debt at sustainable market interest rates, to be followed by Ireland, Portugal, Spain, and Italy among others. Greece had been projecting a government budget deficit for 2009 of 6 percent of GDP, but the new government elected in October indicated an actual figure at least double that amount due to previous misreporting. Levels of accumulated government debt had also been underestimated. Despite austerity measures, restructuring bail-outs from the other European countries and the International Monetary Fund (IMF), and liquidity support from the ECB, Greek government debt would rise to an unsustainable 160 percent of GDP in 2012. Greece was thus forced to write off more than half of its sovereign debt held privately, while the deteriorating situation led to civil unrest, strikes, and the resignation of the prime minister.

Spreading bank failures in Europe starting in late 2008 led to massive, unprecedented bailouts by central governments. The Netherlands, Belgium, and Luxembourg spent $16 billion to bail out Fortis, the Netherlands put $13 billion into ING, Iceland took over its three big banks when they collapsed, Ireland's government guaranteed all of the deposits of its commercial banks as well as their interbank lending, and so did Greece. The Spanish government purchased $70 billion worth of bank assets, and the UK guaranteed 250 billion pounds of bank liabilities, arranged for an additional 100 billion pounds to be swapped with government bonds, and directly purchased 50 billion pounds of equity in British banks. Similar bailouts soon followed of approximately $200 billion in Sweden, $400 billion in France, and $500 billion in Germany, which guaranteed bank debt as well as supplied money-liquidity to banks.

Unlike the Federal Reserve in the US, which injected approximately $1 trillion of liquidity via direct loans into US banks in late 2008, European rules had been generally such that the ECB could not make emergency loans to save a single bank. But, in 2009, what was called a "Grand Bargain" allowed the ECB to make loans to banks so that the banks could purchase bonds from governments that were having trouble raising money in the government bond markets. As governments began bailing out banks and began having debt problems themselves, the ECB began buying government debt in May, 2010—holdings which increased significantly in this Securities Market Program to approximately $100 billion in mid-2011 when the European debt crisis began spreading from Greece and Ireland to Spain, Portugal, and Italy. Ultimately, an increase in risk premiums and therefore interest rates and default risk on government bonds across the eurozone was reversed only when, on 26 July 2012, at the Global Investment Conference in London, ECB President Mario Draghi announced: 'within our mandate, the ECB is ready to do whatever it takes to preserve the euro. And, believe me, it will be enough.'

Also, as a lender-of-last-resort initiative, the euro-countries created the European Financial Stability Facility (EFSF), which from 2010 to 2012 provided financial assistance to Ireland, Portugal, and Greece from its paid-in contributions from member countries (by unanimous agreement) as well as through the issuance of bonds and other debt instruments on capital markets. The more permanent rescue mechanism, the European Stability Mechanism (ESM), started its operations on 8 October 2012. The ESM is currently, along with the IMF, the main mechanism for responding to new requests for financial assistance by euro-area member states. It has provided loans to Spain, Cyprus, and Greece. An 11 March 2011 euro-area summit increased the EFSF's lending capacity from 250 billion to 440 billion euros, and the effective lending capacity of the ESM was set at 500 billion euros.

Despite this assistance, Europe as an aggregate macro-economy recovered more slowly than the US from the 2007– crisis. Real GDP in the US took only until the third quarter of 2011 to surpass its previous peak at the end of 2007. However, in early 2016, total economic output in the 19-country eurozone was still slightly lower than in early 2008, and in Spain, Italy, and Greece it was substantially lower (Greece's GDP was approximately 75 percent of 2008 levels). Problem loans remain high at banks, credit growth is low, and other 'human ecology economics' (as discussed in Chapter 5) challenges remain high, such as the reluctance and inability of governments to coordinate fiscal policy, banking reform and rescue, along with broader social challenges such as rapid immigration and increasing political division that threaten effective unity of purpose in the eurozone itself.

Unlike the extremely expansionary fiscal and monetary policy response to the crisis in the US, many eurozone governments responded by cutting spending and engaging in other austerity economics of budget balancing that reduced economic growth. And, initially, on 9 July 2008, the ECB actually raised its reference interest rate to 4.25 percent, before the next quarter's sharp decline in GDP caused it to reverse course. Finally recognizing the collapse in euro-area income velocity of money in the fourth quarter of 2008, the ECB expanded its balance sheet by 35 percent while expanding bank notes by 13 percent. Yet, even under its president Mario Draghi, who came to power in late 2011, the central bank was unable to mount a stimulus program comparable to the Federal Reserve's until

March 2015, because the bank's Governing Council, coming from the various eurozone countries, disagreed over various courses of action.

C.   Similarities: Japan 1989– versus China 2016–

For the most part, at least initially, China escaped the 2007– US- and European-centered crisis, given that its financial integration and globaliza-tion with the US and Europe was not extensive, and given that it had con-sistently been achieving close to 10 percent annual real GDP growth with trade surpluses. Similarly, Japan in the late 1980s mostly escaped the 1987– Asian financial crises, due to its relatively self-contained financial sector and similarly strong export-driven economic growth. Japan 1989 and China 2016 had both enjoyed 20–30 years of strong comparative advan-tage in a variety of export sectors as supported by high labor productivity, low production costs, and new opportunities allowed by openness and globalization—long booms similar in length to the US and European long boom from 1980 to 2006. Both countries had accumulated large govern-ment reserves of foreign currency from these export-driven successes. By 2016, China's GDP had risen to surpass Japan's, thus making it the second largest GDP economy in the world after the US.

Prior to Japan's and (likely) China's 'financial peaks' in 1989 and 2016, respectively, both economies, especially their export sectors, were slowed, however, by crises and recession in their trade partners, and both economies showed signs of losing some of their labor cost advantage and export-driven success to other emerging nations. Despite an increase in government spending which comprises approximately 50 percent of GDP, China's GDP growth rate dropped significantly from previous averages to below 7 percent in 2016 and both its exports and its imports were falling— in 2015 as a whole, China's total trade dropped by 8 percent, as exports shrank 2.8 percent and imports fell more sharply by 14.1 percent due to a weaker renminbi and falling global (recessionary over-capacity) prices of the primary commodities that China imports.

Possibly at the end of its long boom, in 2016 China showed all the signs of excessive debt, as facilitated both by the big state banks and the recently allowed shadow banks. In March, 2016, People's Bank of China Governor Zhou Xiaochuan announced that 'total social debt' in China had increased to 250 percent of GDP, up from 160 percent ten years earlier. At 160 percent of GDP alone, he indicated that 'lending as a share of GDP, especially corporate lending [at 160 percent of GDP] as a share of GDP, is too high'.[1] China's big state banks reported a rise in bad loans in 2015: Industrial and Commercial Bank of China, the country's largest lender, said non-performing loans increased 44 percent from a year earlier to about 180 billion yuan ($28 billion), and China Construction Bank and Bank of China reported increases of 47 percent and 30 percent, respectively.[2] Along with the Agricultural Bank of China, these four banks are the largest in the world by assets in 2016[3] (they average almost $3 trillion in assets); at the peak of Japan's boom in 1989 its banks were the largest in the world, but now only Mitsubishi remains in the top ten.

China's 'shadow banks' include mainly the country's more than 65 trust companies, which are lightly regulated finance firms that make loans and other investments but cannot collect deposits. However, as counterparties, they often help the state banks skirt rules on deposit rates and loan terms—a practice that happened in the US and Europe with subprime real estate and other loans prior to 2007. The shadow banks also provide wealth-management products, which channel money from better-off investors. Shadow banks were in their infancy prior to 2010, but with surges in credit across the economy starting in 2009 they grew to have assets of more than 30 trillion yuan ($4.9 trillion) by 2014, which was 50 percent of China's GDP and 43 percent of the 73 trillion yuan in assets held by the big five official banks. Assets managed by the trust companies increased five times between 2010 and 2014 to 12.5 trillion yuan.[4] China's total debt, at 250 percent of GDP, is broken down as follows: the state banks hold debt equal to 150 percent of GDP, the shadow banks 100 percent of GDP, and bond markets supply debt equal to 50 percent of GDP.[5]

Although smaller in capitalization relative to Japan in the late 1980s, China's private stock, real estate, and other asset markets have shown similar 'topping' behavior that occurs at the end of a long boom. By 2016, house price-to-income ratios were 17 in Hong Kong and 15 in Beijing, which was between 50 percent and 100 percent higher than San Francisco, Vancouver, and Sydney.[6] The Shanghai Composite Stock Market Index, which had a value of 99.98 at the end of 1990, reached an all-time high of 6,092.05 in October of 2007 and since then it has been volatile with a current value of approximately 3,000. In 2015, deregulations which allowed more foreign investment to flow between Hong Kong's more open stock market and China's main stock market in Shanghai, thus opening China to more foreign investment, did not result in significant net inflows—reflecting rising international concern with valuations and risk in China.

Perhaps the most important common pattern between Japan's financial peak in 1989 and China in 2016 is increasing capital outflows. As discussed in the previous chapter, in Japan's case newly deregulated domestic funds, as well as international funds, flowed out as required by international interest rate parity (IRP) and financial strategy parity (FSP) considerations. These capital outflows were seeking new opportunities, including in developing countries, and they were attracted by seemingly low risk premiums, especially relative to the domestic Japanese market as bad loan problems surfaced there. According to the Institute of International Finance, China accounted for almost 30 percent of total foreign capital inflows to emerging markets between 2000 and the end of 2014, a total of around $3.6 trillion. And, its holdings of US Treasury securities increased to $1.2 trillion over this same time period. Investors removed $674 billion from China in 2015 and are expected to remove $538 billion in 2016.[7] And, like Japan in this comparison period, China is seeing its huge government reserves of foreign currency begin to significantly decrease: from $4 trillion in June 2014 to around $3.2 trillion in February 2016. By another calculation from the IMF, China's cushion between its actual reserves and what could be required has decreased in 2016 to 15 percent from 50 percent in 2014.[8]

II.   COMMON PATTERNS

A 'financial crisis' is generally defined to be 'a wider range of disturbances, such as sharp declines in asset prices, failures of large financial intermediaries, or disruption in foreign exchange markets' (De Bonis et al., 1999). There is a 'crisis', generally speaking, because the real economy is seriously and adversely affected, including negative impacts on employment, production, purchasing power, and the possibility that large numbers of households and firms or governments are fundamentally unable to meet their obligations, that is, 'insolvency'. When an organization is fundamentally solvent but temporarily unable to meet its financial obligations, then the notion of 'illiquidity' is often used, but in practice insolvency and illiquidity are difficult to distinguish. For example, a common pattern is that 'vicious circles' start from a money-liquidity crisis at a few banks, which then extends to an international crisis of investor confidence in certain parts of the financial sector, which extends to a funding or balance of payments problem for the country and perhaps currency devaluation, which extends to, therefore, even further liquidity and, at some point, solvency crises at the banks.

In the cases of large-scale financial crisis discussed in this book, including the recent crisis, a country or region initially benefits from expanded supplies of base money, new 'quasi-moneys' which are created from base moneys, and credit supplies—a financial liberalization and deregulation phase. Typically, the financial sector expands as it captures profit from new efficiencies and opportunities allowed by globalization. The country or region, for a time, may be favored by international investors; thus the banking system, including government, is well capitalized and able to expand money-liquidity. Assets increase in monetary value and interest rates are low, and this wealth effect encourages consumption, borrowing, business investment, and government spending. Productive resources are more fully utilized and economic growth is well supported. There is a 'boom', as measured by (1) increased monetary wealth held by private and public sectors of an economy, such as the value of stocks, real estate, currency reserves, and so on, and/or (2) the current production of merchandise and services (GDP).

Then, in the 'bust phase', typically, the money supply (m) times its rate of circulation or velocity for GDP purposes (v) contracts, and therefore so does the equivalent nominal GDP. The decline in nominal GDP is usually split between its two components: real GDP which is the volume of current production measured in constant prices (q), and the GDP price level (p). By definition, as elaborated in Chapter 2, these variables are linked by the equation of exchange: $(m \times v = p \times q)$. When (q) declines for a sustained period (typically at least six months) we call it a recession, and when (p) declines we call it deflation. After this process starts, monetary policymakers may react by rapidly expanding (m), but this action may be too little too late—individuals and institutions may have non-payable debts, banks may be failing, and confidence in the country or region may already be damaged. In LDCs with weak financial systems, the desperate increase in (m) may reverse the slide in (p) and even lead to hyperinflation (destabilizing, rapid increases in p), but (q) would continue to fall. However, in developed-country cases, such as Japan after 1989 and for the US, Europe, and other developed countries in the recent crisis, deflation is more likely as a weakened financial system is less able to maintain the circulation rate of its money supply for productive activities, especially if people and institutions are hoarding money; that is, the decline in (v) has offset the increase in (m) to such a degree as to be deflationary. Given relative international confidence in the dollar, yen, euro, and other developed-country currencies, they have remained hoarded as 'stores of value' in these situations, and thus unlike crises in developing countries, there has not been the kind of capital flight and 'currency debasement' that triggers inflation scenarios. Even though the 2007– crisis started in the US, demand for the dollar has remained strong; the same has been true for the euro in, for example, German depository institutions where short-term interest rates have remained close to zero.

The initial contraction in 'effective money' $(m \times v)$ in a crisis may be caused by monetary authorities or national and international investors draining money (m) from the country or region, or there may be a decline in (v) for reasons having to do with the inability of the financial system to direct money toward productive activities. A contraction in effective money, a withdrawal of international investment, or bad loan problems (which need not initially affect narrow money supplies) may undermine equity markets, debt markets, bank capital, or government reserves, and monetary wealth is then revalued downwards. General economic or political uncertainty worsens the situation—the resulting austerity-mentality causes a contraction of spending and credit, and an increased 'risk premium' attached to business activity scares away investment and bank lending. Interest rates may rise, the demand for quasi-money and credit— that is, the desire to hold and use the insecure 'monetary float'—declines, and people try to convert the monetary float into more secure base money, Treasury securities, and other more secure assets. No reserve-currency banking system is able to cover all of its monetary float with secure bank reserves if customers try to redeem too much of the float at once, and thus 'runs' on banks can destroy the banks themselves—as in 2008 in the case of Northern Rock in the UK, Iceland's banks, and others. A deteriorating banking sector may be unable to honor its deposits, bad loan problems surface, and a 'lender of last resort' such as the central bank, the national Treasury (taxpayers), or the IMF may need to be found.

Following similar patterns as in Japan after 1989, the acceleration of the recent crisis in mid-2008 in the US was associated with a collapse in broad money supplies (m3). Although the US Federal Reserve took the controversial decision to stop reporting (m3) data (m2 plus a wider range of bank instruments) after February 2006 on the grounds that the modern financial system made this data unmanageable and not useful, estimates compiled by Lombard Street Research show a decline in the US (m3) growth rate from 19 percent in early 2008 to 2.1 percent (annualized) in the period May–June 2008—a decline very similar to Japan's (m2 + CD) decline in 1991–92 as shown in Figure 3.2. A continuing decline in estimated US (m3) in July 2008 by $50 billion was the biggest one-month fall of US (m3) since modern records began in 1959. The US (m1) annualized growth rate, which had fluctuated around 0 percent during 2006 and 2007 and the first half of 2008, was dramatically increased by the Federal Reserve (too little too late in the view of the author) to approximately 5 percent in September 2008 and 15 percent by the end of 2008, and thus it did not initially serve as a base for expanded supplies of broad money as those supplies were instead consumed by financial institutions in distress. Eurozone (m1) growth had also fallen to near-zero growth levels in mid-2008, and (m4), the broadest measure of money in the UK, had actually dipped into negative growth territory. A temporary boom in US estimated (m3) prior to mid-2008 before the acceleration of the crisis did not reflect an economy-wide condition—there was a near total shutdown in much of the American commercial paper market in 2008, and borrowers were forced to take out bank loans (m3) instead. The commercial paper market had yet to recover during mid- and late 2008 while (m3) plunged, thus collectively the economy's broad-bank and near-bank (commercial paper, etc.) money and near-money supplies declined dramatically in mid-2008.

US nominal GDP (p × q) declined at an annual rate of approximately 10 percent in the fourth quarter of 2008, of which approximately 6 percent was a decline in real GDP (q) and 4 percent was a decline in the GDP price deflator (p). The annual growth rate of 15 percent in US (m1) (m) during this same period translates into a severe structural decline in the US income velocity of money (v)—from an (m1) (v) of approximately 10 through much of 2008 to a value of approximately 7.5 in the fourth quarter of 2008, indicating an unprecedented decline of approximately 25 percent, and an unprecedented absorption of money by financial markets away from GDP markets.

Thus, a rapid expansion of (m) by the Federal Reserve in mid-2008 in the US, rather than by late 2008, might have significantly reduced the spread of the recent crisis. Similarly, as argued earlier, the crises in Japan 1989– and Europe 2007– might have been significantly reduced in severity if the Bank of Japan and the ECB had, respectively, moved to more expansionary monetary policies earlier. China, which in 2016 faces the risk of the same kind of turning point toward a deflationary money-liquidity crisis, has shown some signs of moving toward more expansionary monetary policies—the Chinese central bank has reduced interest rates six times since November 2014 and has also reduced the reserve requirement for commercial lenders. Whether any future increases in (m) prove to be sufficient to counterbalance any future decreases in (v), especially before a decrease in (v) becomes severe and temporarily irreversible within a crisis scenario, remains to be seen in China.

And in Japan, after two decades of recessionary and deflationary conditions, on 4 April 2013 the new Bank of Japan Governor announced that there would be open-ended asset buying with the goal of doubling the monetary base to 270 trillion yen ($2.9 trillion) in order to push inflation up to its 2 percent target. This unprecedented degree of monetary easing has yet, as of mid-2016, to translate into strong enough (m) growth to achieve its inflation target—once again, in the view of the author, the translation of an expanding monetary base and other bank reserves into productive loans and therefore expansion of money-liquidity, (m × v), is more difficult when there are such lengthy delays following the onset of financial crisis and recession.

III.   NEW THINKING: ON PSYCHOLOGICAL, SOCIAL, AND 'TRANSCENDENTAL' FACTORS

Recent models of large-scale financial crises are often characterized as 'first generation' models or 'second generation' or, most recently, 'third generation'. First generation models, as pioneered by Krugman (1979) and others, emphasize the importance of a country's foreign exchange reserves, that is, if government budget deficits are excessive, then ultimately a government loses the ability to maintain these reserves, and a speculative attack on its currency exchange rate is inevitable. Second generation models, as summarized by Rangvid (2001), arose during the 1990s when this cause–effect linkage no longer explained various currency crises. In particular, there is now a weaker relationship between economic fundamentals such as public sector deficits and the timing and severity of speculative currency attacks and related instabilities. The timing of government decisions to abandon a currency regime in favor of other political-economic goals has also proved difficult to predict. Second generation models thus tell stories of 'multiple equilibrium' values that key variables might assume, unpredictable or irrational behavior by private investors and governments, and there has been an effort to discover new 'sunspot variables' that will better explain sudden changes in markets.

Third generation models, as per Krugman (1999) and Allen et al. (2002), introduce additional variables and feedback processes, especially the role of companies', entrepreneurs', and government balance sheets, and the impact of international financial flows and exchange rates on those balance sheets. During and after the 1997 Asian financial crisis, the financial condition of firms weakened more than was anticipated by second generation models, which drew attention to these processes. Furthermore, until new entrepreneurs come forward, or until balance sheets return to normal, it has been difficult for economies to return to normal growth and stability.

Second and now third generation models of financial crisis, while simulating many common patterns, do not yet explain sudden movements in exchange rates, interest rates, international investment flows, stock market and real estate values, and other key variables to levels well beyond normal fluctuations. Thus, there is a revival of interest in what Keynes, in *The General Theory*, called 'animal spirits' such as 'spontaneous optimism' among entrepreneurs and others (Marchionatti, 1999). Essentially, Keynes argued that people may have a limited cognitive and informational basis for fully rational decision-making and, therefore, they may rely on less rational social conventions, vague beliefs, and other psychological factors. One implication is that the market will be subject to waves of optimistic and pessimistic sentiment, which are unreasoning and yet in a sense legitimate where no solid basis exists for a reasonable calculation. (Keynes, 1936, p. 154)

As authoritatively summarized by Kindleberger in *Manias, Panics, and Crashes: A History of Financial Crises* (1989), over the long history of market capitalism, the start of an unsustainable financial boom or 'mania' is always linked to a sudden increase in money-liquidity and lending. Unstable and exaggerated expectations, which are quite subjective, play a role:

> The heart of this book is that the Keynesian theory is incomplete [in explaining economic instabilities and crises], and not merely because it ignores the money supply. Monetarism is incomplete, too. A synthesis of Keynesianism and monetarism, such as the Hansen-Hicks IS-LM curves that bring together the investment-saving (IS) and liquidity-money (LM) relationships, remains incomplete, even when it brings in production and prices (as does the most up-to-date macroeconomic analysis), if it leaves out the instability of expectations, speculation, and credit and the role of leveraged speculation in various assets. (Kindleberger, 1989, p. 25)

IV. NEW THINKING: ON EVOLUTIONARY AND COMPLEX SYSTEMS[9]

A. Mainstream Economic Theory and Financial Crises

The neoclassical general equilibrium model has long provided the theoretical rationale underlying mainstream economic efforts to understand macroeconomic fluctuations. This model conceives of an economy as a set of fully connected interlocking markets which can be analyzed like a force field in physics. To make the model work it is virtually imperative to assume that the market participants are homogeneous or nearly so. Prices in this model are not negotiated, they are set by a central authority (the famous Walrasian 'market auctioneer'), who assesses prevailing excess demands and imposes a set of prices that will clear all markets simultaneously. The model presumes strong tendencies toward equilibrium: it would be in equilibrium most of the time unless some exogenous force were to disturb it, in which case it would normally settle back quickly. But nominal and institutional rigidities are assumed to prevent such shocks from being perfectly damped, which generates business fluctuations.

Markets in a model like this satisfy the *efficient markets hypothesis* and, because of the strong equilibrium tendencies, have price changes that are Gaussian (normally) distributed. An important feature of a Gaussian distribution is that very large positive and very large negative deviations from the mean (more than three standard deviations, say) are virtually impossible. Yet price changes of these magnitudes routinely occur during financial crises. This suggests that whatever is occurring during these episodes is not following the processes embodied in the general equilibrium model.

The general equilibrium model also assumes that promises are always fulfilled: when goods are purchased or loans are made, the goods get paid for and the loans get repaid on schedule. This condition is routinely violated in a financial crisis. Leijonhufvud (2004) notes that, despite the obvious importance of understanding better such breakdowns in the equilibrating processes, which can threaten the social order, modern macroeconomics sheds little light on their nature. LeRoy (2004), in his survey of traditional economic analyses of price bubbles, comes to a similar conclusion.

B.   Complexity Theory

Given the inability of standard general equilibrium theory to explain the occurrence of financial bubbles and crises, researchers have explored other avenues. One promising approach is to look at the economic system through the lens of complexity theory. A complex system differs in important ways from the general equilibrium system of neoclassical economics. If an economy is a complex system, all behavior emanates from the bottom, from the actions of individual agents: there is no global controller or Walrasian market auctioneer to set parameters or behavior. Because agent behaviors interact in nonlinear ways, the macro result which emerges can have a life of its own which is not obviously deducible from the properties of the agents: the whole is not only greater than the sum of the parts, it is different as well. Positive feedback loops often exist, which amplify the effects of small changes into large cascades with significant influence. Complex systems are path-dependent, meaning that their present state is determined by what happened to them in the past (history matters). They exhibit perpetual novelty: new behaviors and structures constantly stimulate more of the same. Dynamics dominates statics; the system evolves and adapts rather than just 'running' as general equilibrium models tend to do. As a consequence, a complex system is rarely in equilibrium. It may have long periods of stability, but stability is not the same as equilibrium: it can degenerate into chaotic behavior on short notice without exogenous disturbance. This often signals what is known as a phase shift, whereby the system changes from one way of functioning to a distinctly different way. Financial crises can often be thought of as phase shifts.

Because a complex system does not have strong tendencies to equilibrium, it does not usually generate variables with Gaussian distributions. Instead, it tends to produce power law distributions, which have fatter tails than the Gaussian and thus explain the frequent occurrence of extreme positive and negative values. Benoit Mandelbrot has been a student of financial system prices for many decades and has produced persuasive evidence that they follow power law distributions (Mandelbrot and Hudson, 2004). His work, long ignored and even suppressed by efficient market theorists, is now widely recognized as correct and has been brought to the attention of the general public by Nassim Taleb (2007).

C.   Complex Adaptive Systems

The mathematics of complex systems have been studied for some time now and are reasonably well understood. Although phase shifts and cascades are suggestive of financial crises and power laws are consistent with frequent large price changes, complex systems were originally developed to explain inanimate phenomena such as chemical reactions. The agents in that type of complex system have no volition of their own: they passively respond to whatever natural forces affect them. An economy on the other hand is composed of agents who both perceive their situation and are capable of changing their behavior in response to it. This suggests the notion of a complex *adaptive* system (CAS) in which the agents are active participants. The behavior of a CAS is much more difficult to study, yet reflection suggests that a modern economy is almost surely a CAS, so this is a task which must be undertaken if we are to make progress understanding financial crises.

Foster (2005) has developed a useful taxonomy for complex systems. He identifies four types:

- *First-order (imposed energy)*. Found in inanimate settings when energy is imposed on chemical elements. Characterized by fractal patterns, butterfly effects, and so on. Can be modeled with dynamical mathematics. This is the approach Mandelbrot applied to financial prices. The agents passively react, so this is a complex system.
- *Second-order (imposed knowledge, acquired energy)*. Found in organic settings. Plants and animals receive imposed (genetically encoded) knowledge and also gain knowledge from experience. All of this gets translated into a knowledge structure that permits some control over energy acquisition. Agents both react and adapt to their environment, so this is a CAS.
- *Third-order (acquired knowledge)*. Agents interact not only with their environment but also with images of possible worlds, that is,

mental models. When this happens, some mental models will wind up determining aspects of reality. This is a CAS where 'adaptive' involves creativity. If everyone has a mental model of the market and begins associating with their fellow agents according to market rules, the market gets transformed from mental model into reality.

- *Fourth-order (interactive knowledge)*. At this stage mental models begin interacting with each other. Agents imagine what other agents might be imagining and alter their own models accordingly in a potentially infinite regression. Agents form aspirations and commitments into the future. This type of CAS gets extremely complicated and depends heavily on trust and understanding to achieve the cooperation necessary for the system to function.

In the study of financial crises, the first-order type of complex system is of interest because it provides a realistic description of how prices behave in bubbles and panics. However, it gives us little in the way of a behavioral explanation for these price changes. The fourth-order type does provide a basis for the behavioral explanation we seek—as a way to include the impact of the psychological, social, and 'transcendental' factors discussed in the previous section. The problem is that fourth-order complex systems cannot at present be analyzed mathematically. However, though analytical solutions are at present not possible, such systems are beginning to be studied fruitfully through simulation methods and through certain types of econometric modeling, as detailed below.

The Federal Reserve has gotten interested in a CAS approach to managing financial crises. In the world at large, complex systems abound: weather patterns, tectonic processes, disease contagion, power grids, and so on. Their instability and potential for large, disruptive regime shifts are major social concerns. The ubiquity of such problems suggests that there may be common principles at work. A 2006 Federal Reserve conference on systemic risk (Kambhu et al., 2007) saw experts from fields such as civil engineering, disease control, ecology, national security, and finance discuss their approaches to catastrophe control. The following composite picture emerged: an initial shock (possibly a seemingly insignificant one) leads to a coordinated behavior in the system with reinforcing (positive) feedbacks. A contagion begins, which spreads the original shock. When the pressure becomes too much the system makes a regime shift 'from a stable state to an inferior stable state while shedding energy so that it cannot readily recover its original state, a process known as hysteresis' (Kambhu et al., 2007, p. 7). Research is focusing on factors that increase resistance to regime shifts and hysteresis, and on factors that can help the system recover. Some of this research may prove helpful in managing financial crises.

D. Evolutionary Economics

If an economy is a CAS, then as time passes it does not just run like an electric motor; its form and structure evolve. The machine is the metaphor of the general equilibrium economy; for the CAS economy, the metaphor is the living organism. It is not easy to model an evolving economy using the neoclassical model, which can accommodate growth fairly readily but structural change only with great difficulty. In a neoclassical model of an evolving economy based on past history, the parameter values are always becoming obsolete—slowly and steadily sometimes, or very quickly when there is a structural shift.

The field of evolutionary economics has emphasized these issues for some time and has made efforts to incorporate capacity for structural change into its models. Schumpeter's idea that creative destruction is the essence of capitalism forms the basis of much modern thinking in evolutionary economics. Schumpeter emphasized the role of liberal credit as a driver of speculative booms, and sudden credit contraction as a major contributor to the severity of the ensuing crash (Leathers and Raines, 2004). The version of evolutionary economics that appears most useful for analyzing financial crises is the 'Micro-Meso-Macro' framework of Dopfer et al. (2004). This framework centers around two novel concepts: rules, and meso units.

A rule is a pattern that agents follow in their everyday economic behavior: it may be cognitive, behavioral, technological, institutional, organizational, sociocultural, and so on. Rules may be nested in other rules: we might talk about a motorcycle rule that includes engine rules, tire rules, and so on. or a market rule that includes a double auction rule, a fixed-price rule, and so on. Rules are carried out (actualized) by microeconomic agents (individuals, families, organizations, etc.). A meso unit is a rule plus its population of actualizations (e.g. the motorcycle meso is the motorcycle rule plus all agents who make, sell, repair, or drive motorcycles). An economic system (assumed to be complex adaptive) is a collection of meso units evolving over time. Macroeconomic behavior is the result of interactions among meso units. Economic evolution is the process by which new rules originate and diffuse through the population: very often this process takes the form of a logistic growth path in the new rule's meso unit. Structural change occurs when a new meso rule permanently alters the coordination structure of the meso units of the economic system. Over time, creative destruction occurs: new rules are constantly being originated; the successful ones develop strong mesos which displace previously dominant mesos; the weak ones disappear.

In this framework, a bubble or crisis in the financial sector would be analyzed as a structural change. Foster and Wild (1999a and b) have developed a promising econometric methodology for analyzing such structural shifts in terms of the logistic function, and for identifying early warning signals that the macro-economy may be about to undergo a structural change. A high priority today is to analyze the international growth of money and credit over recent decades using these techniques.

For example, Figure 2.1 shows a structural change in the long-term trend GDP velocity of money (v) in the US, UK, and Canada in the early 1980s that marked the beginning of the boom phase of this recent financial crisis. In each of these countries, corresponding with the particular timing of the break in (v), governments dramatically abandoned financial market protectionism. Policymakers removed ceilings on interest rates, reduced taxes and brokerage commissions on financial transactions, gave foreign financial firms greater access to the home financial markets, allowed increased privatization and securitization of assets, and took other steps that allowed money to move more freely and profitably between international and national markets. As can be seen in Figures 2.2 and 2.3 for the US and UK, in these key 'phase shift' years, there was a corresponding dramatic expansion in the transactions volumes of money-absorbing financial transactions (measured as the combined value of stock, bond, and government securities transactions)—shown as an inverse relationship between (v) and financial transactions volumes. In the US, the major structural break in (v) along with other monetary-transmission relationships occurred in 1982 as participants responded to newly profitable forms of liberalized financial market participation with the aid of new information-processing technologies (Allen, 1989, p. 273). The major structural break in the UK occurred in 1985–86 as participants anticipated the UK's 'Big Bang' of October 1986, which ended fixed commissions for brokers and separation of powers between brokers, and allowed a rush of foreign financial firms into the marketing of British stocks and government bonds and other securities.

V. TOWARD A NEW POLITICAL ECONOMY OF FINANCIAL CRISIS

Research cited earlier indicates that large-scale financial crises have been a regular phenomenon for centuries. Based on historical data, the 2007– crisis is not unusual in magnitude, and if anything 'we were overdue' based upon historical patterns. However, for most observers and participants in the 1980s and 1990s and even into 2008 after the recent crisis started, 'this time was different' and confidence in institutions remained high. As discussed earlier, that level of confidence along with other psychological, social, and 'transcendental' factors were key drivers of the long boom phase of the recent crisis.

Heightened awareness of the likelihood of crisis only began to surface in the mid-1990s. In 1996, the IMF indicated that approximately three-quarters of its more than 180 member countries had encountered 'significant' banking sector problems between 1980 and 1995, one-third of which warrant the definition 'crisis' (Lindgren et al., 1995). Then, in 1997, unexpectedly, the East Asian financial crisis struck, which was followed by the Russian and Brazilian crises in 1998 and various others, such as the Argentine crisis in 2002.

These crises, even prior to the current situation, began to generate a flurry of policymaking activity. Initiatives at the IMF and elsewhere in 2000–05 came close to, but did not realize, a 'bankruptcy procedure' for countries, which was a stark contrast from the famous, and uninformed, quote of less than three decades ago (shortly before the 1982– Latin American debt crisis) from the Chairman of CitiCorp that 'countries don't go broke'. However, there was no agreement within the IMF's Executive Board regarding the best way to proceed. Its Director Anne Krueger had proposed various 'Sovereign Debt Restructuring Mechanisms' (SDRMs), which in some cases would require an Amendment of the IMF's Articles of Agreement in order to extend the IMF's role in resolving crises. She summarizes IMF discussions of the first SDRM proposals as follows:

> Many Directors believe that ... intermediate options could help address concerns about significantly extending the Fund's powers in a statutory approach ... Some Directors, however, expressed a strong preference for a contractual approach not requiring an Amendment of the Fund's Articles, and cautioned against any mechanism that would imply the creation of an international judicial body to oversee the restructuring process, either within or outside the Fund. (IMF, 2002)

Unlike the well-researched national banking crises that have been resolved under domestic regulations, there has been no comprehensive international law or policy that sets out the procedures for the international community to follow in international crisis episodes. The ad hoc rescue fund provided to Mexico after its crisis at the end of 1994 was unprecedented in size—approximately $50 billion—as well as international political scope, given the ways that it involved the IMF, the US Treasury's Exchange Stabilization Fund (normally reserved for other purposes), the Bank for International Settlements, and a variety of independent countries. Mexico's oil export revenues could even be held by the Federal Reserve Bank of New York to guarantee US loans. Ad hoc financial bailouts offered to Korea and Indonesia in 1997, and Brazil in 1998, were similarly large. In Indonesia's case the IMF insisted on a variety of unprecedented restructuring requirements that were viewed by President Suharto as a direct challenge to his leadership, including the winding-up of some domestic monopolies that were associated with his family.

Complicating efforts by the IMF, central bankers, and others to prevent and resolve country crises and to advance a better international financial architecture has been disagreement on how recent financial crises are related to recent 'globalization' of economic activity. When the author published the first edition of *Financial Crises and Recession in the Global Economy* in 1994, a member of the US Federal Reserve Board concluded (in *Choice* magazine, January 1995) that the author 'grossly overstates [that financial globalization] is the principal cause and explanation of various events that Allen exaggeratedly refers to as crises'.

Scholarly journals were launched in recent decades to respond to these issues. For example, in the first edition of *Review of International Political Economy*, the editors state:

> The creation of a global economic order has come to represent the defining feature of our age, as a major force shaping economies and livelihoods in all areas of the world. Globalization, of course, has many aspects . . . The first of these is the emergence of a truly global financial market . . . and the resulting increase in the power of finance over production.[10]

Thus, a 'political economy of financial crisis' is called for in order to give perspective to the key issues and processes that surround recent large-scale financial crises, and in order to identify procedures that will help to avoid and manage crises. Disciplines that this new field should draw on include (the already overlapping) economics, politics, international relations, political economy, and international political economy. In the author's view, literature in political economy and international political economy comes closest to hitting the mark. Prominent contributors to both fields, since the great depression of the 1930s, are also prominent contributors to the study of financial crisis, including John Maynard Keynes, Hyman Minsky, and Charles Kindleberger, who were referenced elsewhere in this chapter.

An excellent review of PE and IPE, including the place within them for research into financial systems, can be found in another relatively new journal titled *New Political Economy*. Regarding the relationship between politics, economics, and markets, this review states the following broad perspective, which is shared by the author:

> [Recent encyclopedias on both political economy and international political economy] treat the concept of a market in an identical manner, stressing that markets are social mechanisms that facilitate the exchange of ownership (or

property) rights within a context of embedded rules and procedures legitimized by some form of organized authority. (Germain, 2002, p. 304)

This broad institutionalist perspective of markets, which draws attention to legal, cultural, political, and social infrastructures, applies on the international level as well as the national level, thus showing the close analytical bonds between political economy and international political economy. Using a principle of parsimony, it thus seems better to title this new field simply *The Political Economy of Financial Crisis* . . . rather than *The International Political. . . .* As a further justification for this choice, not all of the issues central to this field have international dimensions, with 'international' taken to mean 'activities taking place between nations'. For example, how is money created, transferred, and destroyed? And how 'rational' are financial market participants?

The author and others have worked to define the issues and scope of what might be a new political economy of financial crisis (Allen, 2004). The issues include: What is a financial crisis? Can we agree on certain definitions and distinctions—banking versus balance-of-payments versus country crisis? Are the complex factors that lead to a 'country crisis' similar to the well-known factors that lead to a smaller-scale 'banking crisis'? For banks or countries, what is the difference between a 'liquidity crisis' and a more fundamental 'solvency crisis'? What are the early warning signs, which seemed to be so absent before the 1997 Asian crisis as well as the recent crisis? What international, multinational, transnational, global, and so on political and economic systems are involved, as opposed to strictly national systems? What 'international financial architecture' will best prevent and resolve these crises? What disciplines, theories, economic and political processes, current and historical events, and so on, are relevant to the political economy of financial crisis? And, how do all of these issues reflect on the nature of the various capitalisms and other political economic systems that are being practiced across the world?

Of course, a key question arising in the recent crisis is: When should a 'lender of last resort' prudently intervene with fresh funding to resolve bad loans and prevent 'contagion' and the risk of systemic failure? Intervention which is too early, too often, or not ultimately necessary encourages reckless and unproductive activity including the 'moral-hazard problem' that 'the authorities will save me from the adverse consequences of my actions'. And, intervention can be extremely expensive to taxpayers as in the recent crisis.

If, although as a simplification, economics is the study of wealth, and politics is the study of power, then a key issue for 'a political economy of financial crisis' is the broader relationship between financial crisis and the creation and distribution of wealth and power. Thus, the following questions arise: What are money and wealth? How are they created, transferred, and destroyed in the episodes that we call 'financial crises'? How do these crises affect the economic, political, and social power of involved parties? Some research advances the innovative notion that finance capital might sometimes represent the first-round creation of new (rather than appropriation of fully existing) social powers—a conclusion arrived at recently by the author and discussed further below. Similarly, the subjective monetary wealth or 'capital' that is lost or transferred in financial crises might represent the first-round appropriation of broad social powers between affected parties.

The larger political economic system, within which recent financial crises have occurred, includes a variety of competing forms of capitalism, including what has been described as 'Anglo-American economic orthodoxy' versus 'the Asian model' and others. The consummate financial market insider George Soros, among others, has critiqued Anglo-American 'free market fundamentalism' as pioneered by Ronald Reagan and Margaret Thatcher in the early 1980s. Soros suggests that newly deregulated global financial markets are inherently unstable and, in the absence of urgent reforms, they could produce ever greater crises and a powerful backlash against the global capitalist system, especially from the poorer countries on the periphery. He suggests a political-economic framework reminiscent of Keynes' position at the 1944 Bretton Woods conference, including a greater role for an international currency, international credit insurance, and other measures to reduce the natural fallibility and inequity of markets (Soros, 2008).

Susan Strange (1998) provided further context for the political economy of 'the new world of debt' along with global inequality and sustainability issues, including an update to her 1986 assessment of Keynes' 'casino capitalism', which observed:

> The sorry state of the financial system is undoubtedly aggravating the difficulties in the path of economic development for poor countries while conversely the difficulties of the deeply indebted developing countries, so long as they persist, will aggravate the instability of the banking system. (Strange, 1986, p. 181)

In the next chapter, various issues that are central to this new political economy of financial crisis are presented, including the author's views on different forms of 'capital' and the role of 'US money-mercantilism'. A broad 'human ecology economics' framework as coined by the author is used to draw together all of the material from this book, which itself builds on the complex and evolutionary systems framework discussed in this chapter.

VI. CONCLUSIONS

This chapter has characterized the recent global financial crisis as having a long 'boom' phase (early 1980s–2006), followed by a turning point and continuing 'bust' phase (2007–) with many patterns in common relative to other financial crises. It is beyond the scope of this chapter to rigorously model this financial crisis; instead the goal has been to suggest the best analytical framework—some of which is 'new' as applied to financial crises—that might direct more rigorous modeling.

Departing from the neoclassical general equilibrium model and other mainstream approaches, this book proposes an evolutionary and complex systems approach toward understanding the recent crisis (as well as to rethink other large-scale crises). The 1980s' boom in leveraged financial transactions was thus a 'phase shift' in a CAS, and it was a transition to a new 'meso structure' in the language of evolutionary economics. As the author's econometric research has verified, structural changes in normal money supply and demand relationships occurred in the US, UK, and other money centers at this time that were associated with government deregulation, advances in information-processing technology, and other aspects of financial globalization. Although beyond the scope of this book to rigorously simulate, most of the trajectories of financial market data associated both with the 1980s' structural phase shift (Figures 2.1, 2.2, 2.3) and with the recent crisis time period are likely to fit the patterns identified by Foster and Wild (1999b, p. 754) as 'logistic diffusion trajectories' with three self-organizing phases called the 'emergent', 'inflexion', and 'saturation' phases.

As a result of the structural changes identified in this book, financial markets have absorbed newly created money-power beyond levels predicted by any equilibrium models, which in turn were used to inflate asset prices and incentivize production and consumption beyond predictions; then, during the bust phase, these variables moved in the opposite direction more than expected, including a greater than expected fall in stock and real estate prices and destruction of monetary wealth.

Because of the extraordinary magnitudes of these transfers and revaluations of monetary wealth over time and space in the global system, serious real effects have been produced over time and space. These processes, generally not accepted by mainstream, Marxist, and many other economists, can nevertheless account for what the mainstream has understood as 'business cycles', 'debt–deflation crises' including depressions (Fisher, 1933), and so on, and what Marxists have understood as crises of 'underconsumption', 'overproduction', and 'disproportionality' (Clarke, 1994). The ideologies and institutions of finance are not only capable of being 'where the action is', and where differential economic power is determined across the world system, but these institutions are also increasingly key to the sustainability of the current global economic system—a necessary 'infrastructure of the infrastructure' as per Cerny's analysis (1993).

This expansion and globalization of financial market structures that accelerated in the 1980s, which seemed to take on a dramatic life of its own somewhat separate from GDP processes, can be modeled with the help of third-order and fourth-order complexity processes—acquired knowledge and interactive knowledge processes, respectively—as discussed in the previous section. Given the 'animal spirits' of irrational exuberance or fear, transcendental 'laws of compound interest' and no-reserve-requirement money-liquidity creation, and so on, interactive mental models drove financial cycles and monetary-wealth creation and destruction processes beyond the bounds of general equilibrium to levels that required a breakdown in the equilibrating processes—the boom phase and its accompanying meso structure were unsustainable (beyond 2006 or so), and now a new meso structure is in the process of adaptation.

Whether or not financial crises arising from over-indebtedness and followed by deflation—as per Irving Fisher's classic work (Fisher, 1933)—should be systematically expected in modern capitalism has been debated. Mainstream economic thinking has until recently been generally confident that 'hard-to-qualify' lending restrictions, wherein all parties are conscious of systemic risk, can avoid over-lending and debt-failure. In contrast, Marxists (see Clarke, 1994) and others across various disciplines, such as Frederick Soddy (1926), are convinced that these crises are endemic to capitalism. Most recently, as summarized by Reinhart and Rogoff, extending their data set back over eight centuries and 68 countries shows 'a perennial problem of serial default . . . in this respect the 2007–08 US subprime financial crisis is hardly exceptional' (Reinhart and Rogoff, 2008, p. 2).

Given that massive debt-repudiation crises continue to happen in the world system, we have not yet been able to avoid over-lending and periodic disjuncture crises between, on the one hand, the belief system that includes mathematical compound interest, and on the other hand, the ability to generate money from tangible 'real world' processes. Some borrowers and lenders are well informed but reckless risk-takers who know that periodic failures are required in 'casino capitalism' (John Maynard Keynes' phrase), whereas other borrowers and lenders underestimate systemic risk and allow over-lending based upon a mistaken ideology regarding the stability of the system. Thus, on both accounts, the literature generally concludes that debt crises are likely to remain with us as a normal function of a capitalist economy. In this regard, there has been a revival of interest in the work of Hyman Minsky among others (Minsky, 2008). Minsky's financial instability hypothesis explains instability as a result of the normal functioning of a capitalist economy, as compared to the relative stability in neoclassical models. Minsky expanded upon Keynes' general theories by arguing that financial structures in a dynamic capitalist economy naturally evolve from robust to fragile until enough fragile institutions expose the system to the risk of large-scale crisis as per the debt–deflation scenario of the Great Depression.

Understanding the political economy of the new global financial structure further is the topic of the next chapter.

NOTES

1. 'China's Central Bank Chief Sounds Warning Over Rising Debt', *Bloomberg News*, 20 March 2016.
2. 'Bad loans are rising quickly at China's top banks', *CNNMoney*, 31 March 2016.
3. 'Special Report: Finance in China', *The Economist*, 7 May 2016, p. 4.
4. 'A Moving Target: China's Shape-Shifting Shadow Banks Evolve Once More', *The Economist*, 6 September 2014.
5. 'Special Report: Finance in China', *The Economist*, 7 May 2016, p. 5.
6. 'End of One-Child Policy Is Unlikely to Solve China's Looming Aging Crisis', *Forbes*, 29 October 2015.
7. 'China expected to see $538 billion capital exodus in 2016, IIF says', *Reuters News Service*, 25 April 2016.
8. Ibid.
9. For the content of this section, the author is heavily indebted to his recent co-author Professor Don Snyder (Allen and Snyder, 2009).
10. *Review of International Political Economy* (1994), **1** (1), 3.

5.   A human ecology economics (HEE) framework for the analysis of financial instability

'Human ecology economics' (HEE), as recently developed by the author (Allen, 2008) as a new heterodox approach to doing economics, expands upon the evolutionary and complex systems approaches discussed in Chapter 4. In the author's view, HEE is a superior framework for 'the political economy of financial crisis', because unlike traditional economics and other social sciences, HEE (1) allows a very long run time perspective, which can identify structural changes in the system; (2) encourages use of the humanities including a formal role for belief systems and 'ways of being' within the economic system, which are key drivers of financial instability; (3) allows everything to vary within the economic system—including belief systems, ways of being, and social agreements— in complex, co-evolutionary ways; (4) emphasizes global systems; and (5) effectively juxtaposes 'sustainability' and other interdisciplinary issues alongside traditional economic issues. Each of (1)–(5) is needed, in the view of the author, to best sort out and apprehend the 'creative chaos' of financial crisis and related instabilities over recent decades and into the future.

This chapter lays out the HEE framework as it might guide future research and thinking on large-scale financial crisis, and then it uses the HEE framework to elaborate some of the recent transitions and financial instabilities discussed in previous chapters. In particular, it identifies the longer-term role of various kinds of 'capital' in the financial system, including how 'capital' is important for sustainable growth and development. A case study of Eastern Europe is illustrative. Also, drawing on the work of Thomas Piketty, *Capital in the Twenty-First Century* (Piketty, 2014), the long-term effects of financial globalization and related processes of capital accumulation are discussed. Through a process defined as 'US money mercantilism', the US is seen as a major 'winner' in the new structure of the global economy. Finally, conclusions to the book are presented.

I. THE HUMAN ECOLOGY ECONOMICS FRAMEWORK

HEE proposes various structural components or building blocks of 'the human ecology'. Perhaps the most fundamental components are human populations, belief systems, social agreements, and physical environments and resources. From these basic structural conditions other structural conditions emerge, such as organizations, institutions, and, for the purpose of this book, economic systems—that is, the global economic system.

Figure 5.1 organizes the four basic structural conditions into quadrants. 'Belief systems' is shown in the upper-left quadrant, which can be defined as 'ways of organizing alleged truths and convictions'—examples include, but are not limited to, mythologies, religions, faiths, ideologies, philosophies, mathematics, science, and various academic fields. 'Social agreements', shown in the upper-right quadrant, can be defined as 'the structure that humans impose on their interaction'. Social agreements usually reduce uncertainty; they are the formal and informal 'rules of the game'. Examples include, but are not limited to, politics, law, use of money, communications, and norms of culture and etiquette. In the lower-right quadrant is 'human populations' with characteristics that include birth, fertility, and death rates, population age structure, migration, and spatial distribution. In the lower-left quadrant is 'physical environments and resources', which includes land,

BELIEF SYSTEMS	SOCIAL AGREEMENTS
Mythologies Religions, Faiths Ideologies, Philosophies Mathematics, Science Various Academic Fields	Politics, Law Use of Money Communications Culture, Etiquette
	INSTITUTIONS ORGANIZATIONS MESO UNITS
PHYSICAL ENVIRONMENTS AND RESOURCES Land, Air, Water, Energy City/Regional Spatial Arrangement Transportation, other Infrastructure	HUMAN POPULATIONS Birth, Fertility, Death Rates Population Age Structure Migration Spatial Distribution

Figure 5.1   Structural conditions in the human ecology

air, water, energy, city and regional spatial arrangement, transportation, and other infrastructure—both natural endowments as well as human-built.

The four basic structural conditions in the human ecology can also be combined with each other to form new structural conditions. For example, as shown in Figure 5.1, 'organizations' can be defined as *human popula- tions* bound together by common *social agreements*—examples include firms, trade unions, political parties, regulatory bodies, and so on. Of course, organizations use, and interact with, *belief systems* and *physical environments and resources*, but these interactions are not generally neces- sarily in order for organizations to exist as legal entities. In common usage, 'institutions' are sometimes closely synonymous with 'organizations', and sometimes more synonymous with 'social agreements'. A useful definition for human ecology (similar to social agreements) from Douglass North is:

> Institutions are the rules of the game—both formal rules and informal con- straints (conventions, norms of behavior, and self-imposed codes of conduct)— and their enforcement characteristics. (North, 1997, p. 225)

Shown with organizations and institutions in Figure 5.1, from the lan- guage of evolutionary economics from Chapter 4, a 'meso unit' is a rule or pattern that agents follow in their everyday behavior, along with the people who actualize that rule.

Each of the sub-elements in Figure 5.1 can be broken down into sub- sub-elements. For example, maybe we want to understand what a bank is, or what a bank should be—a key question in recent crises involving many debates such as what it means to 'nationalize a bank', what it means to no longer support 'investment banks' in favor of 'bank holding companies', and so on. With regard to belief systems, perhaps a bank relies upon the mathematics of exponential growth (such as the law of compound inter- est) and stock-and-flow-variable models, and maybe there is an ideology of making money as well as an ideology of supporting certain kinds of home ownership or other types of clients (but with what balance between interest groups in recent crises?). In Figure 5.2, these sub-sub-elements of belief systems are shown separately in the belief systems quadrant within the circle called 'A Bank'. From the physical environment and resources, perhaps a bank uses commercial office space and utility infrastructures, which are therefore shown separately in that quadrant. Or, perhaps an electronic or 'offshore' bank does not require a traditional office . . .? Sub-sub-elements from social agreements and human populations are also identified, and when all sub-sub-elements are bundled together, we have the structure of 'a bank'. And what type of organization (human population bound by social agreements) is a bank? As shown in Figure 5.2,

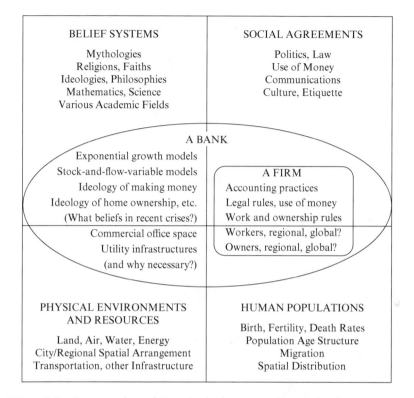

Figure 5.2   Structural conditions in the human ecology: a bank

when the bank structural elements from human populations are bundled together with the bank structural elements from social agreements, then the new bundle is what we commonly call 'a firm'.

Based upon these same structural components of the human ecology, Figure 5.3 shows a possible bundle of structural elements that might be used to describe the economic system. In the author's scheme, economic systems are shown to have important elements from each of the four basic structural conditions. Regarding belief systems, the human ecology approach proposes that the economic system relies heavily on mathematics, science, (traditional textbook) economics, ideals, faith, and myth, among other factors. Also, as discussed in Chapter 4, Section III, an orientation toward philosophical 'materialism' versus 'transcendentalism' might lead to different understandings of how financial markets work, and thus both are listed. The types of social agreements which are important in the economic system include, but are not limited to, the use of money,

BELIEF SYSTEMS	SOCIAL AGREEMENTS
Mythologies Religions, Faiths Ideologies, Philosophies Mathematics, Science Various Academic Fields	Politics, Law Use of Money Communications Culture, Etiquette

ECONOMIC SYSTEMS

Materialism, Transcendentalism Science, Math, Econ., Ideals, Faiths	Money, Policy, Regulation Networks, Culture
Commodities, Infrastructures Natural Resources	Workers, Entrepreneurs Consumers, Policymakers

PHYSICAL ENVIRONMENTS AND RESOURCES	HUMAN POPULATIONS
Land, Air, Water, Energy City/Regional Spatial Arrangement Transportation, other Infrastructure	Birth, Fertility, Death Rates Population Age Structure Migration Spatial Distribution

Figure 5.3   Structural conditions in the human ecology: the economic system

policy, regulation, networks, and culture. From human populations, there are workers, entrepreneurs, consumers, and policymakers, among others, and from physical environments and resources there are commodities, infrastructures, and natural resources, among other tangible goods and structures.

Compared to most economics literature, which minimizes the importance of belief systems, social agreements, institutional change, and the integrity of physical environments and resources, the human ecology framework might allow for a more comprehensive identification and explanation of economic processes. Also, in contrast to much of the economics literature, these structural components are assumed to interact with each other 'endogenously' over time. That is, each structural condition, defined broadly as per Figure 5.3, co-evolves with each of the others in complicated feedback processes, and all structures change. Broadly defined, no structural condition is absolutely fixed or 'exogenous' or serves as a 'global controller' of the others. Of course, human populations cannot exist without physical environments and resources, but human populations rearrange, destroy, and create new physical environments and resources.

Within 'physical environments and resources', the laws of thermodynamics and other laws of natural science might serve as global controllers, as continually debated within the literature. However, the reader should note that 'physical environments and resources' also includes the built environment and what human populations arbitrarily identify as 'resources', which is partly based upon belief systems, the evolution of technology and social agreements, what organizations do, and so on. Similarly, within 'human populations' a certain amount of biological 'hard wiring' might serve as a global controller, as debated in the literature, but clearly birth, fertility, death rates, migration, and other characteristics of 'human populations' are affected by what goes on in the other quadrants.

Figures 5.1, 5.2, and 5.3, along with these dynamic processes, are another way of framing the 'evolutionary and complex systems approach toward understanding the recent crisis' (Chapter 4, Section IV), especially the fourth order (interactive knowledge) complex adaptive system (CAS) approach that the author recommends for modeling financial crises. The privileged role that belief systems and social agreements play in this interactive dynamic framework is consistent with the author's 'new thinking' on psychological, social, and 'transcendental' factors.

This four-quadrant HEE diagram, whether describing a bank, or an economic system, or whatever phenomenon, is also useful in defining 'sustainability'. Essentially the challenge is to fill out the four-quadrant diagram with structural elements—to construct the ontology of a bank, or Europe's possible banking union, or an economic system, or whatever, as one sees it—while determining which elements should be sustained and which elements might have to be eliminated so that preferred elements can be sustained. Often the role of particular belief systems, social agreements, institutions, and so on in the upper two quadrants are not sorted out very well in this way in sustainability studies (Allen, 2008).

In the next section of this chapter, this HEE framework is used to identify the important role played by different kinds of 'capital' in a sustainable economic and financial system—a discussion that extends the common definitions of capital to include more elements from the upper two quadrants of this four-quadrant HEE diagram.

II. DIFFERENT KINDS OF CAPITAL IN THE HUMAN ECOLOGY

For the purposes of this book—including how to support sustainable financial systems within the global political economy—an in-depth look at 'capital' is necessary. As broadly defined in this section, sustainable supplies

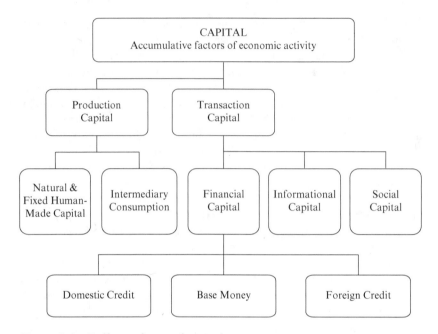

Figure 5.4   Different forms of capital

of various kinds of 'capital' are a necessary condition for sustainable economic systems.

For definitional purposes, 'production capital' is assumed to be composed of 'fixed human-made capital', 'natural capital', and 'intermediary consumption' (Figure 5.4). The common definition of human-made capital is something produced by humans that is used itself in the production of goods and services, such as tools, factories, computer systems, and so on. Human-made capital is typically contrasted with natural capital such as non-renewable resources (oil, minerals, etc.), renewable resources (fish, wood, drinking water, etc.), and other environmental services such as a maintained climate, recycling of nutrients in soils, pollination, biological diversity, and so on. For this book intermediary consumption is similar to 'circulating capital' as used by Adam Smith, David Ricardo, and Karl Marx to refer to physical capital and operating expenses that are short-lived (as in one cycle of production) such as office supplies and inventories—and is thus not 'fixed' for the longer term.

For the purposes of this book fixed human-made capital (including from natural resources) and intermediary consumption—generally accepted by the economics literature as productive—are contrasted with other forms of human-made 'transaction capital' such as financial, informational, and social capital—which are not as generally accepted, at least by mainstream economics literature, as productive. As we shall see, these forms of transaction capital are less tangible and less materially measurable than production capital—even invisible by comparison—and they require careful exposition given that mainstream economics literature as well as Marxism (which has long focused on 'das capital') are most comfortable with a framework of philosophical 'materialism'. In contrast, drawing further from the terms of philosophy, as per Kant and others, transaction capital as identified in this book allows non-empirical, non-observable 'transcendental' human constructs and agreements to also have an important role.

'Social capital' was articulated almost one hundred years ago as:

> good will, fellowship, sympathy, and social intercourse among the individuals and families who make up a social unit . . . The individual is helpless socially, if left to himself . . . If he comes into contact with his neighbor, and they with other neighbors, there will be an accumulation of social capital, which may immediately satisfy his social needs and which may bear a social potentiality sufficient to the substantial improvement of living conditions in the whole community. The community as a whole will benefit by the cooperation of all its parts, while the individual will find in his associations the advantages of the help, the sympathy, and the fellowship of his neighbors. (Hanifan, 1916)

Of course, the values of community life including sympathy, fellowship, and cooperation are discussed from the beginning of literary traditions, but it is worth noting that Adam Smith stressed the importance of innate sympathy as a basis both for helpful social acts and for the sustainability of the social system (Smith, 1759). In the 1980s, the French sociologist Pierre Bourdieu and the German economist Ekkehart Schlicht elaborated their notions of social capital to identify the social and economic resources embodied in social networks (Bourdieu, 1984). Bourdieu, especially, clarified the term in contrast to cultural, economic, and symbolic capital. Many different uses of the term since then include Robert Putnam's *Bowling Alone* (2000), which concludes with a chapter titled 'Toward an Agenda for Social Capitalists' that describes how we might create (or re-create) social capital in the US where, based on many measures, it has been declining over recent decades.

The use of 'informational capital' in this book—as a key factor in economic growth and development—is similar to its recent use by US Federal Reserve Chairman Ben Bernanke, and for our purpose we will emphasize the acquisition of informational capital by financial intermediaries:

A central function of banks is to screen and monitor borrowers, thereby over-coming information and incentive problems [because full information, no trans-actions costs assumptions as often used in neoclassical economics are violated]. By developing expertise in gathering relevant information, as well as by main-taining ongoing relationships with customers, banks and similar intermediaries develop 'informational capital'. The widespread banking panics of the 1930s caused many banks to shut their doors; facing the risk of runs by depositors, even those who remained open were forced to constrain lending to keep their balance sheets as liquid as possible. Banks were thus prevented from making use of their informational capital in normal lending activities. The resulting reduc-tion in the availability of bank credit inhibited consumer spending and capital investment, worsening the contraction. (Bernanke, 2007)

Similarly, insufficient informational capital to support the ontology of new globalized financial markets is a major 'cause' of the financial crises discussed in this book including sudden insolvency of banks and national economies. For example, in Chapter 3, the more lengthy quote describing Sweden's crisis of 1991 included the following:

The banks did not have information systems capable of handling the new situation with rapidly expanding credit portfolios . . . banks lacked an overview over their credit portfolios . . . The large share of lending to finance compa-nies added to the information problem, since borrowers denied credits over a certain limit in banks often had loans with the finance company. (Englund, 1999, p. 96)

Of course, this same informational capital problem applies to secu-ritized, 'exotic', 'toxic', international portfolios that got financial compa-nies into so much trouble in the recent crisis when they lost their grasp over what was in their portfolios and what risks were involved.

Also, lack of sufficient informational capital prevents effective regula-tion and response to crisis. In Mexico's crisis in 1994–95 (Chapter 3), when the run on Mexican assets started, it could not be slowed by negotiations between government officials, the International Monetary Fund (IMF), and large financial institutions. Various mutual fund and hedge fund managers were present at the Federal Reserve Bank of New York on 21 December 1994 to discuss emergency measures with Mexican officials, but they represented only a subset of the exposed investors. Mexican officials wanted to renegotiate terms with its creditors, but they could not identify a sufficient number of them in order to proceed.

As stated by Levine in his exhaustive survey of financial development and economic growth, 'existing theories have not yet assembled the links of the chain from the functioning of stock [and other financial] markets, to information acquisition, and finally to long-run economic growth' (Levine,

1997, p. 695). However, it has long been accepted that information acquisition costs provide incentives for financial intermediaries to form that, compared to individuals acting separately, can economize on the overall costs of processing information about potential investments, selecting and coordinating the most promising firms and managers, and perhaps even stimulating technological innovation: 'The banker, therefore, is not so much primarily a middleman . . . He authorizes people, in the name of society as it were, . . . [to innovate]' (Schumpeter, 1912, p. 74).

Financial capital, as shown in Figure 5.4, is assumed to be the aggregate of base money, domestic credit, and foreign credit—the full 'money and credit pyramid' discussed in Chapter 1. In recent decades until the 2007– crisis, with advances in information-processing technology, government deregulation of financial markets, and globalization, there was a dramatic expansion of financial capital, including base money, domestic credit, and foreign credit as shown in Figure 5.4.

The author's view is that domestic prosperity in the global system depends crucially on the supply of circulating financial capital, and crucially upon the supply of social and informational capital that can direct financial capital, because the main limit to economic growth and development over time is not production but transaction. In the HEE framework, unlike in neoclassical and socialist models, the nature and role of 'transaction', so basic to intra-species negotiation, coordination, and behavior in ecological models, are stressed.

Also, as discussed in the context of 'US money-mercantilism' later in this chapter, the supply of financial capital for the US and various other countries has depended on the sign of the balance of 'invisibles' with the rest of the world, as deficit in the net export flow of goods and services has been compensated mainly by inflows of financial capital from abroad that provide domestic money-liquidity. Using endogenous growth theories, it is possible to show that the external sector can allow a way out of diminishing returns into less-bounded domestic economic growth for financial capital importers.

For example, the HEE framework has been used by the author (in Allen, 2008, Chapter 5), Guillaume Daudin (in Allen, 2008, Chapter 6), and, in a supporting way, by Clark (1998), to show that the industrial revolution was more of an 'industrious revolution' resulting from new workforce participation and coordination—that is, from related build-ups of social, informational, and financial capital, rather than a breakthrough in fixed technology and other fixed human-made capital as per the emphasis of common economics literature.

Although Guillaume Daudin is talking about eighteenth-century France in the following quote, the following processes apply to capital importing regions during recent decades, such as the US, Europe, and others, especially with regard to the importance of financial and other intermediaries, that is, 'traders' who support the growth of financial, informational, and social capital:

> The activity of traders can be divided in three parts. First, they were insuring the actual movement of goods along space and time (the cost of keeping inventories), along with their packaging and their bundling. They had to take precautions in order to insure that each member of the trading network behaved well. They had also to adapt to lack of information—even in the absence of misbehavior—and changing states of the market.
>
> Some of the forms of capital needed by traders for their activity are familiar. On one hand, the exchange activities—especially their transformation side— require what we are used to calling capital in production economies: carts, buildings, that is, fixed capital. This capital is of the same nature as in most economic models; it needs to be produced the usual way, through work and other capital. This is also the case of circulating capital: the wool that is to be threaded, the threads that are to be woven, etc.
>
> They needed also what is usually called 'merchant capital': circulating financial capital to buy intermediary consumption used to package and present goods and the circulating capital embedded in each good as they kept inventories between its purchase and its sale.
>
> They were tackling the problems of misbehavior with work entailed by the inspections and the capital needed to access the legal system that was supposed to enforce proprietary rights. However, they could save dramatically on these operations if they had developed enough social and legal links with their partners. This stock could be inherited by offspring of a trading family; be produced out of social capital, by sending members of their family abroad; be produced in its own right out of their work—during travels or apprenticeship; be produced out of financial capital, by buying lands and offices which were tools of integration in a stable community and hence commitment to good behavior. This stock was also very fragile, and it was a commonplace to affirm that nothing was at the same time more precious nor more fragile than a reputation—the other term for a large stock of social capital . . . However, there is no machinery that can be used to build up reputation capital. One way to do it is to expend part of one's wealth to show the commitment—this wealth only has to be symbolic. This is similar to a 'bond' approach to social capital and reputation.
>
> Tackling the problems of market uncertainties and changeability required traders to spend time in getting information from all their correspondents and interpreting it. Yet, they could also save on this by using their own knowledge of the market. We can represent this by a stock of market-cultural capital: a mix of tricks, best practice and knowledge. Most of this knowledge could only be transmitted with difficulty. Experience of a particular type of network or of market could only be the fruit of day-to-day operations once traders had created the first link. To create this link they had to stake a lot of money, suffer many rebuffs and learn from them . . . Hence, traders were sacrificing the money they could get from operations that they were acquainted with in order to get a larger stock of knowledge capital.

Hence, even though the development of transactions required specific pro-duction factors, they were highly personal and bound to depreciate very quickly. However both social and knowledge capital could be increased through a costly transformation of monetary capital. This capital was not the ideal transaction factor, but it was the easiest to exchange and socially accumulate. Hence, in the absence of institutional transformations, what was crucial for the long-run development of transactions was the accumulation of circulating monetary capital . . . That was actually the case in France . . .. (Daudin, 2008, pp. 171–2)

To summarize, the four-quadrant HEE framework shows that financial, informational, and social capital—collectively called transaction capital—have many structural elements in common from each of the four quadrants (Figure 5.5), whereas fixed human-made capital, natural capital, and inter-mediary consumption—collectively called production capital—reside only in the 'physical environments and resources' quadrant (Figure 5.6).

As per Figure 5.5, the author thus calls for an expansion of the common

<table>
<tr><td>

BELIEF SYSTEMS

Mythologies
Religions, Faiths
Ideologies, Philosophies
Mathematics, Science
Various Academic Fields

</td><td>

SOCIAL AGREEMENTS

Politics, Law
Use of Money
Communications
Culture, Etiquette

</td></tr>
<tr><td colspan="2">

TRANSACTION CAPITAL (EXAMPLES)

| Knowledge of the economy
Ideology of innovation | Relationships, reputation,
money, networks, culture |
| Communication infrastructures | Innate social instincts–good
will, fellowship, sympathy |

</td></tr>
<tr><td>

**PHYSICAL ENVIRONMENTS
AND RESOURCES**

Land, Air, Water, Energy
City/Regional Spatial Arrangement
Transportation, other Infrastructure

</td><td>

HUMAN POPULATIONS

Birth, Fertility, Death Rates
Population Age Structure
Migration
Spatial Distribution

</td></tr>
</table>

Figure 5.5   Structural conditions in the human ecology: financial, informational, and social capital—collectively called 'transaction capital'

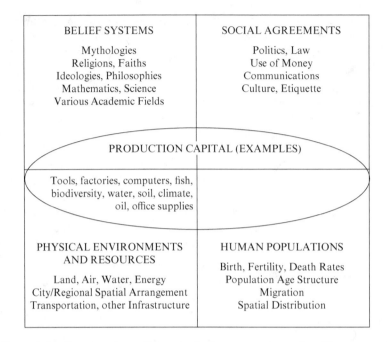

Figure 5.6   Structural conditions in the human ecology: fixed human-made capital, natural capital, and intermediary consumption— collectively called 'production capital'

ontology of capital to include a more important role for various kinds of transaction capital, itself composed from 'human populations': innate social instincts—goodwill, fellowship, sympathy, social powers, and so on; from 'social agreements': relationships, reputation, money, networks, culture, and so on; from 'belief systems': knowledge of the economy, ideology of innovation, and so on; and from 'physical environments and resources': communication infrastructure.

III. AN APPLICATION OF HEE: PRESERVING CAPITAL IN EASTERN EUROPE[1]

As discussed in Chapter 4, in the decade or two preceding the 2007– global crisis, many European nations benefited (more than expected by conventional thinking) from the inflow of foreign monetary wealth. This monetary capital inflow was allocated by information-sharing social capital networks including national and international financial intermediaries to expand domestic money and credit, diverse intermediary consumption, fixed capital, economic growth, and wealth. This rapid expansion of circulating capital allowed economic activity to be better coordinated and more efficient on a large scale in an EU or near-EU context, and it encouraged more intensive production and consumption activities including higher labor-force participation rates, debt-financed home ownership and consumerism, and debt-financed business development. Of course, all of these processes were then reversed (more than expected by conventional thinking) with negative consequences on economic growth and development when financial, informational, and social capital supplies were reduced after 2007. This capital flight was especially pronounced out of the 'European periphery' into the European core, not only the 'Mediterranean periphery' as discussed in the previous chapter, but also the Eastern European periphery. Rather than summarizing the typical financial capital transfers, which are unreliable estimates in the case of Eastern Europe, this section discusses a few examples across Eastern Europe, from Estonia in the north to Azerbaijan in the south, and through Hungary in the middle, whereby it has been hard to sustain supplies of all forms of transaction capital—informational and social as well as financial capital.

The nature and role of 'transaction', so basic to intra-species negotiation, coordination, and behavior in ecological models, is too often ignored in neoclassical and socialist economic models, and also in the practical policymaking of Eastern Europe post-1989—given revolutions and globalization—as well as in the post-2007 crisis period.

Effective transaction capital, as identified in Figure 5.5, is necessary to facilitate economic growth and sustainable development across all dimensions of the human ecology in complex and often intangible ways, including for social and communication networks, for information exchange between small and medium-sized businesses, for innovation and creative learning by doing, for financial intermediation, for better inter-party cooperation at the national level, and so on. In contrast, production capital resides primarily within the dimension of physical environments and resources and its accumulation does not tell us much about the evolution and rationalization of competing belief systems and social agreements and behaviors—an evolution that has been so critically important for Eastern Europe post-1989.

A. Hungary

During the early 1990s, Hungary, alongside the Czech Republic and Slovenia, was one of the more prosperous areas of Eastern Europe. Transitions had been going fairly well after the 1989 revolutions toward more market-based approaches. Some of these transitions had roots in the mid-1980s, such as the introduction of so-called 'Goulash-communism' (Csanádi, 2009). These reforms created a brand new meso structure in the nation: a series of privately owned micro-businesses, frequently run during the owner's free time, after they were done with their 'official' jobs. These changes had a far-reaching effect in the HEE approach. First and foremost, the basic premise of the program—privately owned for-profit businesses—meant a large change in the *social agreements* quadrant. The original promise of the Marxist-socialist structure, that everyone will be able to receive from the common pool based on their needs, was given up by this change: more industrious, more successful businesspeople had inherently greater access to resources; thus even access ceased to exist even theoretically. These reforms also had great impact in the *human population* quadrant, since these changes by definition affected a large portion of the population: micro-businesses sprung up all around the country, at times engaging in real competition, improving the quality of life for many. A lesser, but maybe more important change appeared in the *belief systems* quadrant: the changing social agreements loosened the predominance of the Marxist-Leninist approach, giving way to traditionally oppressed beliefs. Starting from 1986, civil rights movements gained strength and paved the way for the transformations to come (Szabó, 1998).

Then, in 1990s, the free-market 'shock transition' caused large-scale changes in all quadrants—some which were undesired, many that were unintended. The *premise* of the free-market transition was a more competitive economy, balanced budget, and, in the longer run, better quality of life.

The initial changes were expected to happen in the *belief systems* quadrant. People were expected to give up the none-too-embraced socialist-communist ideals and embrace the efficiency of the market. These changes in beliefs would underline, explain, and make bearable the unavoidable changes in the *social agreements*, which would permeate all of society. Sadly, this is not what happened. The original, communist social agreements were torn down, but no alternative was placed in their stead. Healthcare, education, and pension, crucial issues not just for the country but for all nations, have been left in a kind of halfway state, where it is not always clear what one can and will receive, and who finances it. For example, the relatively complex pension reform (clearly analyzed in Palacios and Whitehouse, 1998) is constantly adjusted, thirteenth and fourteenth month pensions are given and then taken away, threatening the liquidity of the government and keeping pensioners in uncertainty.

A further and unexpected change came in the form of the *physical environment*. While borders of the nation remained unchanged, in 1991 the

Comecon trade agreements between the former socialist bloc countries were abolished, thereby greatly changing the available resources and markets for the nation.

These problems did not arise *despite* the reforms in the 1980s, but greatly *because of them*. The new social agreements, although on the surface closer to the market mechanism, reinforced meso structures that are incompatible with capitalistic values. The duality of the economy appeared in a duality of property, reinforcing the belief that when one works for someone else, the best strategy is to conserve personal resources while reallocating shared resources—frequently facilitating the operation of the privately owned businesses from the resources of the communal ones. The expected paradigm shift toward market-based values, therefore, was blocked by these unofficial social agreements and parasitic meso structures, undermining desirable changes in the other quadrants as well.

The most dominant change in the nation happened in politics: as early as 1989 the nation split into two—a split that became a rift around the elections of 1994. Since 1996 the two dominant parties have divided the nation into two uncooperative halves. One of the dominant groups is heavily religious, sacral, and social in nature, the other is technocratic and anti-religious. Both parties have a fixed and roughly even following that place their allegiances mostly historically. This split causes a ceiling to the potential social capital, since the two sides have reduced levels of contact with each other. Social agreements across the macro-economy do not progress, thus limiting economic growth and development.

The combined effect of these peculiarities in the belief systems and social agreements quadrants of Figure 5.1 caused the following anomalies: The government and the entire political culture lost some credibility. The perceived level of corruption stands out in the region (Treisman, 2000), and both starting a business and doing business is relatively difficult. The reduced support for politicians opens another rift in the society: not vertically but horizontally, between the political parties and the people, which causes additional loss in social capital and output. The government supports large international corporations over local firms in many ways. Tax breaks are given to international corporations, whereas the local firms suffer delays in receiving funds. The government is slow to distribute EU funds, and the process is characterized by a lack of transparency (Kincsei, 2009). These practices can cause severe insolvency issues—sometimes firms have to wait 12 to 18 months for payments to arrive, thus shortages of financial capital are caused by shortages of informational and social capital.

B.   Estonia

In Estonia, like Lithuania and Latvia, 80–100 percent of total bank assets are held by foreign banks. In the Baltic States, 70 percent of household debt and 30 percent of corporate debt is in foreign currency. These debt instruments are held by foreign interests who have provided financial capital but little informational and social capital to Estonia and the Baltics—thus an over-reliance on one component of transaction capital which is difficult to sustain without growth in the other two. Furthermore, with reduced supply of foreign credit during the recent global crisis, sustainable growth and development has floundered.

Like Hungary, Estonia embraced globalization and market models in the early 1990s. The government approved the 'Concept of Basic Principles of Privatization' in 1990, which introduced two goals: (1) integrate the new economy into the world economy and (2) attract foreign direct investment (FDI). However, foreign banks primarily supported a real estate boom, which led to a consumer boom, and household savings plunged. Local knowledge and financial capital was replaced by FDI. By 2001 almost 80 percent of GDP was generated through the private sector. After independence was declared in 1991 entrepreneurs were encouraged to bring new ideas and new products to the marketplace. However, since the start of the recent global financial crisis it has been difficult to service the now historically high debt levels because they were incurred without a corresponding build-up of other forms of sustainable domestic capital and productivity.

Estonia struggles to evolve from its historic emphasis on production capital toward social infrastructures that facilitate entrepreneurial innovation. In a 2007 government document titled 'Knowledge-Based Estonia: Estonian Research and Development and Innovation Strategy, 2007–2013', Prime Minister Andrus Ansip portrayed Estonia's weaknesses as low levels of research and development investments in the private sector, too few patent applications, a small number of graduates in natural sciences and technology, and only a modest amount of high-tech export. He outlined three aims of his administration: establish attractive conditions for doctoral studies; build a modern research and development structure; and support high-tech entrepreneurship. The Ministries of Education and Research and of Economic Affairs and Communications are now charged with achieving the following objectives: development of human capital; organizing public sector research and investment more efficiently; increasing innovation capabilities of companies; and policymaking directed toward the long-term development of Estonia. These objectives favor the HEE approach advocating an emphasis on transaction capital.

There is also a need to reverse an increasing migration of skilled workers who have taken informational and social capital to the more affluent EU countries where wages are significantly higher. Political scientist Rein Toomla of Tartu University indicates that unless wages in both the private and public sector are addressed Estonia will be 'emptied out'.

Despite a transparent privatization process and transformation from a command to a market economy, Estonia is another example of an Eastern European country that has done little to motivate small and medium-sized domestic entrepreneurs to experiment with 'new products, processes and new forms of business and commercial organization' (Schumpeter's 1912 definition of innovation) which are key to the sustainable HEE agent-based domestic networks described earlier. Most 'value added' products are imported. Estonia's expenditure on research and development is 0.88 percent of GDP (vs. 1.9 percent in the EU). Estonian research infrastructure is outdated as minimal funds have been expended in this area, and labor productivity is approximately 60 percent that of the EU.

A build-up of domestic transaction capital per the charge given to the Ministries of Education and Research and of Economic Affairs and Communications is vitally important. Research, development, and innovation must be promoted. Young people must be motivated to enter this arena. Students, scholars, researchers, engineers, and scientists from abroad must be enticed to study and work in Estonia as well as traders, agents, and intermediaries of all kinds. Government support for Estonian companies to create and innovate as well as pursue entrepreneurial, risk-taking ventures must be made available. Otherwise, Estonia's once competitive and seemingly sustainable development will deteriorate (Bedford and Leimann, 2008).

C. Azerbaijan

Azerbaijan has seemingly made strides to motivate entrepreneurs to experiment with new products, processes, and forms of business and commercial organization per Schumpeter's (1912) definition of innovation. These initiatives meant changes in the social agreements as well as the belief systems quadrants. As summarized in an International Finance Corporation (IFC) report (IFC, 2008), the country has enacted reforms to help start businesses, employ workers, register property, obtain credit, protect investors, pay taxes, and enforce contracts. These reforms reflect an emphasis on transaction capital. However, the central government dominates the economy and the President exercises strong control over economic decision-making, which is often unpredictable. Such action can disrupt improvements in informational and social capital. In a survey dated 8 September 2008, the Baku-based Entrepreneurship Development

Foundation reported that only 40 percent of entrepreneurs expressed satisfaction with the business climate, 51 percent said they felt compelled to skirt the law on occasion, and 30 percent felt vulnerable to pressure from bureaucrats.

Potential investors in Azerbaijan are concerned over political uncertainties. Exclusionary links between business and politics remains prevalent. Unstable regions surround the country, including Chechnya, Armenia, and Iran to the south. Two-thirds of the money invested in non-oil sectors has been derived from foreign assistance projects. However, the projects have only mildly contributed to spillover development of related economic enterprises.

To test the realities of Azerbaijan's need to emphasize social and informational capital, academic, political, and business personalities were interviewed (Allen et al., 2011). According to Professor Huseyin Baginov, Rector, Qerb University in Baku:

> There are many entrepreneurs in Azerbaijan that have the ability to pursue a business model but are restricted because of: 1) the continuing war with Armenia, 2) the complex legal system and 3) the political situation. Entrepreneurs are frustrated and are leaving the country [taking informational and social capital with them]. These students mainly learn in order to get a certificate allowing them to earn more money and perhaps get a job with a multinational.

Ramiz Mahdiyev, chief of the Presidential Executive Staff stated: 'The success of national modernization, to a great extent, depends upon social activities of the youth. They are often the authors of new ideas.' However, there is concern among the youth that social capital—the goodwill, fellowship, and social intercourse needed to promote innovation—is lacking in Azerbaijan.

Founder and Chancellor Hamlet Isaxali of Khazar University expressed considerable interest in the initiatives to advance informational and social capital. He indicated that there were many small businesses in Azerbaijan. However, he was unable to identify a manufactured product from Azerbaijan in the global market —an indication of little 'import' or 'export' of social and informational capital, that is, little 'openness'. Mohammed Nouriev, Dean at Khazar University, admitted that no one wants to pay taxes and thus reveal their figures to customs, thus there is little incentive to manufacture and export. When Chancellor Isaxali was asked if he felt any of the students were at Khazar University to develop creative and entrepreneurial skills to start a company his response was, 'No'. On the surface it appeared that the students were not prepared to change either belief systems or social agreements.

Izzet Rustamov, Deputy Prime Minister as well as Chancellor of Baku

State University, felt that the major restriction to development in the country was the lack of financial capital for domestic innovation. He acknowledged that the country must look at how best to use local resources, that is, address the physical environments and resources of the HEE approach. He further noted that reforms are being carried out very slowly because of the prolonged war with Armenia and the refugee problem (one million refugees out of a population of seven and one-half million). He felt Azerbaijan has gone through significant ideological changes over the past several years. Now the country has been going through privatization, which has presented its own set of problems directly related to adjustments in belief systems and social agreements. According to an Azerbaijani newspaper:

> The state of affairs in the business and investment sectors is complex. As high level corruption damages the formation of a competitive market foreign investors, except for speculators, avoid investments in Azerbaijan.[2]

Shamseddin Hojiyev, Department Head of International Economic Relations at the Azerbaijan Economic Institute suggested that the lack of adequate laws make social and informational capital formation very difficult.

A sign of progress to improve transaction capital is that policymakers are increasingly being asked to answer questions on TV. The internet is also beginning to surface as an important medium for political communication. The use of both mediums is a positive development toward networking and innovation.

Comments from business and economics students at the universities previously mentioned include:

> Local businessmen do not invest in the country because of the lack of laws and human rights; I would not invest in our country; There is no political stability; The country is too corrupt for manufacturing enterprises; Azerbaijan is a dictatorship and if you say what you think you are in trouble; We do not have adequate technology and managers.

Bahram Khalilov, Head of Azerbaijan's Civil Service Commission, recently stated, 'Further improvement is needed to enhance relationships between civil servants and the public' (UNESCO, 2007). Ilham Saban, Director of the Center of Oil Research, in a 2008 interview with Baku-based news portal Day.az, stated, 'Azerbaijanis show themselves as individuals who are not inclined to collective business management'.

Although there are several reforms that would improve transaction capital within the country, there are also difficult hurdles and serious challenges, to wit: government must partner and not hinder business enterprises. Laws need to be transparent. Entrepreneurship has to be encouraged. Youth must be motivated to succeed. Domestic credit needs to be made readily available. Corruption has to be addressed and the tax system overhauled to allow manufacturing the ability to function in a just environment. Such actions would significantly enhance the transaction capital required for sustainable development within the country.

IV.   RECENT US MONEY-MERCANTILISM

While Eastern Europe and other regions in the new global economy have had difficulty sustaining capital in recent decades, the US has been the major capital importer. For the purposes of this book, the unique role of the US in the core of the global financial system should be discussed.

Supplying a growing international economy with secure currency, so that money-liquidity crises, capital flight, destabilizing currency devaluations, and so on. are avoided, has long been an important concern of political economists. From World War II to the late 1960s, under the Bretton Woods system, the US dollar and gold served as the main international means of payment and source of value for the rapid expansion of international commerce. One problem with this dollar-based international monetary system, as forcefully put forward by Robert Triffin in his book *Gold and the Dollar Crisis: The Future of Convertibility* (1961), was that the US balance of payments deficits, which supplied the needed money to the international economy, would eventually undermine confidence in the value of the dollar and therefore the system itself. However, if the US eliminated its overall financial deficits with the rest of the world and restored world confidence in the dollar, there would not be sufficient gold or other money-liquidity to finance the growing world economy. This dilemma came to be called 'the Triffin dilemma', and it eventually led to the late 1960s break-up of the Bretton Woods system based on gold and the dollar. Attempts were made for several years to re-establish a fixed dollar–gold link and create other supportive international currencies such as the IMF's Special Drawing Rights, but these attempts failed.

Also contributing to the break-up of the Bretton Woods system were arguments by President de Gaulle of France and others that the dollar-based system gave the US an unfair advantage by allowing the US to freely finance itself around the world and then settle its obligations in dollars without limit. To this day the US remains the only large economy that has a majority of its foreign obligations denominated in its own currency.

More recently along these lines, given the weak emergence of regionalism as a counterweight to dollar-based globalization processes (Narine, 2002, and Phillips, 2000), various authors have concluded that capital outflows, devaluations, and use of soft currencies in the 'periphery' of the global economy have pushed the periphery into relative poverty and pushed the dollar-haven core of the global economy into relative wealth. The periphery has included Latin America and Africa since the early 1980s, but in the 1990s the capital-losing periphery widened. The Japanese yen gave way to the dollar, not in terms of the unit-to-unit currency exchange rate, but in terms of the share of the world's wealth that is denominated in yen, which has probably dropped 50 percent since Japan's financial asset market peak in 1989. Also, as documented in Chapter 3 in the 1997– Asian crisis, dollar havens gained monetary wealth from Asian 'dollar colonies' when the Asian crisis hit. The net flow of investment into the US from the rest of the world was $194.6 billion in 1996, $254.9 billion in 1997, and more than $250 billion in 1998.

Millions of private international financial market participants, along with the official international financial institutions (IFIs), have favored 'dollarization' of the international system along with an expanded role for the IMF and its affiliates as 'lender of last resort'. In April 1997, shortly before the Asian crisis, US Treasury Department Secretary Robert Rubin headed a meeting by the finance ministers of the G7 largest industrial countries which issued a statement 'promoting freedom of capital flows' and the deregulation and opening of the financial markets of newly industrializing countries in Asia and elsewhere. Efforts were simultaneously made to amend the charter of the IMF so that it could also promote 'capital account liberalization' of its member countries. However, during negotiations to resolve the crisis, financial liberalization in Asia and elsewhere was increasingly seen as a win–lose game favoring the interests of US financial firms and their multinational affiliates in foreign markets (Wade, 1998–99). For example, the $57 billion restructuring bailout of South Korea in late 1997 did not require US banks with the bad loans to put up significant new money or write off bad debts, but Citibank, J.P. Morgan, Chase Manhattan, BankAmerica, Bankers Trust, and others were allowed 2–3 percentage point higher interest rates and government guarantees that passed the ongoing risk of default from their shareholders to Korean taxpayers. The main 'burden' accepted by the US banks was an extension of these risky loans for up to three years. As stated by Milton Friedman:

> The effort is hurting the countries they are lending to, and benefiting the foreigners who lent to them . . . The United States does give foreign aid, but this is a different kind of foreign aid. It only goes through countries like Thailand to Bankers Trust.[3]

In earlier editions of this book, the author named these processes 'US money-mercantilism'.

Based on wealth creation and transfer processes, the author's research confirms that the US and the 'hard-currency core' of the current global economy can indeed benefit from what he would continue to call 'money-mercantilism' at the expense of the 'soft-currency periphery'. Because of the way that the international monetary system works with the US dollar as the dominant reserve currency, over time various monetary-wealth transfers from the periphery to the core have occurred without any other inherent instabilities in the real economy. 'Dollarization' of the periphery might increase the wealth of the periphery without necessarily affecting the core (a financial liberalization–globalization phase for the periphery), but then dollar-flight out of the periphery back to the core might appropriate new-found wealth from the periphery back to the core. The core might end up wealthier than before the dollarization phase, and the periphery might end up poorer. If world supplies of the dollar are excessively restricted by the Federal Reserve Bank and other financial institutions in the core, as in 1981–82, then both the periphery and the core might suffer a slump, but the core might still gain 'differential wealth' relative to the periphery.

Similarly, despite the fact that the recent financial crisis started in the dollar core of the global system, the dollar core still gained differential wealth relative to the non-dollar periphery of the global system.

Monetary-wealth transfers to the core need not translate proportionally into GDP inflation; they need not be inflationary at all. Whether inflation is affected depends on the production capacity that is currently available in the core, the capacity that can be added, the 'thickening' and 'commodification' of markets as new activity or non-market activity becomes part of the income–expenditure flow, the degree to which new-found monetary wealth is spent domestically, and so on.

These remarkably successful labors in the core by the Federal Reserve Bank, the 'Wall Street–US Treasury complex' (Bhagwati, 1998), and the millions of international financial market participants, as allowed by the dollar-based international monetary system, need not be conscious or conspiratorial, but they have favored US dollar havens. Because the dollar is a preferred 'store of value' and not neutral (which is a social agreement), dollar havens are wealth havens. Wealth havens are power havens where production power, consumption power, and social-process power are gained relative to non-havens.

Ronen Palan (1994, 2002), among other international political economists familiar with offshore finance, began grappling with this issue in the mid-1990s:

Indeed [after World War II] a hierarchy was produced as the new global currency [mainly the dollar] became the core currency of 'hard' to which all other currencies, 'soft' currencies were attached. The 'off-shore' financial markets may be understood as a reproduction of one of the central features of the post-war international financial system, namely, this hierarchy among currencies . . . The whole off-shore market then operates, whether intentionally or not, as a huge transmission mechanism, transferring the accumulated capital of the old periphery to the financial centers of the 'core'.

. . . about 30 percent of third world debt has found its way into tax havens. The figures rise sharply concerning Latin America. By 1981 five of the havens considered by the Caribbean Task Force report (Bahamas, Bermuda, Liberia, the Dutch Antilles and Panama) had approximately 14.3 percent of the total estimated investment stock which had flowed from OECD to all developing countries, although the economies of these five accounted for less than 0.3 percent of the total GNP of all developing countries . . . With current third world debt outstanding at US \$1.6 trillion, these figures imply a net [accumulated] inflow of US \$500 billion into the tax havens. Such figures quite simply dwarf anything traditional theories of third world's exploitation and unequal exchange have managed to come up with. This is arguably the saddest of all aspects of third world plight. (Palan, 1994)

Recent data estimates that developing countries suffered illicit financial outflows—defined as money that is illegally earned, transferred, or used— of at least \$5.9 trillion over the past ten years.[4]

Where do tax havens invest and transfer this wealth? Swiss banks, the earliest modern tax havens, 'rarely squander it [money accumulated from the periphery] or speculate with it. They invest it prudently and cautiously in the rich Atlantic world'—the big three Swiss banks actually made a policy decision in 1957 to invest only in the 'first world' (Fehrenbach, 1966, p. 126). As shown in Table 1.1, as backed up by Brown (1996), flows into tax havens and other offshore markets have as their major counterpart interbank lending into the US.

Historically, 'mercantilism' is the use of restrictive trade policies and colonial empires, especially by the European *ancien régime* of the seventeenth and eighteenth centuries, in order to accumulate precious metals centrally. Various nineteenth-century German historians, especially Georg Friedrich List, gave coherence to mercantilist notions of how wealth is accumulated, and they critiqued the laissez-faire economics of Smith, Ricardo, and Say. The institutional advantage used by powerful and hegemonic European states to appropriate unequal win–win or even win–lose gains from international commerce was recognized by the German Historical School as an important determinant of 'the wealth of nations'—perhaps a more important determinant than the decentralized 'invisible hand' interactions and efficiencies of supply and demand. More recent defenders of the mercantilist perspective include the Caribbean School and the World-System School (Hopkins and Wallerstein, 1982).

What the author would add to the historical mercantilist perspective, in order to make it 'money-mercantilism', is the notion that extraction of money wealth from the periphery, through institutional advantage, does not require GDP trade flows—instead, it only requires dominance in financial affairs. In the *ancien régime* period, there was an international financial system, but it was associated more with national debts rather than with commercial finance. Hence, it was easier for France and England and others to extract money-species from the colonies through favorable trade and exports of goods and services rather than more directly through commercial finance. However, in the current period, well-developed international commercial financial markets allow various trade channels to be bypassed.

The current 'mercantilists', who are typically financial intermediaries, are less government-affiliated, and thus mercantilism is not so intentionally associated with nationalism, but the wealth-enhancing effects obtained for the home country or its currency bloc are mostly the same as with the old mercantilism. The official government 'players' in this process might act as direct or indirect agents or partners for the private financial intermediaries and thus maintain much of the nationalism or core-regionalism that is historically associated with mercantilism. For example, case studies of 'The World Debt Crisis, 1982–' and 'The Mexican Crisis, 1994–95' in Chapters 2 and 3 elaborate the degree to which official US institutions were able to protect the solvency, profits, and capital inflows to private US financial intermediaries. The 1985 US 'Baker Plan' and IMF 'austerity requirements' generated new revenues (often from Latin American populations) and loans to service existing less developed country (LDC) debt so that US banks could continue to receive normal payments and not have to classify a majority of their LDC debt as bad debt.

In recent decades, over 50 percent of all international notes and bonds have been denominated in dollars, and 45 percent of all cross-border bank loans have been in dollars. Economists such as Richard Portes and Helene Rey estimate that this dominance in debt markets has given dollar-issuers such as the US government a 'liquidity discount' or reduced transaction costs of 25 to 50 basis points (hundredths of a percentage point). Non-US holdings of US government debt have averaged approximately $4 trillion recently, which means that the US government has saved $10–$20 billion per year in interest expense on its debt due to the liquidity discount. *The Economist* has estimated that an additional $5-$10 billion per year may be 'earned' from other countries by the US due to seigniorage, which is the profit earned by the monopoly issue of coins and notes.[5] That is, other countries give up real goods and services to holders (and therefore issuers) of dollars in order to obtain dollars for their reserve accounts.

In the author's view, these widely acknowledged money-mercantilist 'profits' are only part of the money-mercantilist benefits that currently accrue to the US. The $200–$250 billion annual net investment inflow into the US in the late 1990s, which rose to $800 billion in 2006 at the peak of 'the long boom', mostly channeled through private markets, is of course approximately matched in the balance of payments accounts by a similarly large US current account deficit in goods and services. However, a majority of the US current account deficit as early as the 1980s was intra-firm or reflects critical component and sub-assembly transfers between global affiliates, and thus the majority of this current account deficit should not be seen as a net profit or wealth loss to the 'real' sector of the US economy—unlike the *ancien régime* period when trade deficits between more separate national economies could more clearly be identified with non-competitiveness and wealth outflows.

In the current period, virtually all of the capital-usage and monetary-wealth enhancement benefit of the now, as of 2016, $400–$500 billion/ year annual net investment inflow supports the US economy; yet some of the monetary outflow due to the current account deficit (an outflow which is often less than the size of the deficit) enhances US multinationals, or at least remains denominated in dollars and builds up the US dollar core of the global economy. As elaborated in Chapter 2, US current account deficits are increasingly not bad for US economic interests, and might even be good due to overseas production, international joint ventures, and international ownership arrangements—it depends on how firms have 'gone global'.

US money-mercantilism is achieved via favorable terms (as per the liquidity premium and seigniorage) on more initiating capital account surpluses, which are recycled through more accommodating current account deficits. On both accounts, but especially on the dollar-rigged financial side, US multinationals and their dollar-based affiliates benefit. In contrast, *ancien régime* mercantilism was achieved through institutionally and militarily rigged current account surpluses that were then used to expand the political-economic power of the regime.

Whichever type of mercantilism is identified, the essential element is the disproportionate accumulation of monetary wealth which is obtained by the institutionally more powerful country or region through international commerce. How does this monetary-wealth accumulation from international commerce enhance the domestic economy of the mercantilist country? Daudin (2008) answers this question for the *ancien régime* of eighteenth-century France. Not only did France use political and military power to exploit wealth from the colonies, but the inflow of precious metals (monetary wealth) actually allowed France a more-than-proportionate increase in domestic economic growth and wealth. Under this mercantilist revision of mainstream economic thinking, France was well justified in sacrificing various free-trade efficiencies in order to centrally accumulate precious metals that could serve as hard currency. The accumulation of gold and silver as reserve currency allowed a non-neutral (wealth-favorable) expansion of quasi-moneys and credit which in turn intensified and coordinated economic activity and further enhanced French economic growth and power relative to the (capital-exporting) rest of the world. During the eighteenth century, there was no real banking system in France, and most money creation was done by commercial agents who issued bills of exchange and promissory notes based upon reputation. The estimated 0.8 percent growth per year in circulating metallic money during 1715–88 made it possible for commercial operators to reliably circulate a much larger volume of commercial paper and exchangeable notes.

Daudin's mercantilist analysis is further supported by Clark (1998), who identifies in great detail how the industrial revolution in Britain was more of a monetary-capitalist-driven top-down 'industrious revolution' supported by the appropriation and use of foreign wealth rather than a bottom-up industrial revolution initially driven by new technologies and greater productivity of the average worker. Enhanced transactions systems brought, especially, under-utilized rural labor into the formal economy in Britain as well as France.

In both the mercantilist *ancien régime* and in present-day mercantilist US, economic growth might thus be largely driven by a 'thickening' and 'commodification' of domestic markets as social agreements and institutions allow foreign and newly created domestic monetary wealth to be spent domestically. Following this pattern, in recent decades the US economy boomed ahead with an unexpectedly great labor-force participation rate (from 60 percent of the population aged 16 and over in 1970 to 66 percent and the longest workweek among industrial countries at the peak of the boom in 2006) despite a much less significant increase in the inherent physical GDP-productivity of the average worker (which has fluctuated around a 3 percent growth rate per year for several decades).

Thus, reflecting these financial processes, recent research, including from the World Institute for Development Economics Research of the United Nations University indicates that a 'widening gap between the global haves and the have-nots in large measure reflects the failure of less-developed countries to develop, while rich countries—particularly the United States—have experienced fast economic growth and a spectacular buildup of assets':

In 2000 the United States accounted for 4.7 percent of the world's population but 32.6 percent of the world's wealth. Nearly 4 out of every 10 people in the wealthiest 1 percent of the global population were American. The average American had a net worth of nearly $144,000, losing only to the average Japanese, who had $180,000, at market exchange rates; the average person in Luxembourg, who had $183,000; and the average Swiss, who had $171,000. By contrast, in 2000 the average Chinese had a net worth of roughly $2,600, at the official exchange rate. China, home to more than a fifth of the world's population, had only 2.6 percent of the world's wealth. And India, with 16.8 percent of the world's people, accounted for only 0.9 percent of the world's wealth.[6]

V.   FINANCIAL GLOBALIZATION AND CAPITAL ACCUMULATION

Given the increased importance, across a larger and more dynamic global political economy, of subjective expectations, leveraged investment as supported by new electronic and derivative money and credit forms, unregulated no-reserve-requirement offshore financial markets, and so on, some current research is consistent with the innovative notion that monetary wealth, or what Marx called 'unproductive finance capital' (as opposed to physical capital or capital goods such as machines and factories), may be a 'driver' of economic instabilities. As elaborated by Philip Cerny, among others, the new global financial markets may even be an 'infrastructure of the infrastructure'. Cerny's initial position, elaborated in debates that began in the early 1990s, was that 'a country without efficient and profitable financial markets and institutions will suffer multiple *dis*advantages in a more open world . . . [and will] attempt to *free-ride* on financial globalization through increasing market liberalization' (Cerny, 1993, p. 338). Helleiner (1995) restrained this position—of a determinist, autonomous, technology-driven financial globalization—by demonstrating that states, especially the US and the UK, have fostered and guided the entire process.

Reversing the causality of Karl Marx's (and many others') philosophical materialism, it may increasingly be true that autonomous, invisible financial processes can drive changes in the physical relations of production, as well as vice versa. As part of this process, central banks and other financial market participants can (usually haphazardly) increase or reduce wealth independently of any initial changes in the production of GDP or other 'real' economic prospects. The Chairman of the US Federal Reserve Alan Greenspan began allowing for this possibility in the late 1990s:

Today's central banks have the capability of creating or destroying unlimited supplies of money and credit . . . It is probably fair to say that the very efficiency of global financial markets, engendered by the rapid proliferation of financial

> products, also has the capability of transmitting mistakes at a far faster pace throughout the financial system in ways that were unknown a generation ago, and not even remotely imagined in the 19th century . . . Clearly, not only has the productivity of global finance increased markedly, but so, obviously, has the ability to generate losses at a previously inconceivable rate. (Greenspan, 1998)

The author would emphasize from Greenspan's quote that 'the capability of creating or destroying unlimited supplies of money and credit' is equivalent to 'the capability of creating or destroying monetary wealth'. Money and credit are 'stores of value', as determined by social consensus within nations and between nations.

These more philosophically 'transcendental' notions of value applied to financial processes need not reflect, or even be compatible with, the observed empirical world. For example, the 'law of compound interest' is a social agreement, which may not correlate with the way that the physical economy grows. Growth in the physical economy is subject to thermodynamics, biological growth processes and carrying capacity, endowments of resources, sunlight and rain, and so on. Perhaps debtors as a group, who are required to pay *exponentially* increasing interest under this transcendental law, can generate goods and services and therefore economic revenues only in *arithmetically* increasing increments beyond some threshold of time. Therefore, perhaps some debtors have to fail, and yield their economic resources to the others, so that the others can meet their obligations.

Invisible belief systems, including those of money-gamblers and optimistic market capitalists, have supported a money economy based on exponential interest payments, and an easing of lending restrictions. The acceptance and growth of offshore finance in the 1980s–90s, without reserve requirements or other significant regulations, is an example of how belief systems—in this case market capitalist ideology—drive institutional change. Offshore market institutions, such as the Bangkok International Banking Facility, encouraged unsustainable over-lending and excessive unprofitable construction of real estate and ultimately contributed to the risk of crisis, recession, and misery in the Asian financial crisis of 1997.

And, this wealth—literally created or destroyed out of thin air (or cyberspace) in some cases—is generally allocated through the arbitrary customs and interest rates concessions of particular social networks. Wealth itself in the global human ecology, in these cases, can thus be derived entirely from 'pure social agreement' depending on how well one can participate in the financial system.

A review of the author's controversial position as italicized here, especially critiquing it from the Marxist and other philosophical-materialist frameworks, appeared in *Review of International Political Economy* (Carchedi, 1996). To the reviewer, the author's approach incorrectly 'privileges financial changes *vis-à-vis* changes in the real economy (production of value)' (p. 532). Furthermore, to the reviewer, any perceived initial creation and distribution of wealth or 'value' that happens in 'the thin air' of financial markets could not be sustained over time without correspondence to supportive GDP activity.

In contrast, to the author, 'money is wealth' in the sense that it gives the holder a claim on the entire social product. The 'social product' includes not only consumption power and production power, but also the power to direct and control large social processes—such as those which are dependent on (gaining access to) the institutions of government, courts, communications, and so on. The accumulation of monetary assets, or what Marxists would call the accumulation of finance capital, represents a social power claim that becomes a key driver in the evolution of the world system. Once monetary wealth is understood as power claims over the social product, then monetary wealth is 'real', and it is limited only by the degree to which power can be exerted over others. Presumably this limit would only be found in the extremely unlikely event that an all-encompassing global monopoly—or the world's super-rich individuals and corporations—have maximized their differential power.

Belief systems and their supporting institutions can thus drive empirical changes in human populations and their physical environments. In the author's view, much of the increase in US net household wealth in the recent boom from $10 trillion in 1980 to $67 trillion in 2007, to $88 trillion in 2016 after recovering from the Great Recession of 2007–09 (even though the recession started in the US), was facilitated through expansion of the global money and credit pyramid, including massive inflows of the 'global savings glut' into the US. The myriad social agreements that facilitated the long boom from 1980 to 2006 were then recast in the 2007–09 crisis by 'waves of pessimistic sentiment where no solid basis exists for a reasonable calculation' (Keynes, 1936). In 2009, declines in average housing prices of approximately 35 percent since their peak and declines in stock prices of approximately 50 percent reduced net value of US wealth down to approximately $55 trillion. But then, full recovery of expectations and money-liquidity measures, in the context of 'US money-mercantilism' have pushed net US household wealth up to this $88 trillion figure in 2016, which is approximately one-third of the world's total net wealth.

Recent data shows that average annual real returns on US and European equities were both approximately 8 percent from 1985 to 2014, despite the 2007– crisis, whereas from 1965 to 2014 those same real returns were both approximately 6 percent.[7] These figures indicate a significant increase in returns to holders of equities in the long boom, relative to the underlying growth in real GDP and income levels in the US and Europe—a differential that was supported by expanded money-liquidity and financial globalization.

The author's econometric work summarized in Chapter 2 supports this new thinking related to the importance of psychological and social/institutional factors—essentially by showing that, under certain conditions, financial markets can both create and 'absorb' a portion of the money supply, such that the absorbed money 'takes on a life of its own' and is not contemporaneously available to support and induce the 'real economy'. While economic literature has examined various demands for money for financial market participation, the author's contribution to that literature was the first to show that the absorbed money was not simultaneously available even to induce or incentivize GDP activity. As discussed earlier, this absorption shows up as a decline in the GDP-velocity of narrow money (v), *ceteris paribus*, and it can also be measured by a divergence in the growth of broad money supply aggregates (such as (m3)) relative to narrow money supply (such as (m1)), *ceteris paribus*. This absorbed money-power might be used at a later date to re-engage GDP production or consumption, or it might be destroyed in a financial crisis before its title-holders can use it. Therefore, money is not a neutral driver of the real economy over time. Furthermore, this absorption process can occur to facilitate the boom phase of a financial crisis cycle, and it can also facilitate the bust phase—by driving asset prices beyond normal or sustainable levels.

Returning to the role of capital in this process, some recent research in the field of international political economy also finds it useful to define 'capital' as an accumulation of more intangible intra-society capabilities and powers—as per the HEE approach—rather than as the 'industrial apparatus' per se:

> Drawing on the institutional frameworks of Veblen and Mumford, our principal contribution is to *integrate power into the definition of capital*. Briefly, the value of capital represents discounted expected earnings. Some of these earnings could be associated with the productivity (or exploitation) of the owned industrial apparatus, but this is only part of the story. As capitalism grows in complexity, the earnings of any given business concern come to depend less on its own industrial undertakings and more on the *community's overall productivity*. In this sense, the value of capital represents a *distributional* claim. This claim is manifested partly through ownership, but more broadly through the *whole spectrum of social power*. Moreover, power is not only a means of accumulation, but also its most fundamental end. For the absentee owner, the purpose is not to 'maximize' profits but to 'beat the average'. The ultimate goal of business is not hedonic pleasure, but *differential* gain. In our view, this differential aspect of accumulation offers a promising avenue for putting power into the definition of capital . . . In the eyes of a modern investor, capital means a *capitalized*

earning capacity. It consists not of the owned factories, mines, aeroplanes or retail establishments, but of the present value of profits expected to be earned by force of such ownership. (Nitzan, 1998, pp. 173, 182)

Building upon this quote, Nitzan argues that wealth accumulation processes allowed by monetary capital have favored pecuniary business activities and owners over tangible industrial productivity and working consumers. He argues that, increasingly, 'the causal link runs not from the creation of earnings to the right of ownership, but from the right of ownership to the appropriation of earnings' (p. 180). This causality is consistent with the writings of Thorstein Veblen, who insisted that the 'natural right of ownership' conferred by society to various people (initially to own slaves, then animals, land, and now capital including ever more symbolic monetary forms) can be used competitively to obtain further social powers at the expense of others (Veblen, 1923).

Defining 'capital' as 'financial capital', or 'net wealth' (assets minus liabilities) but excluding the hard-to-measure informational and social capital, Thomas Piketty finds that, indeed, owners of capital in the US and Europe and elsewhere are increasingly gaining relative to non-capital holders and relative to what might be expected from GDP and income trends. For example, he finds that the world capital (net wealth holdings) to annual income ratio has risen from 3 to 1 in 1970 to 4.5 to 1 today. Given that returns to capital (Piketty's 'r') are likely to remain higher than growth in wage and salary-driven income or output (Piketty's 'g'), he concludes that 'the global capital/income ratio will quite logically continue to rise and could approach 7 to 1 before the end of the twenty-first century' (Piketty, 2014, p. 195; see also: piketty.pse.ens.fr/capital21c). In the leading economies in Europe, North America, and Japan, capital/income ratios are currently higher than the world average and have grown somewhat faster since 1970, and for other continents and countries, including Asia (apart from Japan), Africa, and South America, although data is less reliable, the ratios and growth rates since the 1970s are lower than the world averages.

Piketty cites three sets of factors to explain these self-reinforcing differential gains to holders of capital in recent decades, relative to national income earners: (1) slower GDP and income growth 'g' including from slower demographic growth; (2) the transfer of public wealth into private hands in recent decades; and (3) the rise in real estate and stock market prices and returns in recent decades 'in a political context that was on the whole more favorable to private wealth than that of immediate postwar decades' (ibid., p. 173). These second and third factors are, of course, consonant with the 1970s– financial market globalization processes discussed in this book.

VI. CONCLUSIONS

Although beyond the scope of this book to elaborate further, the author's research, as outlined in Chapters 1–5, thus allows the following conclusions:

- Advances in information-processing technologies and related innovations since the early 1970s increased the profitability of financial market participation and arbitrage across the global system.
- Government deregulation of national financial markets to allow international competition and participation also encouraged the expansion and globalization of financial markets, especially during the 'explosive 1980s'. This government deregulation, based upon the 'free market belief system' and related ideologies and 'social agreements', was championed by President Ronald Reagan in the US in the early 1980s along with Prime Minister Margaret Thatcher in Britain among others.
- Since these structural changes in the 1980s, profit-seeking international financial flows are increasingly the autonomous, initiating, driving force, or 'infrastructure of the infrastructure', that determine the movements of currency exchange rates and thus the direction and magnitude of international trade in goods and non-financial services—rather than vice versa as was historically the case prior to the 1980s. The 'interest rate parity' and 'financial strategy parity' logic of profit-seeking international financial flows, as discussed in Chapter 1, thus explains why countries might sustain long-term imbalances in trade—unlike traditional thinking which relied on the now-obsolete theory that 'purchasing power parity' would restore balances in trade.
- The new global financial markets allowed a remarkable expansion of no-reserve banking and money and wealth creation through offshore markets, new financial products and other ways to securitize and market the ownership of tangible property, which supported the 'long boom' from the early 1980s through 2006, but unsustainably so, thus resulting in a dramatic contraction in this money and credit pyramid starting in 2007. The recent global crisis demonstrates many of the common 'boom–bust' patterns of previous large-scale crises, although this crisis played itself out in a more systematically linked global economy.
- The author's econometric research indicates that significant portions of new money creation through reserve banking, securitization of assets, and other processes, as well as use of the expanded 'float' of purchasing power that is based upon core monies, can be allocated

to people over time and space arbitrarily through 'pure social agreement' within the new financial infrastructure. Wealth and transaction capital can be created, reallocated, and destroyed without necessarily involving (in the first round of system-adjustment) the 'good old' political economy of tangible merchandise, stocks of production capital, non-financial services, GDP productivity of labor, and so on.

- These innovations and processes since the 1970s have helped coordinate and direct the global economy, and they have produced efficiencies and sustainable new wealth. They have also increased instabilities and the potential for loss, as per the financial crises and recessions discussed in this book.
- As a 'money-mercantilist' country, since the 1970s the US and others in the 'dollar core' of the global human ecology have increased their wealth at the expense of other countries in the soft-currency periphery. The US population has held approximately one-third of the world's wealth, that is, 'social power', and, despite the recent global crisis, the US continues to lead world economic evolution through its influence in international financial institutions and markets.
- The 1970s– expansion of global money-liquidity has increased the wealth of those who own financial capital faster than, and sometimes at the expense of, those who benefit from current GDP-derived income.
- Sustaining supplies of financial capital at appropriate levels across all regions of the global economy, in order to avoid periphery-to-core transfers of wealth and widening inequality as well as crises of capital flight, also requires sustaining complementary supplies of informational and social capital across all regions. These other forms of transaction capital, although hard to measure, are also central to sustainable growth and development.

What responses to these developments might improve the 'global sustainability' of the economic and financial system? The author has the following suggestions, based upon the material in this book:

- The basic 'unit of control' for financial policymaking needs to be the monetary good that the global markets, as influenced by official institutions, have chosen. In today's 'one-world financial markets', this currently means that the world, as a whole, needs to cooperatively focus on the quantities of dollar- and euro- and yen- and other-denominated financial instruments, in proportion to their share of various economies and financial markets. Thus, during the recent crisis, Federal Reserve Chairman Bernanke entered into currency swap arrangements with 14 other central banks in order to provide US dollars to international markets—an unprecedented official step (both procedurally and in quantities of international liquidity supplied) toward globalization of central banking money and debt management. Similarly, the Chinese yuan has recently been accepted as a currency in the weighted monetary basket of currencies used by the IMF.

- Central banks should revisit their guidelines for policy. First and foremost, the quantities that are tracked need to be expanded to include all 'monetary goods' and not just narrowly defined domestic money supplies. For example, the Fed should reinstate its measurement of m3 (supplies of cash plus a wider range of bank instruments). As in Japan in its crisis after 1989, the acceleration of the recent crisis in mid-2008 was associated with a collapse in broader money supplies in the US and Europe—in these cases an early indicator of crisis that was not fully considered.
- Governments need to be explicit in their desire to impose regulation on financial markets that recognizes the large degree of economic externalities (positive and negative) that issue from the activities of financial institutions. This regulation needs to insure transparency as well as an internationally agreed-upon system for bankruptcy of financial institutions.
- Regulation is also needed that insures transparency as well as an internationally agreed-upon system in situations when countries are unable to honor sovereign debt (as per Mexico 1994–95, Iceland 2008, and ongoing struggles within Europe). Whether the IMF and others move toward a formal bankruptcy procedure for countries or toward other Sovereign Debt Restructuring Mechanisms (SDRMs), it is clear that nations increasingly need to be coordinated like the 'states' in the US or the eurozone for financial emergency and lender-of-last-resort purposes.
- Along the continuing, irreversible path toward even further globalization of financial markets, encouragement and support needs to be given to the creation of more organized regional currency blocs. If done properly, destabilizing financial flows between currencies can be reduced, and the dominant US dollar core of the global system might gain less money-mercantilist benefits at the expense of other less organized currency areas—thus reducing the risk of financial crises and further inequalities of wealth across the global system. The eurozone case study shows us that 'broadening' a currency zone too fast without sufficient institutional or macroeconomic

convergence, that is, 'deepening' of the union, is also a mistake. Thus, more effective common banking unions and other lender-of-last-resort agreements are needed prior to broadening.

- Governments should foster the development of more stable forward-looking financial markets with larger secure reserve facilities, so that financial market participants of all types can better manage their levels of future risk against destabilizing changes in interest rates, exchange rates, financial crises and recession, and so on. Because of the 'non-identification of troubled assets' problem faced by central banks due to securitization and marketization of financial products, lender-of-last-resort intervention by central banks often needs to flood entire markets with liquidity. Unlike the days of J.P. Morgan, or even unlike the more recent days of the 1982– Latin America debt crisis, intervention targeted only toward 'high-profile' bad asset holders (even if they can be identified) is not likely to be as sufficient; thus, larger reserve facilities are necessary. An analogy here is the use of strong systemic antibiotics to fight infection in the human body versus smaller doses of localized antibiotics. From the example of Sweden 1991– and others discussed in this book, ways to quickly respond and contain bad debt without creating undue 'moral hazard' or longer-term dependence on the intervention need further study.

- Working cooperatively, central banks and governments should maintain better money-liquidity throughout the global system with continued research and better monetary policy responses. The econometric research of the author indicates that greater money supplies have been necessary to accommodate the growth of money-absorbing financial activity as well as non-financial activity. Based upon the quantity equation $(m \times v) = (p \times q)$, changes in the income velocity of money (v) need further study so that appropriate supplies of money (m) can be directed toward appropriate levels of both inflation as measured by changes in the economy-wide price index (p) and growth as measured by changes in real GDP (q). This research should include attention to (m1), (m2), and, as mentioned above, (m3) measures of the money supply. In this regard, there has been a revival of interest in theories of endogenous money creation, as by non-state-based as well as state-based financial institutions (SBFIs), that can be contrasted with the more dominant theories of exogenous money creation by the central banks and traditional SBFIs (Lavoie, 2003, and Kinsella, 2009).

- Regulatory systems should be expanded to include non-SBFIs as well as the SBFIs and be flexible enough to recognize the formation of new financial institutions. This means defining financial institutions by function and not by narrow corporate form or balance sheet structure. For example, in the recent crises, the Federal Reserve purchased more than $1 trillion in mortgage-backed bonds to add liquidity and monetary oversight to the housing market, and the Fed created a 'Term Asset-Backed Securities Loan Facility' (TALF) to supply approximately $200 billion to the student, auto, credit card, and small business loan markets. Also, US reclassification of investment banks such as Goldman Sachs and Morgan Stanley as bank holding companies in the recent crisis brought them into the 'public utility' supervision of the Federal Reserve to a much greater degree.

- Finally, new thinking about the dynamics of the global financial system should be encouraged, including greater attention to evolutionary and complex system approaches, and greater attention to psychological and social factors. In this regard, 'human ecology economics (HEE)', as recently developed by the author, as a new heterodox approach to doing economics, expands upon evolutionary and complex systems approaches and includes a formal role for psychological and social system drivers. In the author's view, HEE is a superior framework for the political economy of financial crisis and central banking, because unlike traditional economics and most other social sciences, HEE (1) allows a long run time perspective consistent with evolutionary approaches; (2) encourages use of the humanities including a formal role for belief systems and 'ways of being' within the economic system; (3) allows everything to vary within the economic system—including belief systems, ways of being, and social agreements—in complex, co-evolutionary ways; (4) emphasizes global systems; and (5) effectively juxtaposes 'sustainability' and other interdisciplinary issues alongside traditional economic issues. Each of (1)–(5) is needed, in the view of the author, to best sort out and apprehend the 'creative chaos' of financial crisis, institutional change, and related instabilities in financial markets over recent decades.

Recent global financial crises have led to more direct market participation and oversight by governments and official institutions. Armed with larger currency reserve facilities, and exercising their roles as more active stakeholders in the financial system, central banks, governments, and other official institutions should be in a better position to achieve the goals listed above. However, as Minsky states at the end of his classic work on this topic:

The analysis argues for a system of changes, not for isolated changes. There is no simple answer to the problems of our capitalism . . . After an initial interval, the basic disequilibrating tendencies of capitalist finance will once again push the financial structure to the brink of fragility. When that occurs, a new era of reform will be needed. There is no possibility that we can ever set things right once and for all; instability, put to rest by one set of reforms will, after time, emerge in a new guise. (Minsky, 2008, p. 370)

NOTES

1. For the content of this section, the author is heavily indebted to his recent co-authors Norman Bedford and Andras Margitay-Becht (Allen et al., 2011).
2. 'The USA Threatened the Aliyevs With "Riches"', *Azadliq*, 22–23 June 2008.
3. 'Global Contagion, a Narrative', *The New York Times*, 15–18 February 1999, p. 1.
4. 'Storm Survivors', *The Economist*, 16 February 2013, http://www.economist.com/news/special-report/21571549-offshore-financial-centres-have-taken-battering-recently-they-have-shown-remarkable.
5. 'The International Euro', *The Economist*, 14 November 1998, p. 89.
6. *The New York Times* (2006), December 6, Section C, p. 3, C1.
7. 'The Great Switchover', *The Economist*, 30 April 2016, p. 66.

References

Allen, Mark, Christopher Rosenberg, Christian Keller, Brad Setser and Nouriel Roubini (2002), 'A Balance Sheet Approach to Financial Crisis', IMF Working Paper 02/210.

Allen, Roy E. (1989), 'Globalisation of the US Financial Markets: The New Structure for Monetary Policy', *International Economics and Financial Markets*, 266–86, Oxford: Oxford University Press.

Allen, Roy E. (1991), 'The New East–West Economics', *Coexistence: A Review of East–West and Development Issues*, **28**, 473–94.

Allen, Roy E. (ed.) (2004), *The Political Economy of Financial Crisis*, Cheltenham, UK and Northampton, MA, USA: Edward Elgar Publishing.

Allen, Roy E. (ed.) (2008), *Human Ecology Economics: A New Framework for Global Sustainability*, Oxon, UK and New York: Routledge.

Allen, R.E., N. Bedford and A. Margitay-Becht (2011), 'A "Human Ecology Economics" Framework for Eastern Europe', *International Journal of Social Economics*, **38** (3), 192–208.

Allen, Roy E. and Donald Snyder (2009), 'New Thinking on the Financial Crisis', *Critical Perspectives on International Business*, **5** (1/2), 36–55.

Artis, M. and M. Taylor (1989), 'International Financial Stability and the Regulation of Capital Flows', Conference Paper (University of Surrey), September.

Bank for International Settlements (1995), *Central Bank Survey of Derivatives Market Activity*, Basel, 18 December.

Bank for International Settlements (2010), *80th Annual Report*, Basel, June.

Bastasin, Carlo (2012), *Saving Europe: Anatomy of a Dream*, Washington, DC: The Brookings Institution.

Batten, Dallas S. and Daniel L. Thornton (1985), 'Are Weighted Monetary Aggregates Better than Simple-Sum m1?', Federal Reserve Bank of St. Louis *Review*, June/July, 29–40.

Bedford, Norman and Jack Leimann (2008), 'Estonia's Challenge: Add Value to the Country's Resources', paper delivered at the 2008 Association for Global Business Annual Conference, Washington, DC.

Bergsten, C. Fred (ed.) (1991), *International Adjustment and Financing:*

The Lessons of 1985–1991, Washington, DC: Institute for International Economics.

Bernanke, Ben S. (2005), 'The Global Savings Glut and the U.S. Current Account Deficit', remarks at the Sandridge Lecture, Virginia Association of Economists, Richmond, Virginia, 10 March.

Bernanke, Ben S. (2007), 'The Financial Accelerator and the Credit Channel', speech at the Credit Channel of Monetary Policy in the Twenty-first Century Conference, Federal Reserve Bank of Atlanta, Atlanta, Georgia.

Bhagwati, Jagdish N. (1998), 'The Capital Myth: The Difference between Trade in Widgets and Dollars', *Foreign Affairs*, **77** (3), May/June, 7–12.

Blanchard, Olivier (1993), 'Consumption and the Recession of 1990–1991', *American Economic Review*, **83** (2), 270–74.

Bogdanowicz-Bindert, Christine (1985–86), 'World Debt, the US Reconsiders', *Foreign Affairs*, Winter.

Bourdieu, Pierre (1984), *Distinction: A Social Critique of the Judgment of Taste* (in French, *La Distinction*), Cambridge, MA: Harvard University Press.

Brown, Brendan (1996), *Economists and the Financial Markets*, London and New York: Routledge.

Carchedi, G. (1996), 'Review Essay: Financial Crisis, Recessions and Value Theory', *Review of International Political Economy*, **3** (3), Autumn, 528–37.

Cerny, Philip G. (ed.) (1993), *Finance and World Politics: Markets, Regimes and States in the Post-Hegemonic Era*, Aldershot, UK and Brookfield, VT, USA: Edward Elgar Publishing.

Clark, Gregory (1998), 'Too Much Revolution: Agriculture and the Industrial Revolution, 1700–1860', paper presented at the 38th Annual Cliometrics Conference, Washington University in St. Louis, 8–10 May.

Clarke, Simon (1994), *Marx's Theory of Crisis*, New York: St. Martin's Press.

Cooper, Richard E. (1965), 'The Interest Equalization Tax: An Experiment in the Separation of Capital Markets', *Finanzarchiv*, **24**, Fasc. 3, 447–71.

Csanádi, Mária (2009), 'The "Chinese Style Reforms" and the Hungarian "Goulash Communism"', Discussion Paper, Institute of Economics, Hungarian Academy of Sciences, Budapest.

Daudin, Guillaume (2008), 'Money and Capital in the Human Ecology: Rethinking Mercantilism and 18th Century France', in Roy E. Allen (ed.), *Human Ecology Economics: A New Framework for Global Sustainability*, Oxon, UK and New York: Routledge, pp. 163–86.

De Bonis, Ricardo, Alessandro Giustiniani and Giorgio Gomel (1999),

'Crises and Bail-Outs of Banks and Countries: Linkages, Analogies, and Differences', *World Economy*, **22** (1), 55–86.

Dopfer, K., J. Foster and J. Potts (2004), 'Micro, Meso, Macro', *Journal of Evolutionary Economics*, **14**, 263–79.

Dotsey, Michael (1985), 'The Use of Electronic Funds Transfers to Capture the Effect of Cash Management Practices on the Demand for Demand Deposits', *Journal of Finance*, **40** (5), December, 1493–1503.

Drucker, Peter F. (1985–86), 'The Changed World Economy', *Foreign Affairs*, Winter.

Englund, Peter (1999), 'The Swedish Banking Crisis: Roots and Consequences', *Oxford Review of Economic Policy*, **15** (3), 80–97.

Fortier, Diana L. and David Phillis (1985), 'Bank and Thrift Performance since DIDMCA', *Economic Perspectives*, **9** (5), 58–68.

Federal Reserve Bank of Kansas City (1997), *Maintaining Financial Stability in a Global Economy: A Symposium Sponsored by the Federal Reserve Bank of Kansas City*, Jackson Hole, Wyoming, 28–30 August.

Federal Reserve Bank of New York (1995), *April 1995 Central Bank Survey of Foreign Exchange Market Activity*, 19 September.

Federal Reserve Bank of St. Louis (1998), *International Economic Trends*, August.

Fehrenbach, R.R. (1966), *The Gnomes of Zurich*, London: Leslie Frewin.

Feldstein, Martin (ed.) (1991), *The Risk of Economic Crisis*, Chicago: University of Chicago Press.

Fisher, Irving (1933), 'The Debt-Deflation Theory of Great Depressions', *Econometrica*, **I**, 337–57.

Foster, John (2005), 'From Simplistic to Complex Systems in Economics', *Cambridge Journal of Economics*, **29**, 873–92.

Foster, J. and P. Wild (1999a), 'Detecting Self-Organizational Change in Economic Processes Exhibiting Logistic Growth', *Journal of Evolutionary Economics*, **9**, 109–33.

Foster, J. and P. Wild (1999b), 'Econometric Modeling in the Presence of Evolutionary Change', *Cambridge Journal of Economics*, **23**, 749–70.

Frankel, J. (1989), 'Quantifying International Capital Mobility in the 1980s', National Bureau of Economic Research, Working Paper No. 2856, February.

Frankel, J. and K.A. Froot (1989), 'Forward Discount Bias: Is It an Exchange Risk Premium?', *Quarterly Journal of Economics*, **104** (1), February, 139–61.

Friedman, Benjamin M. and Kenneth N. Kuttner (1992), 'Money, Income, Prices, and Interest Rates', *American Economic Review*, **82** (3), 472–92.

Friedman, Milton (1970), 'A Theoretical Framework for Monetary Analysis', *Journal of Political Economy*, **78**, March/April, 193–238.

Friedman, Milton (1988), 'Money and the Stock Market', *Journal of Political Economy*, **96**, April, 221–45.

Gates, Bill, with Nathan Myhrvold and Peter Rinearson (1995), *The Road Ahead*, New York: Viking Press.

Germain, Randall G. (2002), 'Feature Review', *New Political Economy*, **7** (2), 299–307.

Goldfeld, Steven M. (1973), 'The Demand for Money Revisited', *Brookings Papers on Economic Activity*, no. 3, 577–646.

Goldfeld, Steven M. (1976), 'The Case of the Missing Money', *Brookings Papers on Economic Activity*, no. 3, 683–739.

Gordon, Robert J. (1984), *Macroeconomics*, 3rd edn, Glenview, IL: Little, Brown and Co.

Greenspan, Alan (1998), 'The Globalization of Finance', *Cato Journal*, **17** (3), Winter, 243–250.

Grundfest, Joseph A. (1991), 'When Markets Crash: The Consequences of Information Failure in the Market for Liquidity', in Martin Feldstein (ed.), *The Risk of Economic Crisis*, Chicago: University of Chicago Press, pp. 62–78.

Haggard, Stephen and Sylvia Maxfield (1996), 'The Political Economy of Financial Internationalization in the Developing World', *International Organization*, **50**, 35–68.

Hall, Robert E. (1993), 'Macro Theory and the Recession of 1990–1991', *American Economic Review*, **83** (2), 275–79.

Hanifan, Lyda Judson (1916), 'The Rural School Community Center', *Annals of the American Academy of Political and Social Science*, **67**, 130–38.

Hawkes, David (1996), *Ideology*, London and New York: Routledge.

Helleiner, Eric (1995), 'Explaining the Globalization of Financial Markets: Bringing States Back In', *Review of International Political Economy*, **2** (2), 315–41.

HG Asia (1996), 'Philippine Figures Hide a Thing or Two', Communiqué, Philippines, Hong Kong.

Hopkins, Terry and Immanuel Wallerstein (eds) (1982), *World-Systems Analysis: Theory and Methodology*, Beverly Hills, CA: Sage.

International Finance Corporation (2008), *Doing Business 2009*, September.

International Management Fund (2002), *IMF Board Holds Informal Seminar on Sovereign Debt Restructuring*, International Monetary Fund, Public Information Notice 02/38, Washington, DC.

Jennergren, P. and B. Näslund (1997), 'Bankkriser och deras hantering' [Handling Banking Crises], report to Riksdagens revisorer.

Judd, John P. (1983), 'The Recent Decline in Velocity: Instability in the Demand for Money or Inflation?', *Federal Reserve Bank of San Francisco Economic Review*, Summer, 12–19.

Judd, John P. and John L. Scadding (1982), 'The Search for a Stable Money Demand Function', *Journal of Economic Literature*, **20**, September, 993–1023.

Kambhu, John, Scott Weidman and Neel Krishnan (2007), *New Directions for Understanding Systemic Risk: A Report on a Conference Co-sponsored by the Federal Reserve Bank of New York and the National Academy of Sciences*, Washington, DC: National Academic Press.

Kaminsky, Graciela L. and Carmen M. Reinhart (1999), 'The Twin Crises: The Causes of Banking and Balance of Payments Problems', *American Economic Review*, **89** (3), 473–500.

Keynes, John Maynard (1936), *The General Theory of Employment, Interest, and Money*, London: Macmillan.

Kincsei, Éva (2009), 'Lassan és átláthatatlanul osztja a pénzt az állam' [The government is slow and not transparent in distributing funds], *Index*, 22 May.

Kindleberger, Charles P. (1989), *Manias, Panics, and Crashes: A History of Financial Crises*, New York: Basic Books.

Kinsella, Stephen (2009), 'Theories of International Money', Working Paper, Department of Economics, Kemmy Business School, University of Limerick, Ireland.

Kochen, A. (1991), 'Cleaning Up by Cleaning Up', *Euromoney*, April, 73–7.

Krugman, Paul (1979), 'A Model of Balance-of-Payment Crises', *Journal of Money, Credit, and Banking*, **11** (3), 311–25.

Krugman, Paul (1999), 'Balance Sheets, the Transfer Problem and Financial Crises', *Journal of Money, Credit, and Banking*, **11**, 311–25.

Laidler, David (1985), *The Demand for Money: Theories and Evidence*, 3rd edn, New York: Harper & Row, Chapter IV.

Lavoie, Marc (2003), 'A Primer on Endogenous Credit-Money', in Louis-Philippe Rochon and Sergio Rossi (eds), *Modern Theories of Money: The Nature and Role of Money in Capitalist Economies*, Cheltenham, UK and Northampton, MA, USA: Edward Elgar Publishing Chapter 21, pp. 506–43.

Leathers, C.G. and J.P. Raines (2004), 'The Schumpeterian Role of Financial Innovations in the New Economy's Business Cycle', *Cambridge Journal of Economics*, **28** (5), September, 667–81.

Leijonhufvud, Axel (2004), 'Celebrating Ned', *Journal of Economic Literature*, **XLII**, September, 810–21.

LeRoy, Stephen F. (2004), 'Rational Exuberance', *Journal of Economic Literature*, **XLII**, September, 801–3.

Levine, Ross (1997), 'Financial Development and Economic Growth: Views and Agenda', *Journal of Economic Literature*, **XXXV**, June, 688–726.

Lindgren, Carl-Johan, Gillian Garcia and Matthew Seal (1995), 'Bank Soundness and Macro-economic Policy', Washington, DC: International Monetary Fund.

Mandelbrot, Benoit and Richard Hudson (2004), *The Misbehavior of Markets*, New York: Basic Books.

Marchionatti, Roberto (1999), 'On Keynes' Animal Spirits', *Kyklos*, **52** (3), 415–39.

Minsky, Hyman P. (2008), *Stabilizing an Unstable Economy*, New York: McGraw-Hill.

Mullins, Mark (1989), 'Meltdown Monday or Meltdown Money?: Causes of the Stock Market Crash', *International Economics and Financial Markets*, Oxford: Oxford University Press, Chapter 3.

Mundell, R. (1987), 'A New Deal on Exchange Rates', presented at the MITI symposium *The Search for a New Cooperation*, Tokyo, January.

Narine, Shaun (2002), 'ASEAN in the Aftermath: The Consequences of the East Asian Economic Crisis', *Global Governance*, **8**, 179–94.

Nitzan, Jonathan (1998), 'Differential Accumulation: Towards a New Political Economy of Capital', *Review of International Political Economy*, **5** (2), 169–216.

North, Douglass C. (1997), 'Some Fundamental Puzzles in Economic Development', in Arthur W. Brian, Steven N. Durlauf and David A. Lane (eds), *The Economy as a Complex Evolving System II*, SFI Studies in the Sciences of Complexity, **XXVII**, New York: Addison-Wesley.

Norton, Robert (1993), 'Offshore Funds Maximise Reward and Minimise Risk', *The European*, 3 December.

O'Brien, Richard (1992), *Global Financial Integration: The End of Geography*, London: Royal Institute of International Affairs.

Palacios, Robert and Edward Whitehouse (1998), *The Role of Choice in the Transition to a Funded Pension System*, Washington, DC: Human Development Network, The World Bank.

Palan, Ronen (1994), 'Tax Havens and the Market for Sovereignty', paper presented at the International Studies Association Convention, Washington, DC.

Palan, Ronen (2002), 'Tax Havens and the Commercialization of State Sovereignty', *International Organization*, **56** (1), 151–76.

Phillips, Nicola (2000), 'Governance after Financial Crisis: South American Perspectives on the Reformulation of Regionalism', *New Political Economy*, **5** (3), 383–98.

Piketty, Thomas (2014), *Capital in the Twenty-First Century*, Cambridge, MA and London: The Belknap Press of Harvard University Press.

Porter, Richard D., Thomas D. Simpson and Eileen Mauskopf (1979), 'Financial Innovation and the Monetary Aggregates', *Brookings Papers on Economic Activity*, **10** (1), 213.

Prudential-Bache Securities (1989), 'The Triumph of Capitalism', Topical Study #17, 1 August, 14.

Putnam, Robert (2000), *Bowling Alone: The Collapse and Revival of American Community*, New York: Simon & Schuster.

Rangvid, Jesper (2001), 'Second Generation Models of Currency Crises', *Journal of Economic Surveys*, **15** (5), 613–46.

Reinhart, Carmen M. and Kenneth S. Rogoff (2007), 'Is the 2007 US Sub-prime Financial Crisis So Different? An International Historical Pattern', *American Economic Review*, **98** (2), 339–44.

Reinhart, Carmen M. and Kenneth S. Rogoff (2008), 'This Time Is Different: A Panoramic View of Eight Centuries of Financial Crises', Working Paper.

Reinhart, Carmen M. and Kenneth S. Rogoff (2009), 'The Aftermath of Financial Crises', paper presented at the American Social Sciences Association Annual Meeting, January, San Francisco.

Schumpeter, Joseph A. (1912), *Theorie der Wirtshaftlichen Entwicklung* [*The Theory of Economic Development*], Leipzig: Dunker & Humblot, translated by Redvers Opie, Cambridge, MA: Harvard University Press, 1934.

Schumpeter, Joseph (1934), *Theory of Economic Development*, Cambridge, MA: Harvard University Press.

Smith, Adam (1759), *The Theory of Moral Sentiments*, Edinburgh, UK.

Soddy, Frederick (1926), *Wealth, Virtual Wealth, and Debt*, New York: E.P. Dutton & Co.

Solomon, Elinor Harris (1997), *Virtual Money*, New York and Oxford: Oxford University Press.

Soros, George (2008), *The New Paradigm for Financial Markets: The Credit Crisis of 2008 and What It Means*, New York: Public Affairs.

Spindt, Paul A. (1985), 'Money Is What Money Does: Monetary Aggregation and the Equation of Exchange', *Journal of Political Economy*, **93** (1), February, 175–204.

Stone, Courtenay C. and Daniel L. Thornton (1987), 'Solving the 1980s' Velocity Puzzle: A Progress Report', Federal Reserve Bank of St. Louis *Review*, August/September, 5–23.

Strange, Susan (1986), *Casino Capitalism*, Oxford and New York: Basil Blackwell.

Strange, Susan (1998), 'The New World of Debt', *New Left Review*, **230**, July–August, 91–114.

Szabó, Máté (1998), 'New Social Movements in Hungary', *Soundings*, Barry Amiel & Norman Melburn Trust.

Taleb, Nassim (2007), *The Black Swan*, New York: Random House.

Taylor, M. (1988), 'Coveraged Interest Arbitrage and Market Turbulence: An Empirical Analysis', Centre for Economic Policy Research, Discussion Paper No. 236, May.

Taylor, M. and I. Tonks (1989), 'The Internationalisation of Stock Markets and the Abolition of United Kingdom Exchange Control', *Review of Economics and Statistics*, **71** (2), 332–6.

Treisman, Daniel (2000), 'The Causes of Corruption: A Cross-National Study', *Journal of Public Economics*, **76** (3), 399–457.

Triffin, Robert (1961), *Gold and the Dollar Crisis: The Future of Convertibility*, revised edn, New Haven, CT: Yale University Press.

UNESCO (2007), 'Roundtable Discussion on "Civil Service Reforms and Good Governance in Azerbaijan"', sponsored by the President of the Republic of Azerbaijan.

United Nations (1986), *World Economic Survey 1986: Current Trends and Policies in the World Economy*, Department of International Economics and Social Affairs.

Veblen, Thorstein (1923) (reproduced 1967), *Absentee Ownership and Business Enterprise in Recent Times: The Case of America*, Introduction by Robert Leckachman, Boston, MA: Beacon Press.

Wade, Robert (1998–99), 'The Coming Fight over Capital Flows', *Foreign Policy*, Winter, 41–54.

Wakasugi, R. (1987), 'Attack the Problem at Its Source', *Look Japan*, July, 3.

Wenninger, John and Lawrence J. Radecki (1986), 'Financial Transactions and the Demand for m1', *Federal Reserve Bank of New York Quarterly Review*, **11** (2), Summer, 24–9.

Index

broad money supply
  and economic growth 39, 103, 104,
    172
Brown, B. 6, 102, 165
Bundespost Telekom 90

Canada
  1987 market decline 78
  deregulation 15
  monetary velocity 38, 134
capital
  adequacy 15, 73, 75
  as power 169–73
  forms of 23–24, 147–54
  returns on 23
capital flight 6, 7, 72, 78, 101, 106,
    108–9, 125, 155, 162, 175
  from Asia 107, 108
  from China *ix*, 123–124
  from Latin America 72
  from LDCs 75, 162–4
  from Mexico 72, 100, 101
capitalism 11, 133, 138, 140, 172, 179
  'casino capitalism' 138, 140
  competing forms 137–8
  state 115
Carchedi, G. *x*, 170
Caribbean School 166
Cayman Islands 4
central banks 11, 37, 38, 65, 77, 105,
    117, 169, 176, 177, 178
Cerny, P. *x*, 140, 169
Chaffee, W. *x*
Chase Econometric Associates, Inc. 64
Chase Manhattan 163
Chile 72, 75
China *ix*, 16–17, 122–4, 127, 169
CHIPS 10, 16
Chirac, J.16, 68
Citibank 9, 163
CitiCorp *xi*, 135
Clark, G. 151, 168
Clarke, S. 139, 140
Clearing House Interbank Payments
  System, *see* CHIPS
Clinton, W.J. 101
collateralized debt obligations 4, 115
Colombia
  foreign debt 75
complex adaptive systems 131–2

computers, *see* information technology
Countrywide Financial 115
Crédit Suisse First Boston Ltd. 14, 50
currencies
  exchange rates 55, 58, 64, 65, 69,
    106, 107, 108, 110, 176
  forward-looking markets for 20–22
  hierarchy among 165
current crisis *ix*, *xiii*, 113–16, 133
  re-regulation in the US, 13
Czechoslovakia 17
Czech Republic 155

Data Resources, Inc. 64
Daudin, G. 151, 153, 167, 168
De Bonis, R. 124
de Gaulle, C. 162
Dean Witter 11
debt-capital, returns on 23
debt-equity ratios 22–5
deflation 12, 13, 29, 30, 36, 54, 65, 68,
    102, 103, 104, 110, 117, 125, 127,
    139, 140, 141,
Depository Institutions Deregulatory
  and Monetary Control Act of
  1980 115
deregulation *xii*, 1, 59, 76, 79, 114, 125,
    151, 174
  and monetary velocity 42–3, 46, 49,
    51, 56, 65, 78, 80, 82–4, 139
  in Africa 114
  in Asia 105, 106, 114, 163
  in Canada 15, 50
  in China 16–17, 123
  in Eastern Europe 17, 114
  in Europe 15, 118
  in France 16, 50
  in Germany 16
  in Japan 15–16, 19–20, 32
  in Latin America 114
  in Sweden 91–2
  in the UK 10, 14, 32, 40, 50, 51, 76,
    118
  in the US 13–14, 43, 44, 59
  in the USSR 17
derivatives 3–4, 117
Deutsche Bank 9
'dollarization' 106, 110, 163, 164
dollars, *see* Eurodollar; US dollar
Dopfer, K. 133

Marxism 139, 140, 149, 156, 171, 176
Maxfield, S. 105
Mead, C. 8
mercantilism, *see* money-mercantilism
Merrill Lynch 15
meso structures *xiii*, 113, 114, 117, 133,
    139, 140, 143, 144, 156, 157
Mexico 71
    and oil revenues 71, 135
    capital flight 72
    financial crisis *xi*, *xiii*, 98–101, 106,
        107, 112, 135, 150, 176
    foreign debt 72, 75
    National Banking Commission 98
    tesobonos 98–9
Microsoft 11
Mieno, Y. 102
Minsky, H. 136, 140, 141, 178–9
Mitterrand, F. 16, 60, 67, 68, 69, 114
monetary policies 39, 40, 54, 63, 77,
    127
    and commodity prices 106, 110
    and recession 66, 70–71, 88, 90, 91,
        99, 102, 104
    and stock market crash 74, 78, 79, 80
    and the world debt crisis 69–75
    effects on Asia 108, 110
monetary velocity 41, 94, 121, 172
    and GDP 12, 38, 125, 177
    and globalization 42–3, 46, 65, 77
    and interest rates 38, 82–6
    and market expansion 43, 44, 45, 66
    and stock prices 44–5, 77–80
    decline 37, 39, 42, 48, 125
    in Canada 38, 50, 134
    in Germany 38, 49, 53–4, 118
    in Japan 38, 39, 103
    in the UK 38, 49, 50–52, 118, 134
    in the US 38, 46–9, 77, 97, 103, 118,
        127, 134
    regression analysis 46, 65, 77, 82–6
monetary wealth processes *xii*, 75,
    95, 100, 113, 114, 125, 126, 138,
    139, 140, 154, 163, 164, 167, 168,
    169–71
money-mercantilism 142, 151, 162,
    164–8, 175, 176
money supply
    (m1) 37–42, 43, 50, 51, 79, 104, 106,
        107, 118, 126, 127, 172, 177

(m1), and growth 37–8, 66
(m1), and inflation 37–8
(m1), regression analysis 43, 44, 45,
    46
(m2) 38, 39, 45, 46, 79, 103, 107, 126,
    177
(m3) 10, 38, 39, 79, 107, 126–7, 172,
    176, 177
(m4) 126
money-liquidity *xii*, 7, 40, 48, 51, 52,
    54, 76, 80, 88, 92, 96, 113, 114,
    118, 120, 124, 127, 129, 140, 151,
    162, 171–2
    see also monetary velocity; liquidity
        crisis
Morgan Grenfell Securities
    International 16
Morgan Stanley & Co. 15, 178
Moseidjord, A. *x*
Mundell, R. 29

Narine, S. 163
narrow money supply, *see* money
    supply, (m1)
NASDAQ 10
Näslund, B. 91
National Bureau of Economic
    Research 64, 93
National Union of Mineworkers 67
Netherlands 27, 118, 119, 120
    1987 market decline, 78
New Political Economy 136
Nippon Telephone and Telegraph 26
Nitzan, J. 173
North, D. 144
Northern Rock 126
Norton, R. 5
Norway
    financial crisis 91

O'Brien, R. 1
OECD 22, 119
offshore banking facilities 4, 5, 109,
    114, 144
offshore financial markets 3, 4–7, 37,
    98, 100, 101, 105, 109, 164–5, 169,
    170, 174
Organisation for Economic Co-
    operation and Development, *see*
    OECD